THINKING PSYCHOLOGICALLy

Also by Patrick McGhee

Accounting for Relationships: Explanation, Representation and Knowledge
(co-edited with R Burnett and D D Clarke)

Thinking Psychologically

Patrick McGhee

palgrave

First published 2001 by
PALGRAVE
Houndmills, Basingstoke, Hampshire RG21 6XS and
175 Fifth Avenue, New York, N.Y. 10010
Companies and representatives throughout the world

PALGRAVE is the new global academic imprint of
St. Martin's Press LLC Scholarly and Reference Division and
Palgrave Publishers Ltd (formerly Macmillan Press Ltd).

ISBN 10: 0–333–73596–X paperback
ISBN 13: 978–0–333–73596–1 paperback

This book is printed on paper suitable for recycling and made from fully managed and sustained forest sources. Logging, pulping and manufacturing processes are expected to conform to the environmental regulations of the country of origin.

A catalogue record for this book is available from the British Library.

Editing and origination by
Aardvark Editorial, Mendham, Suffolk

10   9   8
10 09 08 07

Printed in Great Britain by
Creative Print and Design (Wales), Ebbw Vale

For Marianne

Contents

Part I
Principles

Part II

Applications

List of Figures and Tables

Figures

Tables

Preface

This book aims to help you develop your thinking about psychology. Whether you are about to start a psychology course, are in the middle of a course or need a refresher towards the end of a course this book will enable you to think much more creatively, analytically and critically about almost every type of theory, research, book or article you have ever come across or *will* ever come across during your studies in psychology.

This book seeks to improve your thinking skills so that you can enjoy psychology more, experience a greater mastery of its ideas and methods and eventually contribute to the ever-evolving body of knowledge that we know as 'psychology'. However, let me come clean about one thing straight away: this book should lead to higher grades (I hope that doesn't put you off too much). Your grades should improve not because this book is a glorified list of study tips or exam techniques (it certainly is not) but because *good grades happen to good thinkers.*

Why, you may ask, is there a need for a book on thinking about psychology? Is it not enough that we learn about the great theories and landmark experiments of the discipline? The answer to the first of these questions follows from the answer to the second. Psychology is not simply a body of fixed knowledge like some dead language, which we define, frame, package and pass on. Psychology is a living, evolving process of understanding which depends upon constant debate, discussion, challenges and defences being actively entered into by researchers, theorists, teachers, practitioners and, yes, students too. In order to learn about psychology we need to understand it, and in order to understand it we must actively *engage* with it.

To come back to the first question – why is this book necessary? The problem is that nowadays there is very little opportunity for students to stand back and reflect upon the psychology they read about in textbooks or hear about in the lecture theatre. Three factors have come together to create a set of circumstances which will no doubt be instantly recognisable to you.

First, mass participation in higher education means that class sizes are bigger, and contact with specialist psychology staff is diminished. Tutors do not always have the time to give each student the individualised support required to develop critical thinking skills. A second factor is the changing profile of students. Gone are the days when the typical undergraduate was 18 years old, straight from school and studying full time. Today the typical psychology student is more likely to be a 35-year-old mother with domestic, child-care and work responsibilities, studying part time. Psychology students cannot always find the time to really engage in depth with the theories and studies presented to them. A third factor is the 'bureaucratisation' of learning, for staff and students alike, most obviously apparent in the modularisation of psychology degrees. From day one until graduation (and beyond) psychology students and staff are buried under such an avalanche of record sheets, triplicate requisitions, module choice forms and extension request sheets that it is a miracle that anyone *learns* about memory, vision or personality at all. Part of modularisation is overassessment – so many exams, laboratory reports, essays and seminar papers to prepare, write and submit that there is barely time for the tutor to teach or the student to do any learning for them. Little wonder that students sometimes feel there is no time for thinking in their degree, only time for meeting deadlines.

It is in this context that this book seeks to help you to think psychologically. Thinking is not a luxury, an additional task to do if there is time after reading – thinking critically and productively should be, and can be, an integral part of reading books and articles, listening to lectures and participating in seminars. This book tries to illuminate the kind of thinking that lies behind the arguments of researchers, making those arguments more transparent so that hopefully you will only need to read them once to understand them. This book will help you respond to and engage with the ideas being presented and the claims being made so that you will already have an actively critical and questioning understanding of psychology, saving you time at revision periods. You will have little worry about which questions are going to come up in exams, because your understanding of the topics will be *already* organised around questioning perspectives.

It should be clear now why discussion of the pressures on higher education is relevant to the analysis of thinking in psychology degrees: different forms of institution encourage different forms of thinking. Many aspects of modern higher education encourage surface learning of superficial facts quickly, rather than deeper comprehension – a situation which leads to students not achieving their potential. This book seeks to redress the balance a little.

This book will hopefully encourage you to be an active learner, thinking critically and holistically about psychology, and show you how to do it. You will see in future chapters that being an active thinker involves identifying and evaluating the *claims* made by psychologists whose work you read about. It also involves understanding and questioning the *assumptions* psychologists make about the world and the kind of knowledge we can have about it.

I hope this book helps you become a better thinker, and in so doing, helps you to become a better psychologist. That's why I wrote it, and here it is.

PATRICK MCGHEE

How to Read This Book

This book falls into two parts. Part I, 'Principles', is essentially a toolkit of ideas for thinking about psychology. Part II, 'Applications', is a review of six key areas of the discipline – social psychology, constructionism in psychology, developmental psychology, cognitive psychology, biopsychology and personality and individual differences – using the principles identified in Part I. In our toolkit we shall put together ideas from the psychology of thinking, the philosophy of science and basic logic. We shall also begin assembling ideas from the analysis of research methodology, including techniques from both experimental and qualitative approaches. In Part II we shall not only be applying general principles from Part I, but shall focus on distinctive issues that are relevant to specific areas of psychology.

It will not be possible for reasons of space to apply all the ideas from Part I to all the theories and studies we discuss in the various chapters in Part II. However, you will benefit from considering how ideas from Part I, other than those applied in Part II, can in fact be applied to the theories discussed in the various 'Applications' chapters.

Inevitably, the Applications chapters will only go into individual theories or studies in detail to the extent that it is necessary to illustrate a point. It will be assumed that you have recently or are currently reading a psychology textbook and/or taking a course of study in psychology.

It will not be possible to cover every theory in psychology – standard textbooks are not able to do that either. But the specific theories, methods and concepts analysed in this book are ones which illustrate general issues about thinking productively about psychology, and they are also the ones most likely to figure in a first year university general introductory course in psychology. You will, however, probably find more coverage in this book on ideas related to something called social constructionism than you are likely to come across in a first year psychology course. There are at least three reasons for this. First of all social constructionism would argue that most of the ideas psychology students are exposed to in their courses are just plain wrong. I do not happen to agree with this, but constructionist arguments are very subtle and are well worth looking at alongside more traditional theories and methods. The second reason is that constructionist ideas are influencing many areas of psychology and becoming increasingly popular particularly in the areas of social and developmental psychology. Finally, constructionist claims make us think afresh about some very basic ideas about psychology and that can do us no harm at all.

Although useful links between chapters are made throughout the book, each chapter in itself is largely self-contained. You may want to read the chapters in a sequence different from that presented here. You might be studying biopsychology and cognitive psychology this term and social and developmental next, in which case you could read the relevant chapters in that order. However, it is recommended that you read as much as you can of Part I before moving on to any of the chapters in Part II.

Each chapter has the same general structure. The **Chapter Overviews** are designed to help orientate you to the material in that chapter in a general way by outlining what will be covered and linking the material to what has been discussed in earlier chapters.

The **Learning Objectives** are more specific statements of what you should be able to do when you have completed the chapter. At the end of each chapter you should go back and check whether you have in fact achieved the stated learning objectives. If you have then you are ready to move on, if not you may want to go back to the relevant section of the chapter and look at it again. Within each chapter there are a number of **Boxes** which offer tips, food for thought or irrelevant asides that caught my fancy at the time of writing. The most important of these are the 'Think it Through' boxes which ask you to think through some specific issue raised in the text. It is well worth tackling these 'Think it Through' boxes as they help to consolidate understanding about various key points.

The chapter **Summaries** towards the end of each chapter are designed to bring together the main ideas from the text and serve as a brief reminder of chapters you may have read earlier. However, the chapter summaries will make little sense if read on their own without having read the full chapter. The **Key Terms** boxes contain key words which have been emboldened in the chapter and appear in the Glossary. The **Further Reading** section of each chapter is an annotated guide to some 'next step' books you may find interesting if the ideas in the main text particularly intrigue you. These have been selected as texts which are readily available in any university library and which do not typically assume a great deal of prior knowledge.

The final section of each chapter is **Useful Websites**. The Internet is obviously an immense resource for anyone interested in learning about anything. There is also an awful lot of really useless stuff there too. The sites I have identified are those that anyone interested in thinking about psychology in creative, imaginative and critical ways might find interesting. I do not personally endorse or vouch for any of the sites listed, but I have checked them and trust them to be around for a while. There is also a website to support this book at www.patrickmcghee.co.uk.

Hopefully this book will give you the confidence to take a critical perspective on all psychological research and theory that you come across. You will realise that you do not have to sit back and accept all that you read in a textbook or hear in a lecture. And of course it is essential that you apply to your *own* writing, theorising and research work the critical scrutiny which you apply to the work of others.

Some of the ideas presented in this book are fairly easy to grasp – the notion of parsimony (Chapter 3) should not be giving anyone any headaches, for example. On the other hand the relevance of *modus ponens* to research hypotheses (Chapter 4) may take a bit of careful thinking through to get the full picture. I hope it is also true that the value of this book to you will be partly related to your developing depth and range of knowledge of psychology. It might well be the case that you return to some of the ideas in this book later in your undergraduate career and think them through with your by then extended repertoire of examples of theories and studies.

Acknowledgements

Thanks are due first of all to Frances Arnold at the publishers for her constant support and faith in the project and to Houri Alavi also at the publishers for her efficient handling of everything that came her way. I would also like to thank Jeremy Miles, Dorothy Miell, David Nightingale and several anonymous reviewers who were kind enough to read early drafts of some chapters and provide immensely useful comments at just the right time in just the right way. If any of those anonymous reviewers would like to identify themselves at a conference, I will stand them a drink (Jeremy, Dot and David on the other hand are unlikely to require an invitation). I must also thank David D Clarke who first made me realise that ideas are a psychologist's greatest resource and helped me 'think psychologically' when it mattered most. I need to thank all the students at Derby and Bolton who have made thinking psychologically as well as *Thinking Psychologically* such a joy. But above all my greatest debt of gratitude is to Marianne, Patrick and Ciaran for putting up with me while I wrote this.

Part I

Principles

Introduction

1

CHAPTER OVERVIEW

This chapter introduces some of the key themes of the book including the idea of 'science', the importance of diversity in psychology, and constructivism, a model of how ideas are learnt. The chapter also considers the importance of thinking in everyday life.

LEARNING OBJECTIVES

By the end of this chapter you should be able to:

■ Outline what is meant by 'epistemology'
■ Outline what is meant by 'epistemological pluralism'
■ Outline what is meant by 'constructivism'

Thinking scientifically?

At some point in your studies you will probably find yourself looking at an essay list or exam paper with the question 'Is psychology a science?' staring back at you. The question is a hardy perennial and you should think about what kind of answer you would want to give when you do finally have to confront it. The issue of the scientific status of psychology is an important one, and one which has generated much debate in psychology since the discipline began. The person in the street might well imagine that the precision of science cannot be applied to the complexity of human beings. However, most academic research psychologists in the US and the UK would happily answer the question in the affirmative. But many students of psychology feel rather uneasy about this. Is psychology *really* a science in the same way that, say, physics, chemistry or biology are? What makes psychologists think that psychology is a science?

The issue of whether or not psychology is a science might seem a strange place to start our investigation into thinking psychologically but in a sense it is the only place to start. If psychology is a science then maybe 'thinking psychologically' might just mean thinking *scientifically*. Maybe to be good psychologists we simply have to be good scientists? Oh no. To be good psychologists we have to be good thinkers and there is much more to good thinking than just thinking scientifically. Sometimes psychologists *do* need to think like scientists but we also on occasion need to think like philosophers, anthropologists, historians or therapists.

The perspective of this book is that thinking psychologically is *not* just thinking scientifically. Instead, we shall take the approach that although psychology is *partly* scientific it is not *just* scientific – it is many other things besides. However, we will also be developing our scientific thinking, and thinking long and hard about how science really works.

Ever since Wilheim Wundt opened the first dedicated scientific psychological laboratory in Leipzig in Germany in 1879 psychologists have tried to maintain scientific credibility through the use of controlled observations of various kinds in an attempt to repeat the successes of the better established sciences of chemistry, biology and physics.

However, psychological experimentation as we know it today is influenced not by what scientists actually did but by what *philosophers* of science thought scientists did. Psychology in the 1920s and 30s was looking for a firmer, more systematic, more scientific, footing. At that time psychologists were very diverse in their ways of thinking about the most effective way of investigating human behaviour and experience. There were psychoanalysts who drew upon their clinical experiences and Wundt himself had drawn upon popular accounts of myth and religion in his 'folk psychology' alongside his better known laboratory work. However, psychology did not at that point create a new approach to human science, drawing upon this diversity of techniques and methodologies, this diversity of *thinking* about human development. Instead psychology took a ready-made package of scientific philosophy, not from physicists, chemists and biologists who were actually conducting research, but from philosophers of science who were trying to describe what scientists *should* do.

This 'package' was known as **logical positivism** and was developed by a group of philosophers known as the Vienna Circle (we shall be looking at them in more detail in Chapter 2). Logical positivism emphasised that science could only be based on clearly defined hypotheses (ideally expressed mathematically) which could be verified through rigorous objective observations. Logical positivism was initially adopted most enthusiastically by a group of psychologists known as 'behaviourists' who were researching animal learning as a model of human behaviour. Soon this logical positivist model was being adopted in other areas of psychology. **Behaviourism** came to dominate mainstream psychology in North America between 1930 and 1960 by appearing to show how a scientific model could indeed be successfully applied to psychology. Behaviourists studied animal learning, concentrating only on behaviour that could be directly observed and measured such as lever pressing or maze-running. It was not until the 1960s that cognitive psychologists shifted the focus to perception, memory and thinking, phenomena which could only be measured indirectly.

With the growth of cognitive psychology and the gradual demise of behaviourism, the emphasis on observable behaviour was greatly reduced, but much of the scientific framework of logical positivism remained. Most psychological research journals today still publish articles that adhere very closely to the logical positivist model of science, even though the *topics* of the articles themselves are very different from the behaviourist obsession on observables. The range of research topics is much broader than it was in the 1950s but the *assumptions* about the proper way of doing research in psychology are still in many ways very narrow, constrained by the original boundaries of logical positivism.

Contemporary psychology has developed in many ways since the 1950s and 60s. There would seem to be a broad diversity of phenomena being studied, a range of specialist laboratory equipment used in research (most notably data recording technology such as video, physiological and computer equipment) and many different applications of findings in education, business and health. However, underpinning much of this apparent diversity is a particular set of assumptions about psychological knowledge: how we should develop our knowledge about the mind, what the limits of what we can know are, and how we should assess the quality and meaningfulness of what we know, or think we know. That is to say, underlying this apparent diversity of research activity there is often a more fundamental commitment to just one kind of psychological knowledge, that is, one kind of **epistemology**, the epistemology of logical positivism. This epistemological conservatism has been reduced significantly over the years but psychologists working in certain areas of the discipline still feel somewhat uneasy when asked to step outside the narrow, comfortable confines of straight, traditional scientific thinking. This is unfortunate because there is much to be gained from embracing a spectrum of ideas about psychological knowledge, in other words a form of epistemological diversity or epistemological pluralism.

Epistemological pluralism

Fortunately not all contemporary psychology reflects logical positivism. Since the 1970s psychology has to some extent been reacquainting itself with several earlier connections that were lost during the dominance of behaviourism. Anthropology, sociology, philosophy, linguistics, computer science and biology are all seen as having important contributions to make to a fuller understanding of human experience and behaviour.

In practical terms, however, the legacy of logical positivism is that psychology methods courses at most UK and US universities are still dominated by hypothesis testing, operational definitions and statistical tests. Although we will see in Chapter 5 on experiments that there can certainly be much of value in such an approach, we must remember that it is not the *only* approach. The problem with logical positivism in terms of its use in psychology is that it has been applied to a whole range of questions for which it was never designed. Worse, it has trained generations of psychologists to tackle problems from just one point of view. Psychology's way of thinking about a whole range of issues has been restricted to the way logical positivism can think about it. There is a long history of psychologists coming across complex, serious, curious, challenging problems in social, educational, psychiatric and developmental settings and then failing utterly to solve them because their only way of thinking about those problems was with the mind set of logical positivism. Psychologists, believing that no alternative to logical positivism was sufficiently scientific to be trusted, argued that they *were* applying the right tools to the problems they were asked to tackle. The problem is, of course, that when your only tool is a hammer, every problem looks like a nail, and when your only tool for thinking is logical positivism, every problem looks like an unsolved equation.

The perspective of this book is one of **epistemological pluralism**. That is to say, I suggest that there is no *single* best way of thinking about behaviour and experience, no *single* perfect model for creating psychological knowledge, no *single* solution to the puzzles of mental life. Rather, we should take the view that psychology is multifaceted and requires many different 'perspectives on knowledge'. Consequently, this book will try to help you to think more skilfully in relation to a whole range of epistemologies (including logical positivism). We will discuss how to evaluate theories and how to think imaginatively about them; how to run experiments and when they are likely to go wrong; we will review the process of deductive reasoning and consider what we should and should not be doing with experiments in relation to theory. However, we will be adopting a critical approach to logical positivism. Logical positivism will be seen not just as a technique for psychology but something which itself may need to be put under the microscope.

So much for how psychology has developed over the years – what about the way in which we learn about it? What kind of perspective should we take on what it means to understand psychology? We will be taking the view that learners do not simply receive information and absorb it for future reference in a passive and detached manner. Learners actively produce their own understandings of what they are taught – in short learners *construct* their own version of knowledge.

Constructivism

> Ann and Brenda are two psychology students both in their mid-thirties. Ann is a mother of three children of school age (all girls aged six, eight and eleven), while Brenda has no children and was herself an only child. One of Ann's children (the youngest) was bullied when she initially started school. Brenda's husband is a teacher at an inner city primary school. Ann and Brenda are attending a psychology course seminar on 'educational psychology in the primary school'. Their tutor is outlining different models of the way five-year-olds communicate with teachers.

How do you think the seminar information will be internalised by each of these hypothetical student parents? It is conceivable (but unlikely) that they switch off their own life circumstances and experiences and just 'learn' what the tutor describes. It is much more likely, however, that each will actively try to make sense of the observations in educational psychology in their own way.

In constructing their understanding of the seminar material, Ann and Brenda will draw upon their memories of personal direct experience of school as children, their current beliefs about teachers' competence and motivation and, of course, previous reading and learning they will have done in child and educational psychology. These differences might well mean that one of the two students, say Ann, is motivated to ask specific further questions of the tutor regarding the

> ### THINK IT THROUGH
>
> How do you think Ann and Brenda might differ in the ways they incorporate their seminar into what they already know about children's social interaction? In what ways might they be similar? Which of them would be the more likely to opt to do a practical project on teachers' first impressions of reception class children at primary school?

effect of the sex of the teacher on teacher–pupil communication. The tutor's reply might be to the effect that the sex of the teacher is not as important a factor as, say, the social class of the child. This intrigues Ann as her experience is that her children communicated much more easily with their female primary school teachers than the male teachers. Ann tries to think this through during the seminar while another student comments on ethnicity as a factor. Ann raises the question again, querying the tutor's claim about teacher gender not being a factor. The tutor says he understands her surprise but that there is plenty of research to back him up and, in any case, the effect of teacher gender on teacher–pupil communication quality is caused by variables confounded with gender. Ann does not know what 'confounded' means and does not want to look foolish by asking in front of the rest of the seminar group.

The above scenario is outlined not to illustrate that Ann has a 'biased' view of a particular theory in educational psychology because she has experience of schools in her personal life as a parent. Rather it illustrates *that learners actively contribute to the process of learning*. Ann will have constructed a representation of the process of teacher–pupil communication that builds on what she already knows about such situations – and which is not flatly contradicted by the new information. She has actively sought out further information because the new information did not square with her previous understanding (in this example from the tutor but it could just as easily have been from a library book).

Also illustrated by this example is the central role of language in the construction of the model that Ann has. There were no actual school teachers or pupils in the seminar room being observed, instead language 'stood for' the activities and roles in the real world. The terms 'teacher' and 'pupil' were not used to mean a specific teacher or a specific pupil, but the general categories 'teacher' and 'pupil'. Ann and her tutor would probably accept that what these terms mean, and the categories they are meant to refer to, are shared by them because they share a common culture. But there is a part of Ann's representation which is problematic. She knows that the gender of a teacher is 'confounded' with other variables, and that this confounding is connected to the impact of the teacher on communication, but she is not sure why. Interestingly, later that week at a research methods class, Ann was asked during some group work whether she thought comparing male and female business managers would make a good project. She replied that it was an interesting idea, but that they would all, of course, have to keep a close eye on confounding...

Constructivism is the view that learners actively construct their own understandings of concepts, phenomena and ideas (Sandoval, 1995). The individual is not a passive vessel having small amounts of extra information poured into their mind as they learn. We approach all new information using knowledge structures (sometimes called **schemata**) which we have developed on the basis of past experiences with the world. Usually, we can make sense of the new information within existing schemata, as might be the case when we watch a 'romantic' film (we expect to see the whirlwind romance, the breaking up, the making up, the enforced separation, the dramatic crisis and the happy ending). This process of making sense within existing schemata is sometimes known as assimilation. Of course sometimes our existing schemata do not work and we reconstruct our schemata to accommodate the unfamiliar new information (as when for example we watch an *avant garde* film about relationships between the sexes which does not adhere to the usual romantic narrative conventions). This process is sometimes known as accommodation.

When we are learning about new concepts we are constantly reworking our knowledge structures to incorporate the new information. We are trying to make all the elements of our restructured schema connect properly with other schemata and to the information we are processing. And yet we do not want to restructure our schemata every time we come across a slightly different case. This *balancing* of assimilation (processing information on the basis of what we already know) and accommodation (restructuring or reconstructing what we know, or constructing brand new schemata) is sometimes referred to as equilibration. The child psychologist Jean Piaget initially described these processes in relation to young infants and children, where a schema could be about nothing more complex than a soother. However, the basic principles still apply to more advanced learning, and assimilation, accommodation and equilibration are useful concepts when making sense of how adults learn about quantum mechanics, just as they are when we are making sense of infants making sense of sucking.

This book takes constructivism as one of its basic models of adult learning. However, we should remember that the process of constructing knowledge about psychological theories applies not just to students of psychology *but to researchers also*. Psychologists, when trying to make sense of new data or new insights, also go through a process of equilibration, balancing the desire to interpret information within existing theories with the temptation to create a new, or reconstructed, theory. Psychologists will often go to great lengths to interpret new data within existing theories (curiously enough especially when the existing theory is something that they themselves thought up). Constructivism is essentially the idea that learners actively construct their understanding from balancing what they already know with what they discover. Constructivism emphasises that learning is a process and not an event.

We could use this version of constructivism very usefully without any further amendment. However, we can add a further dimension that will help us to make sense of the way constructions are accomplished during learning (for both students and researchers).

You will recall that Ann was reluctant to ask about 'confounding' in case she was the only student who did not understand but nevertheless she was able to use the term in group discussions later in the week. She had been motivated to quiz the tutor about the research on gender, partly because she wanted to get the facts right for the sake of assessment, but also probably because she wanted to continue to make sense of her children's experience at school. We might also stretch this even further and suggest that Ann, in a culture still unsure about student-mothers, was trying to make her degree relevant to her role as a mother – to provide more ammunition to deal with anyone who had the temerity to challenge the legitimacy of her studies.

Focusing on these aspects highlights a key dimension to the construction of knowledge – the *social* dimension. The roles, relationships, interactions and power (or lack of it) we enjoy, in whatever context we do our learning, have a direct if often subtle influence on how and what we learn. As a consequence of this, the social arrangements for learning (often institutionalised in organisations such as universities) affect the way we think. Not only is learning a process rather than an event, it is specifically a *social* process.

The social dimension to thinking and learning is evident also in the way psychological research reports are written. When psychologists write books and articles about their theories and research, they do not just describe what they believe or what they did, they actively try to encourage the reader to agree with their arguments. As a consequence, scholarly writing in psychology can be said to be **rhetorical** (Billig, 1987), that is, it is constructed to *persuade*. 'Rhetorical' in this context does not mean that psychologists speak or write in flowery or dramatic terms but rather that scientific accounts are always more than just reporting, they are *trying to argue a case*. Part of this rhetorical approach involves the writer anticipating the kind of counterarguments the reader might make against the writer's claims (and then possibly showing how the counterarguments can be dealt with). To some extent, experiments in psychology are designed the way they are precisely to rule out possible criticisms by others. For example, in clinical research, the use of a set of subjects who do not get the trial antidepressant drug (sometimes called a 'control' group) allows psychologists to deal with the potential argument that the improvement in mood would have happened anyway. Thus psychological writings often reflect the fact that they will be mulled over by others and are themselves part of ongoing debates and discussions. In this way learning can be seen to be a social process, not just for individual students but for entire academic communities. When we are 'thinking psychologically', we are not thinking in isolation but as a part of previous, current and anticipated debates in which thousands of psychologists and the psychological community collectively are involved.

Thinking as personal development

Thinking is such a strange phenomenon. In itself it does nothing and yet without it nothing would get done. There is no aspect, good or bad, of human civilisation that is not a reflection of some form of human thinking.

Since the 1960s we have been encouraged to 'get in touch with our feelings' and this advice, stripped of its west coast pseudo-humanist pop psychology, is worth paying heed to – too many relationships freeze over because one partner or the other has repressed or denied their own feelings. But what about getting in touch with our *thinking*? We spend all our lives thinking. Thinking what to do next and what we have done (and what we did not do). We face all kinds of practical problems as individuals and all kinds of challenges as a planet, and thinking is the first step of most solutions. To consider the parallel with feeling a little more: we can all imagine how barren life would be if we never experienced the emotions of joy, surprise, love (and disappointment and jealousy). We would all, I think, consider ourselves substantially incomplete in some significant way if we did not develop our emotional maturity or achieve our full emotional potential (however defined). But is it not also the case with thinking? Should we not also reckon our time in life by the range of forms of *thought* we experience as well as the forms of feeling? And is not cognitive as well as emotional maturity a form of human potential worth developing?

And of course, even if there were a sense in which we felt that emotional development was more important than cognitive maturity, we should remember that feeling and thinking are not necessarily best thought of as two opposing or even separate modes of experience. Our feelings are often a consequence of the conclusions from our thinking, and our feelings in turn motivate some kinds of thought rather than others. Nelson-Jones (1996) for example has advocated what he calls 'pragmatic existentialism' – an approach to personal development which puts thinking at the forefront of coping with life's emotional challenges.

Thinking is central not only to our personal development but also to our participation in society. Thinking has taken over as the new craft skill. In our post-industrial, educated, bureaucratic societies the premium skills are no longer hand skills but *mind* skills. Those who are masters of categorisation, summarising, comparison and imaginative speculation will have more options than those who 'merely' cut, carve or sew. We live in a *cognitive* society which expects thinking skills more than at any other time in the past. And we should never forget that anyone who does not do their own thinking should not be surprised when others start doing it for them.

SUMMARY

In this chapter we have discussed the aim of this book and its general orientation. The aim is to help you think more creatively, more critically and more analytically about psychology, its theories, assumptions and methods. The book takes as its point of departure the idea that individuals construct their own understanding of knowledge in a social context. It advocates diversity and eclecticism in making sense of psychology. The current dominance of logical positivism is seen as being unnecessarily restrictive and other perspectives will be reviewed where they seem to have something interesting to say. We will cover general principles in Part I and then apply them in Part II. Each chapter is structured to support learning and concludes with recommendations for future reading and websites.

KEY TERMS

Behaviourism ■ Epistemological pluralism
Epistemology ■ Logical positivism
Rhetorical ■ Schemata

FURTHER READING

Richard Nelson-Jones' 1996 book *Effective Thinking Skills* (London: Cassell) is a practical guide to taking responsibility for decision making in our lives based on ideas from psychology about thinking clearly and avoiding various rationalisations and biases. The links with existential philosophy are smoothly done and it addresses the emotional and intellectual dimensions with equal thoroughness, a trick not often or easily accomplished.

USEFUL WEBSITES

Each chapter in this book has specific references to websites relevant to that chapter. However, in this chapter some psychology sites of general relevance are introduced.

American Psychological Association (APA)

http://www.apa.org/

The official site of the professional organisation for American psychologists. Interesting in many ways but it has a useful section for students. Various APA policy documents are to be found here.

British Psychological Society (BPS)

http://www.bps.org.uk

A modest but effective site. University subscribers have access to some BPS journals from here. Extracts from the organisation's monthly magazine, *The Psychologist*, are available too.

Australian Psychological Society (APS)

http://www.psychsociety.com.au/

Any organisation which has as its motto 'Good thinking!' just had to be included here.

Canadian Psychological Association

http://www.cpa.ca/

Available in French and English.

American Psychiatric Association
http://www.psych.org
A classy, professional and frequently updated site covering issues affecting American psychiatry.

Colegio Oficial de Psicólogos / Spanish Psychological Association
http://www.cop.es/english/English.htm
The official site of the Spanish Psychological Association. Many of the documents and news items are in English.

Today in Psychology
http://www.cwu.edu/~warren/today.html
A fun, interactive site which enables you to submit any date in the calendar and be told almost instantly which event relevant to psychology happened on that date over the past 100 years or so. Find out which famous psychologist you share your birthday with from their database.

Constructivism Index of Papers
http://carbon.cudenver.edu/~mryder/itc_data/constructivism.html
A useful starting point for anyone wanting to pursue the ideas of constructivism further.

Plomsky's Guide to Writing Research Reports
http://www.uwsp.edu/acad/psych/apa4b.htm
A definitive guide to writing research reports following approved American Psychological Association rules on referencing and format. The good thing about guides like this on the web is that you can use keywords to search for the paragraph you need. There are also 'hyperlinks' which help you jump through the document to find what you want.

Electronic Reference Formats Recommended by the American Psychological Association
http://www.apa.org/journals/webref.html
This web page explains in detail how you should cite web pages if you refer to them. You should find this useful if you want to refer to information you find from the web pages mentioned in this book.

The Thinking Psychologically Website
http://www.patrickmcghee.co.uk
A website devoted to supporting and enhancing your understanding of this book. You will find links to all the websites mentioned, worksheets, quizzes and much more.

The Science of Thinking, and Thinking about Science

CHAPTER OVERVIEW

This chapter begins the process of putting together our Part I toolkit in preparation for the analysis of theories and studies in different areas of psychology in Part II. We begin by asking what research into thinking generally might tell us about how to think about psychology itself. We shall see that different psychologists have conceived of thinking in many different ways. What, if anything, each of these approaches can offer us will be critically examined. This chapter also introduces a key distinction between analytic ('logical') thinking and synthetic ('creative') thinking which will help us to put the positivist model of experimental research in context. We shall consider the nature of analogies in some depth, as they are commonly encountered in many areas of psychology and need to be thought about very carefully. We conclude the chapter with a review of some of the major developments in the philosophy of science over the past 80 years, in order to identify useful constructs with which to assess and comprehend psychological research practice later. In particular, we shall see what developments there have been since the original logical positivist formulation of the 1920s and 30s was embraced by behaviourists.

LEARNING OBJECTIVES

By the end of this chapter you should be able to:

- Give examples of the ways in which Sternberg and Billig have approached the study of thinking, and indicate the applicability of such approaches to the study of psychology itself
- Define and distinguish analytic and synthetic thinking and associated concepts
- Outline and illustrate what analogies are and how they can be assessed

---

LEARNING OBJECTIVES (cont'd)

■ Describe the main developments in the philosophy of science since logical positivism, and demonstrate their relevance to contemporary psychology

■ Explain Popper's notion of disconfirmation and how it differs from Ayer's notion of verifiability

■ Describe and illustrate Kuhn's idea of a paradigm and explain its relation to 'normal science'

■ Outline Feyerabend's concept of 'epistemological anarchy' and what its implications might be for psychology

---

Psychological models of thinking

Before we go any further into the business of thinking about psychology, we would do well to consider the psychology of thinking. What have psychologists said about the nature of thinking? Can we learn anything about how to think about *psychology* from their observations and studies? While many different psychologists have analysed everyday thinking in ways which would be helpful in the process of thinking about psychology, we shall limit ourselves to two. One, Robert Sternberg, is a researcher working within a traditional logical positivist (scientific) context, the other, Michael Billig, is more interested in culture, language and philosophy. Both provide food for thought regarding how we can think about psychology.

Sternberg: thinking as problem solving

Sternberg (1995) suggested that there are seven steps in successful problem solving: problem recognition, definition of problem, strategy construction, representation of information about the problem, resource allocation, monitoring and evaluation. Table 2.1 illustrates this framework in relation to:

1. a student revising for an exam
2. a psychologist preparing to study bullying
3. a critical thinker reading psychological research about divorce among the elderly.

We can see that there do appear to be similarities across the three domains.

Sternberg's work provides a useful initial starting point for organising our thoughts about learning as a problem-solving activity, where the learner is actively assembling, assessing and applying information, while constantly monitoring processes and outcomes. We shall see later in this chapter, however, that scientists are not always as rational in solving scientific problems as Sternberg seems to suggest.

Table 2.1 Sternberg's problem-solving cycle applied to exam preparation, scientific research programmes and critical thinking in psychology

Step	As applied to student preparing for an exam	As applied to scientific research	As applied to thinking about psychology
1. Problem recognition	Calendar reminds student that child psychology exam is six weeks away and he doesn't know enough about Piaget	Specific cases of children being bullied at school hit headlines	Theories of relationship dissolution do not seem to explain why older couples get divorced
2. Definition of problem	There is a section in the exam on Piaget which has to be passed	How can psychologists intervene in schools to minimise or eradicate bullying?	Develop a critique of existing relationship dissolution theories
3. Strategy construction	Get relevant information from books, journals and lectures about Piaget's theory	Identify possible effective interventions, apply and assess them (for example review attempts by other psychologists elsewhere and interview teachers at schools with a low rate of bullying)	Identify all relevant theories of relationship dissolution Identify the assumptions used about relationships Assess extent to which these assumptions are in fact more applicable to young and middle-aged couples
4. Representation of information about the problem	Exam questions in the past have tended to ask for comparisons of Piaget with one other theorist	Which kinds of schools seem to have the worst problem? What is the set of factors identified as affecting bullying?	Draw up a table listing theories in column 1 and assumptions about different aspects of relationships in subsequent columns
5. Resource allocation	60% of revision time to be spent getting to grips with Piaget 10% of revision time doing extra revision on Freud 30% of revision time allocated to carrying out systematic comparisons	One researcher reviews previous research One researcher visits low bullying schools Two researchers design practical, ethically acceptable programmes based on identified strategies Two researchers design ways of randomly allocating participating schools to different intervention programmes	30% of available time on assembling articles and books describing the relationship dissolution theories 40% of available time reading and making notes on theories 20% of time constructing table of assumptions 10% of time writing up conclusions for possible project proposal

(cont'd)

Table 2.1 Sternberg's problem-solving cycle applied to exam preparation, scientific research programmes and critical thinking in psychology (cont'd)

Step	As applied to student preparing for an exam	As applied to scientific research	As applied to thinking about psychology
6. Monitoring	Is the strategy delivering information on Piaget?	Do the participating schools remain happy to be involved in the study?	Are new insights being generated about the existing literature?
	Is the strategy sufficiently focused on comparisons?	Are the different programmes being implemented properly?	Is there a clarity emerging of the overall picture (rather than further confusion)?
	Is the strategy compatible with other resource allocation demands (for example passing Cognitive Psychology exam)?	Is the project spending money faster or slower than expected?	Is the original problem definition still the most useful one?
7. Evaluation	Do I feel better prepared for the exam? Does the tutor feel I am better prepared for the exam? Do I pass the exam?	Do statistical comparisons indicate that there are differences between schools with a programme and those without?	How well does the new theory account for existing data? How empirically testable is the new theory?
	Is the strategy transferable to other problems?	Do statistical comparisons indicate that there are differences in the degree of effectiveness among anti-bullying programmes?	Does the new theory help us understand divorce among the elderly better?
	Are there unexpected gains from the strategy (for example good grounding for Year 2 Lifespan Psychology module)?		
Return to Step 1 with the output from Step 7	Revision for next exam to be planned better	Results become starting point for next study	Theory becomes object of analysis and critique for next researcher

---

THINK IT THROUGH

Draw up a table similar to Table 2.1 above but replace the headings in the main columns with 'recent practical problem', 'recent emotional problem' and 'recent academic problem'. Try completing the boxes for all three types of problems and all seven steps of problem thinking in relation to how *you* thought through a recent problem in your life. Do there appear to be similarities in your thinking style at each stage? Do you seem to have problems at the same stage across different domains? Consider whether thinking more clearly about a *particular* step might help your *overall* problem-solving effectiveness.

Billig: thinking as rhetoric

Michael Billig, an English psychologist influenced by **social constructionism**, suggests that one useful way of making sense of thinking is to see it as an inner form of 'argumentation'. He does not suggest that we are always experiencing some inner conflict of the kind suggested by Freud but rather that we internalise the external world of dispute, persuasion and pursuing alternatives as a basis for thinking. Billig is concerned to demonstrate that the approach of cognitive psychology to thinking is flawed because it is incomplete. For example, he argues that most research on perception emphasises how we categorise incoming data into predefined categories according to category membership rules (for example 'if it barks, it's a dog'). This is a one-sided view for Billig because it ignores the way we *split* categories, *bend* cognitive rules and *create* new categories.

> The categorisation approach gives the impression of telling only one half of the story, for in stressing the constraints of schemata, it ignores the capacity for transcendence. Human thinking may express prejudice, but tolerance is not an impossibility; we can shut unpleasant truths from our mind, but we can also face up to them; we may behave like timid rule-following bureaucrats, but rule-creation, rule-breaking and rule bending can also occur; we may process information but that is not all we can do. …What is needed, therefore is… putting the other side to the categorisation approach. In this way the one-sided image can be opened out into a two-sided one. (Billig, 1987: 130)

Billig argues that many ideas from Greek philosophy still have a lot to teach contemporary psychologists, both in terms of how we understand the business of theorising, researching and publishing but also in terms of offering substantive ideas about the workings of the mind itself. Among the many modern applications of ancient ideas that Billig pursues is the exploration of Protagaras' so-called reversal maxim. This states that 'in every question there [are] two sides to the argument exactly opposite to one another' (Billig, 1987: 41). Possibly the most significant and far-reaching application of Billig's work is the application of this maxim to the idea of categorisation in cognitive psychology. The usual assumption is simply that when we process perceptual input, we 'place' information about different objects or persons into the same category. For example, if we see a leather chair we categorise it cognitively as falling into the *general* category 'chair' and therefore expect that object (the leather chair) to possess various properties that we know chairs in general have. As Billig says, there is no doubt that our minds do this sort of thing all the time and interaction with the world would be impossible if we did not. But Billig's point is that cognitive psychology only emphasises this kind of cognitive processing and generally ignores the reverse. Specifically, cognitive theories emphasise categorisation at the expense of **particularisation**. Particulari-sation is the cognitive process of treating some perceptual stimulus as an individual case and not a member of a category (for example 'this chair which has just been delivered is not the same one as I saw in the shop and paid for yesterday').

The dialectic processes of categorisation and particularisation are to a very large degree mediated by language, which as well as providing a means for naming dissimilar objects by the same name, also provides the means of differentiating between broadly similar objects. Arguments in courts, religious circles, politics and most certainly in academic psychology often depend upon either side's ability to present a specific case as a member of a category (for which rules on treating that category exist) or as a special case (to which the rules do not apply).

Billig's work alerts us to the need to think rhetorically. That is to say, we need to interpret the claims we read about, not just as statements about the way the world is but as attempts at persuading us about a particular way of understanding the world. General assertions about human behaviour can, and should, be turned on their head. This may seem intellectually perverse but Billig is suggesting that psychology is perhaps essentially an enterprise in creating understandings about the world rather than discovering essential truths about it. In this kind of context, every understanding put forward will emphasise one aspect at the expense of another. Billig's view is that we should continually assert the undeclared. It is rather like the second law of Newton's physics – 'for every action there is an equal and opposite reaction' – only here it is 'for every assumption about the world, there is an equal and opposite counter-assumption'. It is not so much that one of these assumptions is right and the other is wrong, nor even indeed that they are 'both right'. It is rather the case that the *awareness of this dual reality* is 'right', the *processes* of engaging with a phenomenon, intellectually or practically, that is 'right'. Billig's work puts this idea, the process of *contradiction*, at the centre of psychological epistemology and methods.

The rational individualistic approach of Sternberg and the rhetorical social approach of Billig represent two very different sets of ideas about how psycholo-gists deal with research puzzles. Sternberg emphasises structure and logic, while Billig emphasises creative argumentation and contradiction. We shall see examples of both approaches throughout this book.

Thinking about psychology

Modes of thought

It useful to distinguish between at least two different modes of thought – the **analytic** and the **synthetic**. The analytic mode of thought involves drawing and

Table 2.2   Features of analytic and synthetic thinking

Analytic thinking	Synthetic thinking
Structured	Fluid
Rigorous	Expansive
Constrained	Unconstrained
Convergent	Divergent
Formal	Informal
Critical	Diffuse
Evaluative	Creative
Problem solving	Problem finding
Deductive	Inductive
Vertical	Lateral
Closed	Adventurous
Conventional	Imaginative
Algorithm	Heuristic
Literal	Analogical/metaphorical
Cautious	Risky
Aims to test proposed ideas	Aims to generate new ideas
Syntactical	Semantic
Seeks to be valid	Seeks to be informative

assessing logical inferences, while synthetic thinking is more free-flowing and imaginative. Nickerson *et al.* (1985) suggested that many of the differences between theorists interested in teaching effective thinking were more apparent than real, simply because each theorist was using different terminology for what were largely the same phenomena. Table 2.2 lays out some of the connections made by Nickerson *et al.* (1985: 50), along with additional pairs of terms that you might come across elsewhere.

This framework provides a useful way of making links between different types of ideas about thinking that we might come across. We now need to look at these two modes of thinking in more detail. After initially considering the logical and deductive forms of analytic thinking, we shall consider some recent developments in the role of synthetic thinking in research.

Analytic mode of thinking

Analytic thinking is the logical, structured and rigorous mode of thought which characterises, for example, the deduction of formal proofs in logic or the systematic testing of claims in mathematics. Generally speaking, analytic thinking and reasoning involve the application of general formal principles to a specific case in order to demonstrate the truth or falsity of some claim about that case. Thus deciding if an individual is or is not a schizophrenic involves (supposedly) the application of strict tests by a psychiatrist on symptoms in order to determine whether or not that individual should be classified as 'schizophrenic'. In this example, the application of the general rules about diagnosing schizophrenia allows a decision to be made one way or another about this particular case. Similarly, a good experiment is designed to allow the researcher to rule out all incorrect explanations and this is done through the application of deductive logic. The application of analytical rules, while sometimes long-winded, is usually designed to get a definitive answer one way or another. Such rules are referred to as algorithms, which are procedures for getting to a valid logical outcome eventually (as opposed to heuristics that get us to an *adequate* answer fairly quickly).

We shall return to how the analytic, deductive mode of thinking is used in psychology later, when we discuss the idea of the hypothetico-deductive method. We should note here, however, the relationship between analytic thinking and philosophies of science. Analytic thinking has historically been seen as the *only* respectable mode of thought for scientists. As a result, psychology, from the 1920s until the present day, has tried to stick to these rules of logical thought when constructing theories, designing experiments, testing hypotheses and carrying out statistical tests on results. The standards of proof and evidence implied by analytic thinking have been used to define 'proper psychology' and distinguish it from the more 'woolly', unscientific approaches of psychoanalytic, humanistic and sociological forms of psychology. Qualitative research in particular has been, and still is, criticised on the grounds that it is not scientific enough, not systematic enough, too subjective and too speculative.

Whatever the force of these criticisms, we need to be aware that they are essentially criticisms to the effect that qualitative research does not meet the standards of a particular mode of thought, namely the logical analytic mode of thought. Whether that mode is the *appropriate* one from which to draw on for criteria to assess qualitative research is something we shall return to at various points throughout this book. For now we will note only that scientific thinking involves a particular mode of reasoning about data, discovery and theory. Supporters of the scientific approach to psychology argue that the analytic mode of reasoning is the only valid kind of reasoning (and anything which does not make sense in those terms should be rejected). However, others argue that there are other modes of thinking and reasoning which do make qualitative research valid.

Synthetic mode of thinking

It is sometimes thought that scientific thinking should involve only the characteristics of the 'analytic' column. The popular image of the scientist is that of someone who is highly disciplined and unwilling to think outside well-defined rules and boundaries. However, good science, and for that matter good scholarship of any kind, requires creative thinking just as much as it requires formal thinking. It is the imaginative leaps carried out by Copernicus, Albert Einstein or Stephen Hawking that set them apart from their merely excellent peers. In psychology today, however, there is still a strong emphasis on analytic thinking as the defining quality of rigorous and proper psychology. Much of this emphasis comes from the enduring influence of logical positivism, even though behaviourism, which introduced it to psychology, has effectively been abandoned by mainstream researchers.

The synthetic mode of thought is characterised by fluid, expansive and divergent thinking styles. We are all capable of this way of thinking but it is not a form of thinking routinely encouraged or trained in all disciplines in universities. This is partly because it is seen as an *inferior* relation to analytic thought (not true) and because, to the extent that it is seen as important, it is seen as *unteachable* (also untrue). Students are often uneasy when encouraged to be imaginative and original in their thinking about psychology. Surely it has *already* all been said and done? Surely it is *presumptuous* to forward my ideas as better than those that have gone before? The first response to this is that imagination and originality can be worthwhile even if done on a small scale. It is perfectly valid for example to observe that a certain theory in psychology has not been tested in children, cross-culturally or in a non-urban sample and that such a study might yield interesting conceptual insights. Such an observation is a modest contribution to the sum of knowledge in psychology, but contribution it is. Another aspect is that there are an incalculable number of novel *links* between topics, concepts and theories that are just waiting to be made. Additionally, all sorts of methods can be applied to all sorts of research problems but in practice research methods and their topics go hand in hand. Thinking about the ways in which alternative methodologies can throw light on existing problems is an important aspect of synthetic thinking in psychology.

The logical positivist philosophers were convinced that the analytic dimension was the important part of doing science. For that reason, research methods courses today are much more likely to contain sessions on structured, deductive reasoning for *testing* hypotheses than they are to contain sessions on imaginative, lateral, creative thinking for *generating* hypotheses. More recently, however, some psychologists have recognised that synthetic thinking is a key component to theory building in the discipline. In particular, William McGuire has proposed a detailed scheme for encouraging and organising discussion in psychology about synthetic thinking in research. We shall be considering McGuire's ideas for improving synthetic thinking in more detail in Chapter 3. It is important to note, however, that creative thinking should also be subjected to critical evaluation. **Analogies** are examples of creative thinking and are very common in psychology. We turn now to consideration of some of the issues involved in evaluating analogies and related synthetic thinking in psychology.

Analogies – rigorous creative thinking

You have probably come across the idea that the mind 'is like' a computer. This kind of analogical thinking is a particularly important form of synthetic thinking in psychology. Psychologists are often faced with complex, multifaceted and amorphous phenomena that do not always lend themselves to simple explanation in highly structured mathematical or formal ways. As a consequence, psychologists use a whole range of analogies to clarify their thinking about those phenomena. An analogy (or metaphor) is simply an attempt to claim that one thing is like another and that both share common features at a certain level of abstraction. Analogies can be dangerous, however, if they blind us to some aspects of the original phenomenon or lead to us to make silly inferences on the basis of irrelevant parts of the analogy. Analogies can serve many purposes. At the beginning of a research programme, they can serve as an initial orientation to generate hypotheses for preliminary enquiries. Later in the programme, they can serve to bring together disparate findings. For example, there are many different analogies in the area of the development of romantic relationships. Relationships have been characterised variously as contracts, games, journeys and growing organisms (see Baxter, 1992).

There is plenty of research indicating that thinking analogically is a powerful way to develop understanding of particular areas of enquiry (Dagher, 1995; Sandoval, 1995). In discussing analogies, psychologists often refer to the **target domain** and the **source domain**. The target domain is the problem we are trying to solve or the psychological phenomenon we are trying to explain. The source domain is the area that provides the analogue model. For example, if we are trying to understand the mind (target domain), we might try using the analogy of a computer (source domain). The trick is, of course, in knowing *which* source domain to apply to which target domain. We should remember that an analogy is the *mapping* from a source domain to a target domain. However, we must always think critically about analogies and consider exactly how adequate they are in each case. When assessing the adequacy of an analogy or metaphor we should think about a number of issues (see box below).

Nine things to think about when thinking about analogies

1. Is the target domain clearly defined?

2. Is the source domain clearly defined?

3. Which features of the source domain are being *explicitly* applied to the target domain?

4. Which features of the source domain are *explicitly* not being applied to the target domain?

5. Which features of the source domain are being *implicitly* applied to the target domain?

6. Which features of the source domain are not being *implicitly* applied to the target domain?

7. What specific new features of the target domain are illuminated by the source domain?

8. What kind of relations between (old and new) features of the target domain are implied by the source domain?

9. Taking into account the features of the target domain which are illuminated by the source domain, is the analogy useful?

Research on the identification and use of analogies in everyday reasoning is sparse and generally pessimistic. On the whole, people are poor at spontaneously identifying potential analogies and need to have the key aspects pointed out to them explicitly. In terms of transferring learning from one domain to another, people find it difficult to think beyond the features of the source domain once they have taken it on board (see Garnham and Oakhill, 1994, Ch. 11 for a review). It is probably the case that psychologists are poor at spontaneously spotting interesting analogies to employ and when they are used they are sometimes used rather uncritically. If you are thinking psychologically, you should seek to be open to new analogies but assess their clarity and relevance ruthlessly.

It is time now, however, to review the development of the philosophy of science. Much contemporary psychology still aspires to a traditional model of scientific practice, in particular the model of science developed by logical positivists in the 1920s. However, we will see that the philosophy of science has moved on significantly since then and that there are many viable alternatives to logical positivism.

Philosophies of science

It is important that we review modern philosophies of science, since they have served to set the rules for how psychologists have thought about their research for the past 80 years. In other words, if we want to understand what psychologists think they are doing when they carry out scientific research, we need to understand their philosophies of science. However, as we shall see there are many different models of the scientific endeavour apart from those used by most psychologists. The evolution of ideas about how to do science indicates that some psychological research is still stuck in an earlier framework which has been supplanted by more recent, and arguably more challenging and liberating, models of how to carry out empirical investigations.

Philosophies of science are ultimately concerned with the question of how we should carry out scientific research, given our understanding of the nature of knowledge. Originally, philosophers of science sought to explain how science should be conducted by looking at successful scientists such as Einstein. More recently, the philosophy of science has moved on to consider how most scientists actually work, given the social and practical circumstances of their research.

Reality, knowledge and science

We all have questions about the world around us. What is real and what is fiction? What do we know and how do we know it? How can we find out more about the world? Philosophers analyse these questions intensively. They are interested in the relationship between **ontology** (the study of what *actually* exists), **epistemology** (the study of what *knowledge* is, what we can know and what the limits of knowledge are) and **methodology** (the study of the *ways* in which the world can be studied) (Table 2.3).

Table 2.3 Ontology, epistemology and methodology in physical science and in psychology

	Definition	**Example in physical science**	**Example in psychology**
Ontology	The study of what actually exists	Is space infinite?	Is the mind part of the brain?
Epistemology	The study of the varieties, foundations and limits of what we can know	What are the limits to our understanding of the relationship between time and space?	What kind of limits are there on our understanding of the link between the brain and consciousness?
Methodology	The study of the means of investigating a phenomenon	How should we study time and space?	How should we study the effects of drugs on consciousness?

It should go without saying that the kinds of assumption we make about what exists affects what we consider we can know about it, which in turn affects how we think it is best to study it. Thus our *ontological* assumptions affect our *epistemological* assumptions, which in turn affect our *methodological* assumptions. For this reason, we cannot really choose a methodology arbitrarily since each methodology brings with it epistemological and ontological assumptions, which is why psychoanalysts use couches rather than microscopes, and why behaviourists use Skinner boxes rather than questionnaires. Many philosophers have tried to clarify the possibilities and limitations of science in terms of ontology, epistemology and methodology and it is worth looking at some of the more influential ideas and considering their implications for psychology. This is the area of the philosophy of science and we need to review it.

But what is the point of looking at the philosophy of science? How is it relevant to psychology? It is useful to acquaint ourselves with the philosophy of science for several reasons. First, we can see what a can of worms a question like 'Is psychology a science?' really opens. There are many different definitions about what counts as science and psychology meets the criteria for some of these, but not others. Second, when we come to consider forms of psychology carried out outside the traditional logical positivist mode, we can think more clearly about ways of evaluating those theories and studies if we have a more flexible idea of what science might entail. When we come to review qualitative research later we will see that we have to be so flexible that we might need to rethink our ideas about 'science' altogether.

Comte, Ayer and logical positivism

We need to begin with the philosophy of science known as **positivism** which was originally advocated by the French philosopher Auguste Comte (1798–1857). He argued that humankind had gone through three great phases of searching for understanding: the *theological* (involving a search for God and spirituality), the *metaphysical* (the search for philosophical truths) and now the *positive* or *scientific* phase (involving the search for facts). This third phase involved scientific exploration and the objective collection and judgements of facts, in order that humankind might arrive at 'positive' truths, as distinct from theological or metaphysical truths. Positivism argued that all sciences should depend upon the same foundation of the study of facts about the physical, material world. In that sense, there were no important differences between biology, physics or chemistry – all would use the same methods for discovering positive truths about the real world – the so-called 'unity of science project'. Facts should be collected and summarised through a process of **induction**. If psychology could adopt that method, it could be accepted as a science.

It was with the emergence of the group of philosophers known as the Vienna Circle in the 1920s that positivism became the recipe for psychology to follow in order to produce acceptable science. Renamed as 'logical positivism', there was now an emphasis on theories, and the logical **deduction** of hypotheses to test those theories as well as the collection of facts. The Vienna Circle were heavily influenced by the success of Einstein and other physicists in making significant progress in quantum mechanics and relativity. Psychologists followed the writings of the logical positivists because they believed that these philosophers accurately described what natural scientists did. However, this belief was mistaken – what the logical positivists described is what they *thought* the natural scientists did, when in fact the natural scientists were doing something rather different. What did the logical positivists say was the recipe for real science? The most clear and influential statement of the Vienna Circle's position was given by Alfred Ayer (1910–89, later Sir Alfred) in his *Language, Truth and Logic*, first published in 1936.

The first claim of logical positivists was that a statement can be true only if it is a self-evident analytic, deductive truth of the kind found in mathematics and formal logic (for example $2 + 2 = 4$) or because the statement matches reality precisely. A consequence of this latter point was that statements had to be **verifiable** to be meaningful. For logical positivists, the meaning of a statement *was* simply the conditions under which it could be verified. That is to say, if a statement did not describe an 'experiential proposition' (that is, a sensation or objective sensory event reflecting some feature of reality) then it could carry no significance. The consequence of this position was to render all philosophical speculation about ethics, religion and aesthetics meaningless, since none of these areas had propositions that could be verified by experience. Philosophers, they said, could and should analyse the way language was being used in these areas but there could be no serious attempt to show that any particular ethical, moral or aesthetic position was 'true' or 'false'.

The upshot of all this was that statements such as 'force equals mass times acceleration' were seen to be meaningful because we can agree on how to define 'force', 'mass' and 'acceleration', we can measure them and we can test this proposed relationship. In other words, the statement is verifiable and a science can be built on that basis. However, a statement such as 'truth is beauty, and beauty truth' is not verifiable because we cannot define 'truth' and 'beauty' or measure this relationship. Statements such as 'childhood trauma leads to adult neuroses' were seen to be too vague and imprecise and therefore were not verifiable, and as such had no place in science (so thank you and goodnight, psychoanalysis). By contrast, the statement 'an animal given food pellets for pressing a lever will increase the frequency of lever pressing' just might be verifiable and just might form the basis of a science of behaviour (so, good news for behaviourism then).

Thus in logical positivism there is a fundamental commitment to **empiricism**, that is, checking ideas against the world. Claims that had no empirical consequences were treated as meaningless. Building on this, the logical positivists argued that science should seek to describe the regularities of cause and effect in order to explain the world. All that was required was a theory to be expressed as a set of axioms (that is, basic assumptions) with rules to link these systematically to objective measurements of the real world. An extreme example of this point of view in psychology was the behaviourist research of Clark Hull, who conscientiously constructed elaborate, formal, internally consistent sets of propositions about animal learning (Hull, 1951). The Vienna Circle argued that as long as a discipline formulated claims about the world that could be translated into physical actions to verify those claims, then that discipline could be called scientific and could be counted as a part of the unity of science programme.

Crucially, logical positivism was clear that the scientific theories were theories about *actual* objects, processes and structures in the *real* world. It is through logical positivism that psychology took on this assumption of **realism** which has characterised the discipline ever since. Thus terms such as 'intelligence' and 'attitude' have until recently been taken as referring to real features in the psychological world rather than just useful models.

It is important to note that logical positivists had little or nothing to say about *how* one constructed these axioms or *which* of the many possible testable hypotheses that could be derived from them should be derived. In other words, they had nothing to say about the *process* of discovery per se. They were simply interested in specifying what should be *permitted* as scientific, without trying to recommend which of the permitted ideas should be pursued. In that sense, logical positivism was conservative, more interested in distinguishing between the correct and incorrect forms of science, rather than between the good and the outstanding.

Now, while some disciplines, such as physics, clearly met the logical positivist criteria, other disciplines such as, say, theology, equally clearly did not. But what about psychology? Psychology seemed to be a borderline case. Some areas of psychology, such as physiological psychology, seemed to meet this criterion of verifiability quite comfortably while other areas, such as social psychology, did not. Ever since, psychology has been like one of those wretched towns where an unthinking (or mischievous) government cartographer has drawn a border down the middle of the main street with the effect of turning neighbours into 'foreigners'.

Logical positivism was picked up by the school of psychology which came to be known as behaviourism. Behaviourism emerged in the West with the work of John B Watson, who developed the findings of the Russian physiologist Pavlov into a full psychological theory. Essentially, behaviourism argued that psychology should focus *only* on that which could be observed because only phenomena that could be observed could be measured objectively and reliably.

Objectivity and reliability enabled different observers to check each other's findings and thus laid the foundation for a science of psychology. So physical body movements and actions were in, while feelings, thinking and free will were most definitely out.

Partly for historical and partly for practical reasons, behaviourists worked on animals, observing how they could learn, defining learning as enduring changes in observable behaviour patterns. Behaviourists emphasised how learning depended on forming an association between a significant event and the signals that came before it. Thus a dog would become conditioned to the sound of a bell indicating that food was on its way, as a consequence of the bell being rung each time the food was about to appear. The bell was thus referred to as a conditioned stimulus and the response to the bell was referred to as the conditioned response. Later these principles of associative learning were supplemented by the ideas of B F Skinner, a radical behaviourist who showed, using pigeons, that animals would learn complex, subtle discriminations and behaviour sequences if these behaviours were rewarded correctly. This reinforcement learning emphasised that animals would initially perform behaviours randomly but then repeat those which were rewarded and not repeat those which were not rewarded. For example, a pigeon could be trained to 'learn' the difference between a triangle and a square by being rewarded only when it pecked a lever for a food pellet reward when a square was presented.

That these studies of canine anticipation and avian snacking could become a blueprint for a whole school of psychology that could dominate the discipline for some 40 years seems outrageous now, but dominate it did. And while it was dominating, it laid down the rules for scientific enquiry that shaped the training of several generations of psychologists. The culture of encouraging experiment, control, objective observation, meticulous recording, precise definitions of behaviour and statistical analyses of results which is held in such regard in psychology today can be traced back to the emergence of behaviourism in the US in the 1930s. Not that there is anything wrong with that culture in principle, but it does reflect only one particular way of thinking about mind and behaviour. Behaviourism sought to exclude all other forms of analysis but some psychologists felt that there might be other methods which were more appropriate to other problems. As we shall see, philosophers of science have also come round to the idea of 'horses for courses' in terms of methods.

Popper and disconfirmation

Sir Karl Popper (1902–94) provided the first major attack on logical positivism. He had himself originally been a member of the Vienna Circle but grew to question some of its assumptions. His most famous work is *The Logic of Scientific Discovery* (originally written and published in 1935 in German but more influential after its English translation appeared in 1959) in which he criticised the Vienna Circle and offered his own model of effective scientific thinking.

Popper (1959) argued that the logical positivist emphasis on verifiability only encouraged *confirmation* of theories rather than genuine discovery. In his youth Popper was both an active Marxist and a support worker for Alfred Adler, the psychoanalyst, but rapidly became disillusioned with each in turn. By contrast, he was inspired by the discoveries of Einstein and, more importantly, the open, self-critical attitude to research which Einstein displayed. Popper felt that Marxism and psychoanalysis were deficient as scientific theories in ways in which Einstein's theory of relativity was not. Popper saw these cases as part of the general issue of 'demarcation', that is, what makes some areas of enquiry scientific and others not?

Both Marxism and psychoanalysis could point to all sorts of evidence that was *consistent* with their theories (for example that the poor were exploited and reacted to that exploitation or that some people did have sexually founded neuroses). These theories were thus 'verified' in the traditional logical positivist sense. But Popper realised that consistent evidence did not in itself amount to decisive support for a theory – it was at best merely corroboration. Popper was concerned too about the capacity of Marxism and psychoanalysis to interpret *every* piece of evidence as consistent with its theoretical positions – even those pieces of evidence that appeared on the face of it to be completely inconsistent with them. Popper sought to answer the question: what is it about powerful theories such as Einstein's that sets them apart from the pseudotheories of Marxism and psychoanalysis? Popper answered this question decisively: a good theory is a theory that is capable of making predictions that could in principle be found to be *false*. Thus, Popper argued that **falsifiability** rather than verifiability was the hallmark of good science.

The problem with verifiability for Popper was that any theory can find evidence that is consistent with it. Ostensibly, most theories are initially constructed on the basis of thinking *inductively* – bringing together all known cases and drawing out a generalisation that covers all of them. Simply seeking to verify a theory amounts to finding more of the same. Much more powerful, according to Popper, is to think *deductively* and actively seek disconfirming cases, because just one counterexample will show the problem with the whole theory. If the theory survives this test then it can be seen to be robust and is worthy of continued support. Popper also pointed out another problem with the logical positivist point of view – that theories can make very *cautious* predictions (that possibly several other theories make too) which even when confirmed are not very surprising, and do not help scientific progress. Predictions are better if they predict the *unexpected* and novel, in short, if they make intellectually risky predictions which Popper called **bold conjectures**.

Popper thus identified several problems with logical positivism. He argued that logical positivism was wrong in claiming that theories are constructed by objectively synthesising all the 'facts' that are known to be true ('verified'). For Popper, no facts or search for facts exist without being part of a theory or similar 'motivated' inspection of the world. Further, once hypotheses have been derived from theories, observations of the world which test those hypotheses are not neutral, they are intimately bound up with the theoretical terms that generated them. For the logical positivists, objective measurements were passive sensory experiences, which just happened *to* scientists or their instruments. Popper rejected the idea of theories and observations being either independent from each other or neutral and was much more aware of science as a practical business than the logical positivists. He considered science to be a process of finding the best answer to a problem rather than the sombre application of logic as the Vienna Circle seemed to suggest. For Popper, science should proceed in four stages (Popper, 1958: 32–4, 1963; Thornton, 1997), which we can label as follows:

1. *Logical consistency stage.* At this stage the theory is checked for internal consistency to make sure all the axioms (assumptions) and associated deductions are in place that need to be in place and that there are no logical contradictions between them. This stage is consistent with the logical positivists' ideas on formal specification of theory.

2. *Logical form stage.* At this stage the scientist should separate out those propositions which have empirical consequences from those which do not. Again still largely consistent with logical positivists.

3. *Comparison stage.* This is a radically new stage. Here the new theory is compared with existing theories which attempt to cover the same phenomena. If the new theory, assuming all its propositions to be true, explains the same or less known facts than the existing theory, *then the new theory should be abandoned.* This makes sense – if there is already another theory which does all that the new theory does (and more), the new theory has no contribution to make to scientific progress. For Popper, the greater the empirical content (that is, the wider the range of phenomena explained) the better the theory is.

4. *Empirical testing stage.* At last the theory can be tested. But which propositions of the theory should we test? Logical positivists had nothing useful to say about this. Every proposition was part of the logical architecture of a theory. Popper went beyond this, however. He argued that everything else being equal, the hypothesis we should test is the one which is the *least likely* to be true. This seems perverse but is entirely consistent with Popper's general ideas about informativeness. If a prediction that can be derived from a theory which seems to contradict all other theories (and also our general 'background knowledge') *does in fact turn out to be supported by empirical test,* then our theory will have been shown to be extremely informative. In any event, an empirical examination (for example an experiment) needs to be set up in order to show that the prediction is supported or not supported by the data. If the predictions are supported then the theory is corroborated (not 'verified'). But all we have in a corroborated theory is a *best* theory, not a true theory. And it is only best until some facts emerge which are inconsistent with the theory or a better theory comes along. What happens if the prediction is *not* supported? According to the logical positivists, we should abandon the entire theory. Not so, argues Popper. If a prediction is found to be unsupported the theory is falsified *but it is still our best guess* so we should hold on to it until a better theory comes along (as a better theory surely will).

THINK IT THROUGH

From Popper's point of view which of the following predictions are likely to be *informative* if found to be accurate?

- The sun will rise tomorrow
- Some drugs are bad for you
- Some drugs are good for you
- Some people can communicate with each other via ESP

Popper's ideas have been immensely influential, both in terms of philosophical discussion on the nature of scientific knowledge and its influence on practising scientists. For the first (and arguably only) time in the history of the philosophy of science, scientists actually read philosophy of science books and believed the ideas were genuinely useful to them.

Nevertheless, Popper's ideas have not gone without criticism. In particular, it has been argued that scientists do not in practice abandon their theories even after they have been falsified and a better theory has come along. The reason why scientists are able to get away with this is because they propose 'auxiliary hypotheses' to account for the falsification of some 'minor' parts of the overall theory. An example of an auxiliary theory in psychoanalysis would be if there were a claim that people who experience trauma and associate it with dogs will grow up to fear dogs. If it turns out that there are a significant number of people who associate trauma with dogs but grow up to *like* dogs, this would seem to blow the theory out of the water. However, the imaginative psychoanalyst might propose an auxiliary hypothesis along the lines of 'some people with fears overreact by denying and embracing them' and thereby salvage the theory (well, salvage it among people of a gullible disposition at any rate). These kinds of auxiliary hypotheses insulate the main theory from falsification since they can always act as a buffer against damaging data.

What are the implications of Popper's ideas for how we think about psychological research? Most studies in psychology do construct hypotheses which in principle can be found to be false. If there is a prediction, for example, that training helps performance on intelligence tests, and if the experiment provides training for one group of subjects but not another, and if those two groups are equivalent in other relevant features and abilities, in principle the results of the experiment could go either way. The trained group *might* perform better on the test or *they might not*. The hypothesis is thus capable of being disconfirmed. The difficulty arises in psychology when it comes to considering theories rather than hypotheses, that is, the general model which inspires particular hypotheses. Theories that are clearly thought out with well-defined theoretical constructs that are linked to each other in coherent ways will generate clear-cut hypotheses. Theories that are internally inconsistent are incapable of being disconfirmed, since whatever the result of an experiment one part of the theory will probably seem to get it right. When we look at Freud's theory of personality in more detail in Chapter 12, we will be thinking further about falsifiability and theory.

Kuhn and revolution

The way in which scientists *actually* carry out research rather than how they *should* carry out research became the main focus of analyses of science after Popper. In particular, the work of Thomas Kuhn (1922–96) highlighted the reluctance of scientists to modify or abandon theories when they fail to receive empirical corroboration. Kuhn contended that scientific progress could not be understood as a purely rational process (Kuhn, 1962). Rather than a steady accumulation of knowledge, there are, argued Kuhn, peaceful interludes punctuated by violent intellectual revolutions. These peaceful interludes were characterised by what Kuhn termed **normal science,** during which scientists shared a common framework for understanding and tackling problems which Kuhn labelled a **paradigm**. In psychology, the dominance of cognition and the model of the computer as a way of 'seeing' the mind could, for example, be called a paradigm. Similarly, the methods and assumptions of behaviourism in the 1950s and 60s could also be said to have formed a paradigm. Kuhn was keen to counter the idea emphasised and encouraged by Popper that scientists were imaginative, sceptical, open to new ideas and completely rational.

According to Kuhn, most scientists are conservative, seeking to apply existing methods and theories to new problems rather than seeking to develop new and better theories. Kuhn argued that when data emerge which seem inconsistent with an established and respected theory that is part of a dominant paradigm, the scientist does not abandon or revise the theory (as Popper says they should do) but rather finds a reason to dismiss the *data* as an artefact or as coming from an unreliable source. It is only when the inconsistent data build up and some new radical paradigm is offered that there is a revolution in science, with more and more scientists abandoning the older paradigm in favour of the new one. The old paradigm is never decisively shown to be wrong but simply withers away as fewer and fewer experiments are carried out within its frame of reference. Within psychology, the behaviourist paradigm dominated from 1930 to 1960 until the new cognitive paradigm effected an intellectual revolution.

What might be the implications of Kuhn's ideas for how we think about psychological research? Kuhn's work suggests that the relationship between evidence and theory is framed by the overarching paradigm in which the research is carried out. If we are thinking about a study and its implications, we would do well to consider whether the theory is part of a long established paradigm which is taken to be above criticism or a newly emerging paradigm which is still trying to gain new converts. In the former case, there is likely to be an undue conservatism when inconsistent results are discovered, while in the latter case there might well be a reckless enthusiasm to champion the new revolutionary framework, whatever its failings. Kuhn in his writings often made the point that younger researchers, who have not yet been 'indoctrinated' into the existing paradigms, were the ones most likely to see its faults and to suggest new paradigms. By contrast, more established researchers tend to have extended commitments to older paradigms. Consideration of the paradigm to which a theory belongs will help us to make sense of the battlelines and alert us to the kinds of assumption being made by both detractors and advocates. For further discussion on how paradigms can influence the course of science in psychology, see the discussion in Chapter 5 on 'institutional threats to validity'.

Feyerabend and epistemological anarchy

Paul Feyerabend (1924–94) was one of the most controversial philosophers of science to have been writing since the war. Influenced initially by both the logical positivists and Popper (whom he studied under in London in the 1950s), Feyerabend was to offer increasingly more radical, alternative models of scientific enquiry throughout his career (Preston, 1997). Feyerabend gradually rejected his original commitment to realism, preferring instead a form of **relativism**, which emphasised that in principle all forms of theories are worthwhile. Feyerabend argued that scientists should go beyond Popper's simple 'comparison' stage where a small number of theories are carefully compared with each other to assess their relative informativeness. In particular, Feyerabend argued for **theoretical pluralism**, whereby scientists should be encouraged to construct, defend and test *as many different theories about the same thing as possible*. However, Feyerabend rejected the idea that theories could be compared with each other in any formal or logical way, as Popper seemed to imply. This arises for Feyerabend as a consequence of his concept of **incommensurabilty**, which states that no theories that are genuinely different can be meaningfully compared with one another. Theories that have different theoretical terms have no common foundation on which an independent assessment can be built. Unlike the positivists but agreeing with Popper, Feyerabend argued that theories give meaning to facts, not vice versa (Preston, 1997).

For Feyerabend, logical positivism was too cautious and did not really explain how scientists made important discoveries, while Popper's falsificationism was fine as far as it went but for him was not radical enough. Kuhn's conception of revolutionary change made sense but did not fully explain what was necessary for progress in science. What, Feyerabend was asking, are the rules of scientific enquiry that make scientific progress likely? In 1975, in his book *Against Method,* Feyerabend made the final break with all the other philosophies of science which had gone before. In *Against Method* he finally answered the question about what the rules are for scientific progress – *there are no rules for scientific progress* – anything goes. There may be tactical principles that are often relied upon but they all have exceptions. As far as Feyerabend was concerned, science, far from being unified by method, has any number of methods for different types of problem. Thus Feyerabend disputes that there is any systematicity in scientific research that can be turned into a *general* methodological procedure for all science. If scientists had tried to follow any one set of rules, they would not have made the progress they have. In rejecting the application of any single method as correct above all others, Feyerabend happily declares himself an advocate of **epistemological anarchy**.

It would be wrong to interpret Feyerabend as arguing that all techniques of enquiry are equally good or bad in any context. Rather he is saying that no method should be ruled out if it *works*. He is concerned to avoid any one system being taken as the only or best universal system of scientific enquiry, arguing that such an approach would inhibit progress in science.

In his very late writings, some of which have been published posthumously, Feyerabend turned to broader themes including the significance of science in society, arguing that science is no better or worse than any other form of knowledge. He argues that 'science' itself is a hotchpotch of many practices and activities, some of which are logical and objective, while others are cultural, personal and political. Feyerabend ultimately aligns himself with a form of social constructionism (see Chapter 8), emphasising that the 'world' is not singular but plural. Scientific inquiry (or any other kind of inquiry) *constructs* the objects it inquires into, scientific objects such as 'force' or 'mass' are not out there in some directly knowable and independent world but created by the very practice of investigation itself.

What might be the implications of Feyerabend's ideas for how we think about psychological research? Feyerabend's ideas have currently had limited direct influence on psychology but the spirit of 'anything goes' is starting to affect the discipline. Feyerabend's work demystifies the position of logical positivism. If there is no single correct method for doing science for all problems at all times in all places, then every research project has to find its own method. We cannot take for granted the idea that a particular experimental method will always give us the result that will help us to make scientific progress. His incommensurabilty principle forces us to think about each theory in its own terms. His shift from realism to relativism and eventual advocacy of constructionism emphasises the doubts that surround logical positivism's fundamental claim to be studying the real world out there. We should not start supposing that Feyerabend is a licence to do research in just any old way good or bad, that is not what he means by epistemological anarchy. What he means is that the methods and thinking appropriate for progress and understanding in one area of science may not be the right methods for another. He means that the methods for understanding pigeons might not be the right methods for understanding people.

SUMMARY

In this chapter we have looked at the psychology of thinking, the role of analogies in thinking and some basic principles of the philosophy of science. These sources provide ideas that we can apply to theories and studies of psychology in later chapters. Thinking can be seen to be structured *and* rhetorical, algorithmic *and* heuristic, literal *and* analogical. We have also considered the crucial distinction between analytic (formal) and synthetic (creative) thought along with parallel distinctions. This distinction helps us think more clearly about the relationship between 'scientific thinking' and psychological research generally. Analogies are characteristic of scientific and informal thought and, while potentially fruitful, need to be thought about carefully. Philosophies of science clarify why experimental, scientific psychology adopts the practices that it does, but also that there are other models which can be adopted. While according to Popper, all theories would seem to need is to be capable of disconfirmation, Feyerabend's work suggests that there is never a set of rules which guarantee scientific progress in relation to disconfirmation, or anything else.

KEY TERMS

Analogies ■ Analytic ■ Bold conjectures ■ Deduction
Empiricism ■ Epistemolgical anarchy ■ Epistemology
Falsifiability ■ Incommensurability ■ Induction ■ Methodology
Normal science ■ Ontology ■ Paradigm ■ Particularisation
Positivism ■ Realism ■ Relativism ■ Social constructionism
Source domain ■ Synthetic ■ Target domain
Theoretical pluralism ■ Verifiable

=========== **FURTHER READING** ===========

Robert Sternberg is a prolific writer and researcher and has produced many outstanding contributions to the study of thinking and creativity. Two of his most recent books provide exhaustive accounts of recent research and his own distinctive theoretical contributions: Sternberg, R J (ed.) (1998) *Handbook of Creativity* (Cambridge: Cambridge University Press) and Sternberg, R J (1997) *Thinking Styles* (Cambridge: Cambridge University Press).

A recent collection of articles on thinking as a social and cultural phenomenon is Olson, D R and Torrance, N (eds) (1996) *Modes of Thought: Exploration in Culture and Cognition* (Cambridge: Cambridge University Press). The contributors to this volume provide readable analyses of the diversity of different forms of thought in different historical periods and cultural contexts.

George Couvalis (1997) *The Philosophy of Science: Science and Objectivity* is one of the few recent readable texts which manages to cover philosophies relevant to the social as well as the physical sciences.

=========== **USEFUL WEBSITES** ===========

The Karl Popper Web

http://www.eeng.dcu.ie/~tkpw/

An excellent website devoted to Sir Karl Popper covering his life, ideas and publications.

The Ism Book: A Field Guide to the Nomenclature of Philosophy

http://www.monadnock.net/ismbook/

A useful guide to all the 'isms' in philosophical, religious and social theorising. Very user friendly and reliable.

Evaluative and Creative Thinking about Theories in Psychology

CHAPTER OVERVIEW

In the previous chapter we reviewed ideas from the psychology of thinking and the philosophy of science to give us a better view of how we can think about the research process in psychology. We found that there is a range of ways of conceptualising thinking and that theories need to be carefully constructed if they are to be useful. We noted that traditional models of scientific enquiry emphasised logical 'analytic' thinking at the expense of creative 'synthetic' thinking. In this chapter, we will be looking in some detail at what we should be looking for in a good psychological theory and trying to integrate both modes of thinking. We shall identify seven main criteria which should be central to our critical thinking about any theory in psychology. These criteria will be used in future chapters in Part II to help us to evaluate theories in different areas of psychology. In this chapter we shall also be considering how we can *generate* good ideas by applying some suggestions of William McGuire, an experimental social psychologist. We shall think critically about McGuire's principles, however, and ask what assumptions about 'good research' are being used.

LEARNING OBJECTIVES

By the end of this chapter you should be able to:

- Define what is meant by 'theory' in psychological research
- Understand the difference between 'theoretical constructs' and 'relational propositions'
- Distinguish between realist and pragmatic uses of theories
- Identify and apply seven key criteria for assessing theories in psychology
- Outline McGuire's tools for creative thinking about psychological theory
- Identify the assumptions and limitations of McGuire's approach to idea generation

What are theories?

You have probably seen the following sort of courtroom exchange in a film or television drama:

Expert scientific witness:	…and that is why the body turned yellow.
Defence counsel:	Are you absolutely certain about that, Professor Smith?
Expert scientific witness:	Well, no, not certain. But my theory of accelerated discoloration explains why when a body is left…
Defence counsel:	I'm sorry Professor Smith – 'theory'? Did I hear you correctly? Did you say '*theory*?'
Expert scientific witness:	Er…. Yes. My theory…
Defence counsel:	So this is just a *theory*? You are asking this court to accept a *theory*? I thought you had hard facts. Clear evidence. Something more than just a pet *theory*.

'Theory' is sometimes held up to ridicule as some sort of idle conjecture or groundless speculation. In science, including those parts of psychology with aspirations to scientific status, theories (or at least good theories) are, however, much more than this. A theory serves many functions and needs thinking about in several different kinds of ways. In particular, we need to understand the relationship between theory, hypothesis and data.

A **theory** is typically a model which tries to explain in a structured way how some part of the world works. It is not just a description of what happens but a statement of the underlying reason for why it works in the way it does. For example, in physics, Newton's law of gravity did not simply list how different objects are attracted to each other but argued that there was force, a *gravitational* force, whereby objects attract other objects to a greater or lesser extent dependent on their relative masses and the distance between them. We cannot see this force but it can be measured. Newton's theory gained widespread acceptance because it explained all the data available at the time relating to the attractions between objects. The theory also allows new predictions to be generated about new situations involving new objects. Thus this theory explains all previous data, and allows **hypotheses** to be derived about what *would* happen if, say, a comet flew near a planet. The theory has its own specific terms such as 'force' and 'body' and the relationship between them. These terms are in general known as **theoretical constructs** and the relationships between them **relational propositions**. Similarly, in Einstein's theory of relativity there are various theoretical constructs (such as 'mass' and 'energy') and particular ways in which these constructs are linked to one another in the theory – most famously in the equation $E = mc^2$.

In psychology, examples of theoretical constructs might include 'attitude', 'frustration', 'aggression', 'trace', 'depth of encoding', 'learning' and so on. The relational propositions between these might include 'increases', 'decreases', 'requires', 'inhibits', 'controls' and so on. In psychology, the relational propositions typically specify some kind of *causal* relationship between two theoretical constructs and this specification provides the basis for a hypothesis that can be tested in an experiment. Theory then can be thought of as a model, a representation of an underlying process which captures all the important features of that process but only the essential features. Hypotheses are then derived (through deduction) from the proposed model. For example, if a theory states that frustration causes aggression, a hypothesis that could be deductively derived from this might be that a reduction in frustration should lead to a reduction in aggression. This hypothesis could then be tested in an experiment.

Theory spotting in psychology

Not all theories in psychology are called 'theories'. Some are called 'views', 'perspectives', 'models', 'accounts', 'frameworks' or even 'ideas'. These are all generally slightly looser versions of theories, in that they might not explicitly define all their terms or the relationships between them. Nevertheless, all these conceptualisations are trying to provide a general statement about the way some aspect of the psychological world works. The criteria for evaluating them are the same as for theories but the relative importance of each criterion will vary somewhat. In particular, 'views', 'perspectives' and so on may be more appropriately assessed in terms of their *heuristic* value rather than, say, their *clarity of constructs*. Of which more in a moment.

Theories in psychology have traditionally come in all shapes and forms. Some theories are specified, such as theories in physics, in terms of the mathematical relationship between variables, as in Fechner's law which seeks to explain the relationship between stimulus intensity (for example the decibel level of a noise) and experienced sensation (for example rated loudness of that noise). Other theories draw upon striking analogies, such as Eric Berne's game metaphor which suggests that much human social interaction can be best understood by considering it to involve game-like features. Freud's psychoanalytic theory is also full of metaphors and analogies with, for example, the story of Oedipus (who killed his own father) used as a way of illuminating the sexual conflicts in the relationships between father, son and mother. In cognitive psychology, many theories of human information processing since the 1960s have evolved around the idea of considering the mind as though it were a kind of computer.

Theories in psychology are often **reductionist**. By this we mean that theories for phenomena refer to more 'fundamental' or basic levels of the system than the level at which the phenomenon is observed. For example, theories about marital breakdown might refer to the underlying ways in which the couple *think* about each other (possibly specifically in terms of who they think is responsible for bad things happening in their relationship). Thus the *interpersonal* phenomenon of relationship breakdown is explained at the *cognitive* level of thinking processes.

Similarly, in abnormal psychology, theories try to explain mental disorders such as depression by referring to neurochemicals and their operation on neurones. In this case, the *emotional* phenomenon of depression is explained at the *biochemical* level of neurotransmitters. Thus a phenomenon at one level can be, and often is, explained by reference to processes or structures at a lower level. Table 3.1 indicates how different levels of explanations might be used to account for extramarital affairs.

A common form of reductionist explanation in social, developmental and cognitive psychology is to explain processes in terms of constituent subprocesses which go to make up the larger process. In social psychology, processes such as attitude change, altruism and aggressive behaviour have several different types of theories, many of which involve specifying a sequence of shorter underlying processes. For example, Pettigrew (1998) presents a theory of how prejudice is reduced through contact in his intergroup contact theory by specifying the subprocesses of:

1. learning about the other group
2. changing behaviour
3. establishing affective ties
4. reappraising the other group.

In developmental psychology, the processes of intellectual, emotional and moral development are often explained in terms of substages, such as Kohlberg's account of moral development which is broken down into the substages of preconventional, conventional and principled morality. In cognitive psychology, the complex process of reading is broken down into subprocess of letter recognition, word recognition, sentence construction and so on. Since these processes do not always occur in a fixed sequence, theories often specify possible sequences of processes through the use of flow diagrams. An example of this will be discussed in Chapter 7, when we review theory construction in social psychology.

Table 3.1   Levels of explanation in psychology

	Levels of explanation	**Possible explanation at that level for an office affair**
Social level	Sociocultural	Weakening of taboos against infidelity
	Organisational	Groups working in isolation from each other in small units
	Group	Work group cohesiveness leading to trust, dependency and support
Individual level	Interpersonal	Reciprocal sexual attraction between two individuals
	Intrapersonal	Need for self-esteem
	Cognitive	Miscalculation by one of the individuals of risk of getting caught
	Biochemical	Levels of adrenaline during sex

It is possible for a theory in psychology to come from any of these levels. The reductionist tendency is reflected in the preference within psychology to look for explanations at *lower* rather than higher levels in the hierarchy.

The alternative to reductionism is **holism,** whereby explanations are sought in terms of the overarching structures in which the phenomenon to be explained is located. So for example, instead of trying to explain how group conflict might be caused by the tendency of the mind to think in terms of either-or categories, we might try to explain group conflict as a consequence of conflicts of interest within local social structures. Nevertheless, such theories are the exception rather than the rule in psychology, with reductionist theories being much more common.

But what are theories *for*? Theories serve many functions. A good theory will summarise data that are already known and will suggest hypotheses that can be tested through future research. Ultimately, a good theory should provide a clear and concise explanation of why things are they way they are, and not otherwise.

There are two ways of looking at theories. The realist approach asserts that theories are attempts to explain the way the world really is and that the constructs in a theory can and should refer to *actual* things, processes and structures in the world. The alternative, more pragmatic, approach is to consider theories as useful fictions, interesting ways of describing the world that help us make sense of it – even if the things, processes and structures we describe do not necessarily exist and are only constructions to give us a fix on the world around us. The realist approach is perhaps most evident in biopsychology where, for example, neurotransmitters and synapses are considered real things and not just 'ways of thinking' about the brain's biochemistry. The pragmatic approach is more evident in the social and developmental areas, where 'schemata', 'attributions' and 'repression' are seen as ways of thinking about psychological experience rather than necessarily as actual objects or mechanisms. Of course, the pragmatic approach is more consistent with the constructivist view of personal learning and academic research outlined in Chapter 1.

In this context, we can consider how we should think about theories in psychology. There is a set of criteria often applied to theories in psychology which help us assess whether a theory is useful or not. To a large extent, these criteria reflect the concern that theories must relate to data in sensible ways. The reason for this is simply that, if properly collected and used appropriately, data from empirical enquiry can help us to assess theories very effectively and thereby help us to better understand the phenomenon in question.

Thinking critically about theories in psychology

Some theories are better than others, even though in science generally and in psychology in particular it is not the case that some theories can easily be said to be 'true'. We want theories that help us to make sense of the world by helping us to make sense of the data that we can collect about that world. Theories that can do this for us are likely to be complete, concise, clear, coherent, consistent, testable, supported and thought provoking. In other words they should meet the standards implied by the criteria of comprehensiveness, parsimony, clarity of constructs, internal consistency, testability, empirical support and heuristic value.

Table 3.2   Criteria for assessing theories

Criteria	Questions to ask about theories in relation to the criteria
Comprehensiveness	Does the theory cover everything it should?
Parsimony	Is the theory concise?
Clarity of constructs	Is the theory clearly expressed?
Internal consistency	Do all the bits of the theory hang together?
Testability	Can the theory be tested?
Empirical support	Is there evidence to support the theory?
Heuristic value	Does the theory help us think in new and interesting ways?

Comprehensiveness

For a theory to be useful it needs to be comprehensive. However, this depends on what it sets out to explain. A theory of children's reading development cannot be criticised because it does not explain the development of children's conversational ability. However, a theory that tries to explain children's *language* development should say something about conversational development. A theory should try to explain (or at least be consistent with) all the known data about a certain phenomenon and should address all the aspects of the problem. The idea here is that, everything else being equal, a theory which addresses the whole problem is better than a theory which addresses only part of it.

In modern psychology, theories tend to be more specialised and seek only to be comprehensive within a specified domain. For example, while the classical psychodynamic, behaviourist and humanistic theories of personality sought to explain all human personality (and in some cases all human society and culture too), modern theories of personality typically limit themselves to just one dimension such as 'aggressiveness'. However, as we shall see when we discuss personality theories later, theories that set out to be comprehensive often in fact redefine the problem quite narrowly and offer an explanation for a particular definition of 'personality'. Thus our evaluation of how comprehensive a theory is will depend on how satisfied we are with the adequacy of the definition of the problem to be addressed.

Parsimony

It is generally considered that the more concise a theory the better a theory it is. There are several reasons for this.

First of all, if a theory keeps the number of theoretical constructs and relational propositions to the minimum possible while remaining informative, it is easier to see what that theory is claiming and it is easier to derive hypotheses to test it. Having collected data about the hypotheses, it will be easier to work out the implications for the theory if it is specified concisely rather than with some elaborate Byzantine mess of endless propositions, subpropositions, qualifications, alternatives and ever multiplying new constructs.

Second, the principle of parsimony also reflects the idea that the simpler theory is probably the right one (everything else being equal). Nature *seems* to be efficient and elegantly economical. Of course this idea might be entirely false. Nature (human or physical) might not be simple at all, it might be complex. Indeed it might be, well, *unnecessarily* complex. Or at least it might seem to us to be so, in terms we might never be able to comprehend. There are some fundamental ideas in biology in relation to evolution suggesting that simpler structures are probabilistically more likely to evolve than functionally equivalent, more complex structures. So maybe simplicity is a good bet. But what about gravity? Newton's theory of gravity is much simpler than Einstein's but Einstein's explains more phenomena.

And what of thoughts, emotions, learning and personality? Just how complex do our theories of these need to be? This is not the sort of question we can answer in general terms. Much will depend on what is already known at the time the theory is constructed. And how do we *assess* parsimony? Do we *count* the number of theoretical constructs and relational propositions? Some concepts can be parsimoniously expressed, yet what they refer to is complex and possibly excessively so. For example, Guildford's model of the structure of intelligence could be described as a three-dimensional array representing the five operations, six contents and five products of intelligence (Guildford, 1956). But this structure implies 150 building blocks of intelligence. Is this model parsimonious (because we can describe it concisely) or unparsimonious (because it is a concise description of 150 factors)? The answer to this question depends on the reason for asking it. If we are interested in parsimony for the sake of deducing hypotheses, Guildford is parsimonious, but if we are considering the overall economy of the model, then we would have to say that, even when organised neatly, 150 factors are still an awful lot of factors. Having said all of this, it remains the case that the more concise the theory is, generally the more scientifically useful it will be.

Clarity of constructs

Clarity of theoretical constructs

It is essential that theoretical constructs are clear. This clarity might not always involve a formal definition being articulated but some attempt at spelling out what is meant by key concepts makes a theory a better one that it would otherwise be. Defining constructs can be a tricky business. For one thing the terms used in the definition have themselves got to be clear. If the terms used in defining the theoretical constructs themselves need defining, then the theory is starting to unravel. There are no simple rules for deciding definitively if any given definition is clear or not. *We* might say that a concept is too woolly, but the researcher says it is not. *We* might say it is narrow, the theorist might say it is quite broad enough. Nevertheless, the debate about the clarity of constructs is worth having. Many researchers have found themselves in the middle of arguments about whether theory A or theory B is correct, with further data collection only making the problem worse. In these circumstances, researchers often go back to the original theoretical constructs and realise that the constructs have not been defined clearly enough. Here are some common difficulties with the clarity of theoretical constructs:

- *Obscurantism* – the definition is opaque because it uses unusual or vague terms, some of which themselves require, but typically do not receive, further clarification.

- *Overly technical* – the definition includes *unnecessarily* complex mathematical or computational terms. Of course, when used appropriately (for example in the study of sensation or animal learning), mathematical models can add to clarity by incorporating parameters that are already well defined.

- *Overinclusive* – the definition includes more than it should, for example 'Reasoning: all processes carried out by the mind' is a definition that would include memory and perception, which seems excessive. It is important to make sure that the definition, in its attempt to cover all possible examples of the phenomenon, does not go so far that it includes examples that are inappropriate.

- *Underinclusive* – the definition is too narrow, for example 'Bullying is any behaviour involving physical contact where one pupil causes another pupil harm'. The 'physical contact' element would exclude verbal aggression or surrogate bullying. This would also rule out ostracism, name-calling or forms of victimisation. It is important that definitions, in their attempts to only include examples of phenomena that are clearly examples of the category in question, are not so cautious that they rule out instances of that category which should in fact be included. For example, in psychology, underinclusive definitions of bullying of the kind mentioned here have led to the mistaken assumption that female bullying is rare.

- *Circular or tautologous* – the definition simply restates the definition, for example 'A reinforcer is any reward which leads to an increase in the frequency of the rewarded behaviour'. The limitations of this sort of definition become apparent if we also claim as a 'prediction' that 'reinforcement will increase the frequency of specified behaviours'. The definition ensures that the prediction is always true.

- *Self-referential* – the definition contains reference to the very thing being defined. This is normally a very bad thing but there are exceptions. It is bad on the whole because it does not provide useful new information, for example 'An attribution is when a responsibility for an action is attributed to a person'. The exception to this rule is known as recursion and does not really apply to the definitions that occur in theories, but is worth knowing about (see Chapter 10 on cognitive psychology).

Clarity of relational propositions

Relational propositions are the proposed *links* between theoretical constructs. We need to bear in mind that *both* the theoretical constructs and the relational propositions need to be clear in psychological theory. That is, not only do the concepts themselves need to be clear but so do the specified relationships between those constructs.

The clarity of relational propositions often depends upon the clarity of the specification of the *causal* relationship between theoretical constructs. Having defined two theoretical constructs as part of a theory, we might simply say that theoretical construct A (for example frustration) 'causes' theoretical construct B (for example aggression) to increase or appear. So far so good – we have defined the theoretical constructs and now we are specifying the relational proposition that defines how those two constructs are related. However, the problem is that we have not specified the 'causal' link clearly enough. Do we mean that frustration *always* causes aggression, no matter what? Do we mean that frustration *alone* can cause aggression? Do we mean that the only time aggression ever happens is when frustration has caused it? These issues relate to considerations of **necessity** and **sufficiency**. It is important to understand these concepts, as many psychological theories play fast and loose with them when they shouldn't.

'Necessity' refers to the idea that a cause is always required for an effect to occur, that is to say, the cause is *necessary* for the effect to occur. For example, knowing your PIN number is *necessary* for you to get money out of the cash machine (that is, ATM) but it is not sufficient (you need your card with you too). Is frustration necessary for aggression? No, since, for example, soldiers fight in wars, and muggers jump passing pedestrians with no immediate sense of frustration (although the breadth of our definition of 'frustration' might be an issue here). 'Sufficiency' means that the cause is enough on its own to bring about the effect. Is frustration sufficient to bring about aggression? If someone is frustrated, will that person always act aggressively? No, they will not. Frustration typically only leads to aggression if the frustrating experience is seen as avoidable and when there are no other channels for dealing with the barrier to the goal. For example, a hockey player will be 'frustrated' by an opposing defender but the player will not get aggressive for that reason alone – because opposing teams having defenders is perceived as a perfectly valid barrier to have to face. Similarly, a player will not usually get aggressive when fouled by an opponent so long as the referee awards a penalty against the defender. However, aggression might well occur if the player faces invalid (that is, unfair) barriers and no other remedy is provided.

Many factors, originally theorised to be necessary and sufficient causes, often turn out (after many experiments) to be nothing of the kind. For example, it was thought for some time in psychology that temporal contiguity (that is, closeness in time) between stimuli (for example a light and a shock) was a necessary *and* sufficient condition for an animal to learn an association between those two stimuli. That is to say, it had been claimed that temporal contiguity *had* to happen for learning to occur and temporal contiguity on its own was *enough* for learning to take place. However, empirical studies showed that this was not the case. Animals will learn associations between stimuli separated in time – for example when a toxic foodstuff in their diet causes feelings of nausea 24 hours later. This shows that temporal contiguity is not necessary. Other studies showed that temporal contiguity is not sufficient either. If stimulus 1 (say a red light) occurs before stimulus 2 (say a mild electric shock) only intermittently, then stimulus 1 does not operate as a good *predictor* of stimulus 2 and the animal will not learn the association. Even if the red light immediately precedes the shock on 20 occasions, if those 20 only account for five per cent of the shocks, the animal will not make any association (Rescorla, 1988). This shows that temporal contiguity is not sufficient for associative learning. It is in general a very powerful criticism of a proposed explanation for some phenomenon to demonstrate that it is in fact neither necessary nor sufficient for it.

THINK IT THROUGH

Look through any psychology textbook and find an explicit statement about how one variable causes another. Is the cause specified as necessary or sufficient or both? If it doesn't say, then work out for yourself what the answer is, or specify what experiment would need doing. Do you get the sense that necessity and sufficiency are often underspecified in psychological theories? So do I.

Thus, it is of the utmost importance that we think carefully about precisely what a theory is claiming about the links *between* constructs. If the theory does not have clear relational propositions, including clarity about necessity and sufficiency, then it is not a good theory.

Internal consistency

When a concept is clearly defined, we need to check that the concept is used consistently throughout the presentation of that theory. Some theories are two sentences long and only a very dim theorist could be inconsistent in that context. On the other hand, Freudian psychodynamic theory is about 24 *books* long and the possibility of inconsistency is therefore very real. Many theories (or 'views', 'models' and 'frameworks') are presented in book length form. It is possible, therefore, to identify changes in the use of theoretical constructs. Inconsistency makes testing theories very difficult, if not impossible. However, we need to remember here that although the *initial* statement of a theory might be internally consistent, subsequent applications and modifications (in the light of data) start to corrupt the integrity of the original impeccable formulation. A theoretical construct modified here, a relational proposition tweaked there, and before you know it the whole thing is a monument to contradiction. It is necessary, therefore, to think about how the author 'refines' and 'develops' a theory in the light of new data and conceptual critique and that our evaluation is not limited to the original formulation only.

Testability

If we cannot derive hypotheses from a theory to test, then we will not be able to assess the usefulness of the theory. In particular it is essential that the theory is capable of not just being tested, but tested in a manner that in principle its claims could be disproved. In other words, it is not enough that a theory lends itself to verification (that is, to the collection of data in its favour) but also lends itself to disconfirmation (that is, the collection of data that would lead to the rejection of its claims, and hence the theory itself). In Chapter 2, we discussed how Popper castigated logical positivists for demanding only data that were consistent with a hypothesis. Popper pointed out that even vague theories or theories with many qualifications to the main claims could collect consistent data without any problems. For Popper, the real engine of scientific progress was the idea that theories could enable hypotheses to be derived from them with which the data might be inconsistent. These hypotheses would be rejected and so in principle would the original versions of the theories from which they were derived. As data come in which appear to be inconsistent with the theory, the theory is usually amended – sometimes through the addition of extra propositions or constructs that deal with these irritating anomalies. As these new elements are added to the theory the theory becomes less testable in the sense that it is difficult to discon-firm a theory with so many qualifications (and the internal consistency suffers as we noted earlier). As the modifications multiply, the theory starts to creak under its own weight and finally, as Kuhn pointed out, it gets unceremoniously pushed aside when a brand new theory comes along which deals with all the data in a radically different way.

Empirical support

Assuming a theory is adequately parsimonious, clear, internally consistent and has been tested, what then? If the data are consistent with the claims made by the theory and, crucially, if there are no data inconsistent with the theory *and* there are no theories which cover the same data more parsimoniously, we can take the theory as being the best theory available (see Popper's empirical testing stage discussed in Chapter 2).

Sometimes there are two or more theories attempting to explain the same phenomenon. The proponents of each theory will argue that the data support one side more than the other. There will be accusations from the supporters of theory A that the studies presented as support for theory B do not really test theory B and therefore cannot be held up as evidence for it. Various methodological flaws and conceptual ambiguities will be pointed out in the other side's theory. Thus the assessment of the evidence for and against a particular theory is rhetorical. That is to say, the evidence is not usually taken as self-evidently or intrinsically for or against any particular theory but is disputed by those who wish to argue for one side or the other (see our discussion of Michael Billig's work in Chapter 2 on this point).

What an unseemly business I hear you say. In fact, the disputes themselves can fuel further refinements of methodology and theoretical models on both sides, which should on the whole be productive for the discipline's general understanding of the phenomenon. The trouble is that as these theoretical disputes between opposing camps become increasingly more focused on precise features of some laboratory procedure or concept, the debate takes on a technical and introverted turn, leaving outsiders, including other psychologists, scratching their heads and wondering what the original dispute was actually all about. The rest of psychology loses interest and the debate is taken outside. At some point many years on, psychologists will turn to each other and say – 'what ever happened to the so-

and-so debate?' Perhaps later still one of the survivors of the bloody encounter writes a definitive review of the debate, concluding that maybe both camps were asking the wrong question in the first place.

When assessing evidence in favour of a theory, we need to think about the following:

■ Is the definition of the construct in the experiment the same as specified in the theory?

■ Is the study methodologically sound?

■ Have the results of the study been assessed appropriately? Is the conclusion going too far if the support is only qualified?

■ If the evidence is only partially supportive of the theory, can the theory be modified or does it need complete rejection?

Conceptually, we need to think about whether or not the pattern of data regarding the behaviour being explained (behaviour X) is properly addressed by the theory. Often in psychology, a theory claims to explain behaviour X in *general* (be it 'aggression', 'spatial ability', 'colour vision' or 'helping'), when in fact, on closer inspection, we find that it only deals successfully with one aspect of X or just one definition of X.

Generally speaking, theories in psychology, when initially proposed, tend to overestimate the *homogeneity* of the behaviour in question. As more studies are carried out, often stimulated by the initial theory, the *heterogeneity* of the behaviour in terms of its diverse expressions, varying prevalence, cross-cultural differences and historical variations becomes clear. Typically these new studies then make psychologists sit back and reconsider the original definition of the behaviour in question.

Therefore, we should always consider the following questions in order to determine how adequately a theory is dealing with the phenomenon in general. For the sake of illustration we can consider what any theory of aggression would have to take into account.

Eight questions about the heterogeneity of behaviour for general theories

1. Is the diversity of expression of behaviour X addressed by the theory? (For example aggression comes in many shapes and forms – physical violence, verbal abuse, wilful deprivation of another and so on)

2. Is the prevalence of behaviour X addressed by the theory? (Generally people are aggressive infrequently compared to other behaviours – so any general theory of aggression would have to explain why people are not aggressive most of the time)

3. Are the differences and similarities between males and females, young and old and across species addressed by the theory? (Males are more aggressive than females, some species fight more often than others)

4. Are the cross-cultural differences of behaviour X addressed by the theory? (Some cultures have more murders per head of population than others)

5. Are the historical differences of behaviour X addressed by the theory? (Although data are sparse, some periods of history have been more violent than others)

6. Are the differences in the criteria for identifying examples of theory X addressed by the theory? (Some people would define verbal abuse as 'aggression', while some would not)

7. Is behaviour X a composite behaviour which requires its components to be explained first? (Violence in public places requires knowledge of physical layout, location of victim and local rules about levels of acceptable aggressiveness)

8. Is behaviour X an individual behaviour, dyadic behaviour, a group behaviour or societal 'behaviour'? Are all these levels addressed by the theory? (Individuals, couples and communities can all be aggressive, albeit in different ways)

If we find ourselves concluding that the answer is 'no' to some of these questions we will have found the limits or 'boundary conditions' of the theory. A theory with too many boundary conditions is of little value, of course. While these questions are relevant to all areas of psychology, we shall explore them in more detail in Chapter 11, when we consider evolutionary psychology. Although assessing the adequacy of a theoretical account in terms of how well it addresses the diversity of behaviour is an example of analytic thinking, considering how *then* to design a broader study which better captures the richness of the category in question would be an example of synthetic thinking, since that involves a more imaginative perspective on the issue.

Heuristic value

The heuristic value of a theory relates to its capacity to capture the imagination of researchers and provide stimulating ideas about what kind of future research might be interesting to do. A theory that is parsimonious, clear and consistent will attract researchers more than one which is long-winded, opaque and incoherent because researchers do not have the time to waste testing poor theories. Freudian psychoanalysis is a theory which in many ways is hopelessly elaborate, obscure and inconsistent and yet has been influential within psychology. Although the number of studies attempting to test Freudian hypotheses *directly* are small, many psychologists have been inspired by it to construct simpler, clearer theories in their own particular areas of enquiry. An example of this is research on mother–child attachments, which has a good reputation for inventive and yet very rigorous tests of hypotheses. Thus some of Freud's ideas on development, although untestable in themselves because of their irrefutability and lack of clarity, still had a significant heuristic influence on psychology.

In assessing the heuristic value of a theory the proof is very much in the pudding – if interesting, valuable and informative studies can be carried out because of the theory, then that theory has high heuristic value. Sometimes theories achieve this heuristic value by being controversial or linked to some ongoing social problem or policy. It is possible, however, to ask what kind of theories are *likely* to have high heuristic value. Conceptually, theories are heuristically worthwhile because they are either novel or counter-intuitive, or both.

Novelty

Theories which present new theoretical constructs are likely to be more influential than theories which are essentially rehashes of old ones. Of course, in a sense, nothing is new under the sun, but some theories have been more imaginative than others. There is also significant heuristic value in identifying new uses for old constructs, For example, Hazel Markus's idea that we possess a *self*-schema (that is, an internal structured mental representation of *ourself*) generated a lot of research because previously the idea of schema had generally only been applied to external objects and other people. Often ideas from outside psychology have a degree of originality which stimulates psychological researchers. Noam Chomsky's ideas about an innate 'language acquisition device', which allows children to learn language rapidly and systematically, have generated a great deal of experimental research by psychologists. It is not enough for the theory simply to be new – it also needs to explain important data and make surprising predictions (see Popper's 'bold conjectures' discussed in Chapter 2). If it does this using new ideas, then it is much more likely to attract and retain the interests of psychologists.

Counter-intuitiveness

Counter-intuitiveness is the extent to which a theory provides explanations and makes predictions that as psychologists or as human beings we find remarkable and surprising. Often theories make claims which on first inspection are counter-intuitive but which on closer inspection make sense. Counter-intuitive theories are interesting because they hold out the promise of making us rethink what we already know. Counter-intuitive theories force us to look carefully at what we take for granted both scientifically and informally.

Examples of theories which have a counter-intuitive ring about them would include Moscovici *et al.*'s theory of minority influence, which predicted that just two people in a group of six or seven can persuade that group to shift its views under the right conditions (specifically when the minority is consistent in expressing its position; see Moscovici *et al.*, 1969). This was a counter-intuitive conjecture on two counts. First of all, most research on social influence had followed Asch in suggesting that majorities influenced minorities. Second, in everyday life we take it largely for granted that minorities yield in their attitudes to the majority opinion, and not vice versa.

THINK IT THROUGH

Overall, the criteria of comprehensiveness, parsimony, clarity of constructs, internal consistency, testability, empirical support and heuristic value are important ways of thinking about theories. It is worth making sure that you have a good grasp of these criteria, because we shall be using them extensively in Part II of this book as we consider specific areas of psychology in turn. It might be a useful exercise to identify a theory in psychology that has caught your imagination and then assess it in terms of the seven criteria. Which criteria are most difficult to apply? Why?

McGuire's heuristics for thinking creatively about theories

So much for assessing theories which have already been established – but how can we *produce* interesting hypotheses to test theories? On the basis of this chapter so far, we now have in our critical thinking toolbox a whole set of criteria for thinking *evaluatively* about theories – what we need now are some ideas for thinking *creatively* about theories.

Recently there has been a series of attempts to codify the creative side of theory generation. We will review this attempt now and link it to some of the discussions in this and previous chapters. Having reviewed the ideas, we will assess them critically – but for now we will consider them in their own terms.

The various methods for testing hypotheses, once they have been generated from theories, are relatively well worked out and involve the more or less mechanical application of statistical tests to well-worn experimental designs and involve logical, deductive and analytic thinking. These methods, because they are generally comprehensive and designed to give the correct answer every time, are sometimes referred to as **algorithms**. Most methods courses spend most of their time teaching students about those algorithms relevant to testing hypotheses, and very little time on how to generate hypotheses in the first place.

However, William McGuire (1997) has suggested that insufficient attention has been paid to documenting and discussing the **heuristics** by which psychologists come up with new ideas to test. You will recall from Chapter 2 that a heuristic is a 'rule-of-thumb', a way of thinking about a situation that gives us a *useful* answer, if not necessarily the most 'correct' one. According to McGuire, there is insufficient attention being paid to synthetic, inductive, *creative* thinking in psychology. McGuire proposes no fewer than 49 creative ways to generate hypotheses. He claims that all of these have been used in psychological research and, if used effectively, can lead to more useful forms of scientific investigation in psychology. These ideas demonstrate how we can be imaginative in explaining psychological phenomena and how we can think about old theories in new ways. These heuristics can be classified into 14 subtypes and five major categories. We will begin by reviewing these five categories and considering their application in our thinking about psychology.

McGuire's heuristics are all examples of how to generate a hypothesis to test in relation to an observed phenomenon or research puzzle. The techniques also enable us to think through new angles on established theories. It is important to understand these heuristics because they illustrate the thinking processes which lie behind how psychologists come to derive new hypotheses to test. In order to get the most out of them, you should consider the techniques in any practical research work you are expected to do in your degree. The heuristics will be especially useful when preparing your honours project or dissertation for your final year. However, the heuristics are important in another way, which will be useful to you right from the beginning of your studies in psychology. When reading about the research carried out by other psychologists, you can ask 'Was this the only way of conceptualising this problem?' You can put the studies you *read* about in context by considering alternative forms of the same analyses. Many of the heuristics presented by McGuire are extremely helpful in thinking imaginatively about existing psychological theories, even if we do not intend to do any empirical work in the near future ourselves. Although presented as ways of generating new hypotheses, these heuristics offer a recipe for imaginative thinking about the state of research and theorising in psychology generally.

The five categories identified by McGuire (1997) are:

1. heuristics sensitive to provocative natural occurrences
2. heuristics involving simple conceptual analysis
3. heuristics involving complex conceptual analyses
4. heuristics demanding reinterpretation of past research
5. heuristics involving the collecting of new data or the reanalysing of old data.

Do not be put off by some of the names McGuire gives to the categories of heuristics, as the labels are not really important and you certainly do not need to memorise them. Table 3.3 hopefully provides a simpler account of what the heuristics actually involve.

These heuristics are all designed to generate new ideas which might help explain some form of behaviour which is under scrutiny (or which should be).

Table 3.3   McGuire's heuristics for generating new hypotheses

McGuire's term	Subcategories	What it involves
Heuristics simply calling for sensitivity to provocative natural occurrences	Recognising and accounting for the oddity of occurrences	Looking at cases that buck the trend
	Introspective self-analysis	Imagining what you yourself would do
	Retrospective comparison	Applying solutions from earlier, similar (even dissimilar) problems to current problem
	Sustained, deliberate observation	Creative thinking from immersion in problem through participation

(cont'd)

Table 3.3 McGuire's heuristics for generating new hypotheses (cont'd)

McGuire's term	Subcategories	What it involves
Heuristics involving simple conceptual analysis	Simple conversion of a banal proposition	Considering effects of reversing traditional predictions
	Multiplying insights by conceptual division	Thought experiments on taking variables to the extreme
	Jolting one's conceptualising out of its usual ruts	Expressing the problem and/or possible solutions in novel forms
Heuristics calling for complex conceptual analysis	Deductive reasoning procedures	Looking for as many possible explanations as possible, exploring the implications of basic assumptions about the problem
	Using thought-diversifying procedures	Using checklists, matrices, tree diagrams and formal logic to encourage closer processing of key concepts
	Using metatheories as thought evokers	Considering how grand theories would tackle the problem
Heuristics demanding reinterpretation of past research	Delving into single past studies	Looking for simpler solutions to earlier data patterns
	Discovery by integrating multiple past studies	Reviewing sets of studies to identify differences and similarities
Heuristics necessitating collecting new or reanalysing old data	Qualitative analyses	Inviting open comments from subjects, pitting variables against each other
	Quantitative analyses	Exploring and reworking statistical relationships including subtracting large but theoretically insignificant factors

Category I: heuristics sensitive to provocative natural occurrences

In this category, McGuire places recognition of 'odd' occurrences, thinking about or acting out one's own behaviour in the situation, reviewing solutions to similar problems and sustained observation of the phenomenon.

Accounting for deviations from the general trend. For the sake of brevity and clarity we can refer to this as the *anomaly heuristic*. The idea here is to look for unusual cases which 'buck the trend'. For example, whereas most children who are traumatised in childhood experience difficulties of integration in later life, some traumatised children grow up to be particularly well adjusted. We need to explain the general trend but the exceptions need to be interpreted also. In particular, the presence of exceptions to the rule, depending on how numerous and significant they are, casts doubts on the explanation for the population in general. The anomalies might suggest an additional psychological mechanism is involved.

Juxtaposing opposite problems to suggest reciprocal solutions. The idea here is that when trying to explain why psychological phenomenon X occurs, we turn to any knowledge we have about when X refuses to occur no matter what. McGuire's example is that of trying to explain why some people do not take their prescribed medicine to manage their hypertension, by thinking about why some people overdose. This seems completely counter-intuitive initially but we should consider it simply as a way of thinking imaginatively about the general underlying dynamics of a phenomenon.

Category II: heuristics involving simple conceptual analysis

Accounting for the contrary of a trite proposition. In this heuristic McGuire advocates simply identifying a general claim or theory in psychology, either something which has emerged from traditional research or everyday popular ideas and then thinking about the conditions under which the *opposite* of that banal proposition might be true. For example, it might be taken to be true that the more likeable the source of a persuasive communication the more likely persuasion will result. There can be little or no questioning that this proposition is true under most circumstances, but McGuire suggests we should think about the conditions under which the *reverse* might be true. For example, when would a likeable source lead to less, and not more, persuasion? (see also Billig's work in Chapter 2).

Another heuristic technique advocated by McGuire under this heading is *pushing an obvious hypothesis to an implausible extreme.* In this case the idea is to take a sensible hypothesis and as a 'thought experiment' speculate on what would happen if one or other of the variables was maximised. For example, argues McGuire, liking is correlated with increased eye-contact between strangers but what if there was a very high degree of eye-contact? At what point does the eye-contact become excessive and the standard traditional relationship break down? Exploring these limits to psychological variables provides ideas for new experiments that test existing theories.

Also in this general category is a set of heuristics based on the idea of *multiplying insights by conceptual division.* By this McGuire means rethinking the variables in an existing formulation rather than the link between them. The most interesting of these heuristics involves considering linguistic synonyms for either the cause or effect side of a theoretical claim and seeing whether the theory still makes sense or whether it identifies the limits of a hypothesis.

For example, one might be reviewing the idea that similarity leads to attraction, as initially highlighted by Byrne (1971). Synonyms for similarity in my dictionary include 'resemblance', 'correspondence' and 'mimicry'. This does indeed throw up interesting facets to a very tired hypothesis in psychology. 'Resemblance' seems to raise the issue of what happens when two people are so similar they remind people of each other or worse (better?) they remind each other of each other. Clearly the degree of similarity that borders on resemblance is an example of taking the relationship between variables to extremes. But no one to my knowledge has ever researched attraction between individuals who resemble each other. The heuristic value of 'mimicry' as an alternative concept for similarity is perhaps rather more obscure. The possibility of engaging another's affection by walking behind them and mocking the peculiarities of their accent and gait can, I fear, only lead to tears. What this analysis does is help us to think about *what it is about similarity* that is psychologically important for the theory. It also reminds us of the fragile links between the language of psychology and the language of everyday life (see Chapter 7).

Category III: heuristics calling for complex conceptual analysis

Category III heuristics are those which call for more complex conceptual analyses. The first of these involves making use of deductive reasoning to some extent even though the overall goal is still to *generate* hypotheses from previous research rather than work out how to test them. A good example of this category of heuristics is the 'generating multiple explanations heuristic'. This heuristic is particularly relevant when we come across an interesting, unexpected or unexplained relationship between two or more variables. McGuire recommends here that we seek to propose several possible explanations for a hypothesised link rather than agonising over how to determine what 'the' correct or most convincing explanation might be. Taking this approach ensures that several roads of enquiry are investigated rather than just one (which might turn out to be a cul-de-sac) and that future researchers are able to consider a wide range of possibilities and not just the one that you preferred or pursued.

The next type of Category III heuristic which McGuire suggests we should use to be creative in our thinking of hypotheses testing involves the use of what he calls 'thought-diversifying structures'. By this he means the use of various conceptual frameworks to 'propel and diversify one's thinking on a topic' (1997: 19). McGuire suggests using checklists of key concepts and subconcepts, each of which can be the basis for a hypothesis. Combining lists and classifying them into subdivisions over and over again in different combinations can bring out unexpected features of the relevant psychological constructs. Also useful, according to McGuire, are matrices (that is, grids), tree diagrams and flow charts.

The final heuristic from this category of thought diversification is that of using *metatheories* as thought evokers. This involves looking at psychological research puzzles from the point of view of one of the 'big theories' in psychology such as evolutionary biology and asking, for example, 'What evolutionary advantage does the behaviour confer on the individual?' or 'What basic adaptive skills are being brought to bear here?' Other examples might include asking 'What would a Freudian psychoanalyst say about this behaviour?' In none of this are we necessarily trying to find an evolutionary or psychoanalytic theory to explain behaviour, but rather we are trying to explore the concept from every angle and at every level to get as good a feel for it as we can. Again, *it is the process of thinking rather than the end product of that thinking* that is significant. And, paradoxically, it is useful to apply theoretical positions you *do not* like to a problem as it still gives you another angle on the issue. If you are clear about why you are unconvinced by a certain theory, then you will have a good idea why some of the ideas about the phenomenon you are examining are not going to be worthwhile pursuing. In much the same way I suppose that if your dreadful next-door neighbour heaps endless praise on some holiday resort you make a mental note not to bother going there.

Category IV: heuristics demanding reinterpretation of past research

The fourth category of sources of inspiration suggested by McGuire is the reconsideration of previous studies. Essentially McGuire advocates a search for simpler explanations of complex results possibly overlooked by the original researcher who may have been focusing on complex relations among variables. This subcategory McGuire calls 'delving into single past studies'. In particular he argues that complex patterns of results may be broken down into more sets of more simple underlying patterns. A good example of this is the curve for recall of items on a list as a function of their place on the list (Figure 3.1).

The overall pattern is what is often referred to an inverted U-curve, a function found in many areas of psychology. What the graph shows overall is that when the independent variable on the x-axis is low (in this case items appearing at the beginning of a list), the dependent variable on the y-axis is high (in this case high levels of subsequent recall). As we move to intermediate values of the independent variable (for example items in a middle position), the dependent variable is low (that is, poor recall). However, when we get to high values of the independent variable (that is, items at the end of the list), the dependent variable

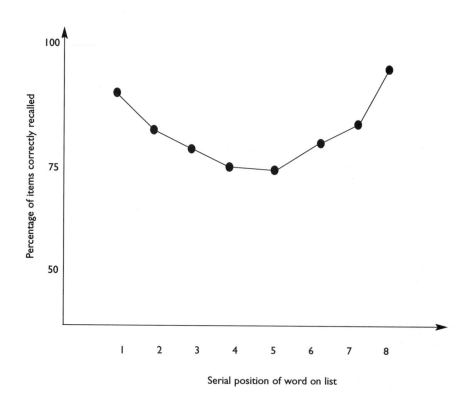

Figure 3.1   Serial position effect curve

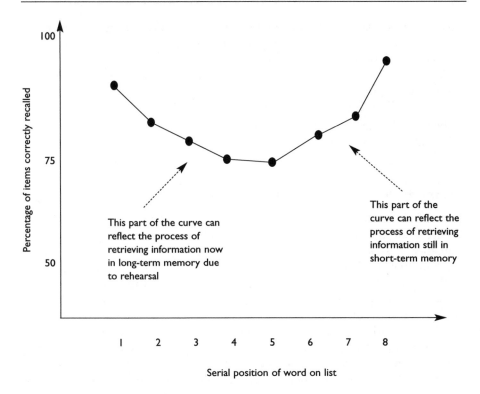

Figure 3.2   Underlying processes in serial position effect curve

value goes up again (indicating high recall of items at that position in the list). We could look at this curve and just conclude that recall from lists is a complex process. However, if we look more closely at the function we can explore whether or not some more basic fundamental processes are occurring which give rise to this characteristic inverted U-shape. It is in fact the case that the serial position curve masks two underlying functions (Figure 3.2).

Thus we can see that the original **curvilinear** function is in fact in part the product of two underlying **linear** functions. The lesson from this is that when we come across a study which has claimed to find a complex curvilinear function, we can ask and explore whether or not there is in fact a simpler set of separate linear functions underneath.

Category V: heuristics necessitating collecting new or reanalysing old data

This final category of heuristics brings together a range of techniques which involve looking at data as a source of original and practical ideas for generating new hypotheses about theories. McGuire breaks these down into qualitative and quantitative types of heuristics. The qualitative techniques include the use of post-experimental questionnaires which involve asking open-ended questions after experiments as a way of getting a participant's view of the study. A further technique here is 'pitting confounded factors against each other'. That is, if your reading around an area suggests that two factors tend to work against each other, it is interesting to include both of these in the same experiment to observe how they trade off against each other. For example, you might find that interpersonal attraction is increased by similarity of attitude but decreased by being interrupted. So what happens if someone keeps interrupting to *say how much they agree with you*?

Assessing McGuire's heuristics

It should be clear from the attention I have given McGuire's heuristics that I believe them to be useful – or else I would not have filled your head with all that Category II , subdivision 3 nonsense, obviously. However, it is worth reflecting on the *limitations* of his scheme to make sure we get a balanced view of his ideas.

We should begin by noting that much of McGuire's framework is located within the assumptions of logical positivistic research, with a strong emphasis on the importance of discovering cause and effect relationships. Although McGuire's heuristics encourage imaginative reflection on psychological theories and research puzzles, generally speaking the mark of success of all this reflecting is the extent to which the application of the heuristics *leads to better positivist models of behaviour*. There is nothing intrinsically wrong with this and it is a major step forward to be thinking about how we should be more bold in our synthetic thinking about theories, hypotheses and experiments – but there are other kinds of research in addition to experiments.

Another limitation of McGuire's approach is that it places a strong emphasis on limited practical solutions to the psychologist's equivalent of writers' block. If you have a research report to submit in three months' time and you are reading the *Journal of Personality and Social Psychology* for the nth time looking for inspiration and getting nowhere, then McGuire's framework is a godsend. However, this tactical approach to research can be overdone. Maybe what is required is some more extended thought rather than quick fixes. The one heuristic McGuire *does not* offer is *do not do any research on this topic*. Some years ago Serge Moscovici, the French psychologist, suggested that all data collection in psychology should *cease* until psychology tidied up some of its conceptual confusions. I think *that* is going just a little too far but nevertheless the assumption in McGuire's model that the only productive responses to theoretical puzzles are *empirical* ones can be challenged. Sometimes the best and only response is a conceptual clarification, resolving some of the contradictions and clarifying what some of the questions might actually mean.

Having said all of that, McGuire's system of heuristics is a major contribution to the practical business of building on previous research and theorising in imaginative and creative ways, and I commend it to you.

SUMMARY

A theory is an attempt to explain why things happen in the way that they do. In psychology, theories are important because they organise our thoughts about behaviour and experience and allow them to be put to the test. Theories involve theoretical constructs (the proposed concepts) and relational propositions (the links between the proposed concepts). Assessing the quality of theories involves consideration of many aspects of their construction and usefulness. It is often useful to think about theories in relation to seven generic criteria: comprehensiveness, parsimony, clarity of constructs, internal consistency, testability, empirical support and heuristic value. Applying these criteria, however, can turn out to be a rhetorical rather than a technical enterprise. There will be those who will want to argue that a given theory *does* meet a criterion while others will want to argue that it does *not*. Nevertheless, the ensuing debates are usually worthwhile. The synthetic (creative) thinking side of theorising has generally been neglected but recently McGuire has suggested five types of heuristic for generating novel theoretical ideas in psychology. Although a useful heuristic itself for imaginative theorising, McGuire's framework is essentially positivistic in nature and is less useful for generating theoretical ideas outside an experimental framework.

KEY TERMS

Algorithms ■ Curvilinear ■ Heuristics ■ Holism ■ Hypotheses Linear ■ Necessity ■ Reductionist ■ Relational propositions Sufficiency ■ Theoretical constructs ■ Theory

FURTHER READING

There are many sources of information on creative, critical approaches to theory. One interesting text is McKenna, R J (1995) *The Undergraduate Researcher's Handbook: Creative Experimentation In Social Psychology* (London: Allyn & Bacon) which goes beyond the usual frame of reference of standard methodology textbooks.

An alternative historical case-study approach is provided by Howard Gardner in his (1993) *Creating Minds: An Anatomy Of Creativity Seen Through The Lives Of Freud, Einstein, Picasso, Stravinsky, Eliot, Graham, and Gandhi* (New York: Basic Books).

========================= **USEFUL WEBSITES** =========================

Creativity Web – Resources for Creativity and Innovation

http://www.ozemail.com.au/~caveman/Creative/index.html

A popular interactive site designed to showcase interesting exercises and ideas about creativity. Plenty of links to other creativity sites.

Relativity on the World Wide Web

http://math.washington.edu/~hillman/relativity.html

Given that Einstein's theory of relativity is often held up as a good theory, it might be an idea to have a look at it.

Game Theory

http://www.economics.harvard.edu/~aroth/alroth.html

A page that deals with a theory that has had considerable impact in biology, economics and more recently psychology. Game theory attempts to explain how two or more rational individuals try to anticipate how each other will act.

Inductive and Deductive Thinking in Psychology

CHAPTER OVERVIEW

In the previous chapter we considered the nature of analytic (evaluative) and synthetic (creative) thinking in relation to theoretical models. In this chapter we consider the basics of formal reasoning in order to get a complete understanding of the logic of experiments and to guide our evaluative thinking about arguments and claims in psychology generally. We shall consider the nature of both inductive and deductive arguments, look at how they come together and indicate their importance to psychological research. We shall concentrate on how inductive and deductive arguments appear in the psychological literature and identify what focus our critical thinking should have when we come to assess the soundness of both.

LEARNING OBJECTIVES

By the end of this chapter you should be able to:

- Define 'induction' and give examples of inductive reasoning
- Specify the main issues to be considered when assessing inductive arguments
- Illustrate how inductive arguments are presented in research and theoretical reports
- Define 'deduction' and give examples of deductive reasoning
- Explain the relationship between inductive and deductive reasoning and the hypothetico-deductive method in experimental psychology

Thinking critically about studies in psychology depends greatly upon appreciating **inductive** and **deductive** reasoning and the relationship between them. Psychological research is often based on a particular combination of these two modes of thinking. Specifically, inductive reasoning relates to identifying the general patterns that need explaining, while deductive reasoning relates to deriving what predictions must be true if a theory is true, and actually going out and testing whether that prediction is supported or not. This combination is known as **hypothetico-deductive** reasoning and is often taken to be the defining characteristic of scientific practice. In order to understand the hypothetico-deductive process overall we need to look at its component parts before putting them all together. We shall begin with induction.

Induction

Induction is often described as 'going from the specific to the general'. We might observe 30 children in our clinic and note that all girls initiate more conversations than the boys do. We might then inductively infer that 'girls are more confident communicators in healthcare settings than boys'. That is to say, by considering a range of specific cases we make a general statement that tries to sum up all those specific cases. This does not only occur in research environments, we make inductions all the time in everyday life, for example, when we give our opinion about all the albums of a particular band, or about all the sandwiches from a particular delicatessen. We have listened to a number of specific albums by the band and come to the general conclusion that 'they are quite a good band' or having sampled a range of sandwiches conclude 'it is a dreadful delicatessen'.

Induction can be presented in the form of a **syllogism**, or formal argument, as follows:

> *Premise 1: Patient 1 was observed in healthcare setting x at time y... and she was confident*
>
> *Premise 2: Patient 2 was observed in healthcare setting p at time q... and she was confident*
>
> *Premise 3: Patient 3 was observed in healthcare setting b at time c... and he was shy*
>
> *Conclusion: Girls are more confident than boys in healthcare settings*

Note that the statements about the observations are called the **premises**, meaning essentially the (alleged) facts on which the conclusion is based. The **conclusion** is the claim or inference being made on the basis of the premises presented. This conclusion is an attempt not only to summarise what is already known but also to describe the way the world is generally (note that the conclusion does not say 'The girls observed in our clinic during this set of observations are confident' but that girls, in general, are more confident in healthcare settings) (Figure 4.1).

How can induction be relevant to real life? Although induction might sound a dry and rarefied activity, it is essential to our everyday lives, and the limitations of inductive reasoning are the limitations of human development. This is because we are processing information about the world all the time in our everyday lives. We come to learn as children that fire is hot, that ice cream is pleasant and that toys are fun. We did not need to touch all fires, taste all ice creams or play with all toys

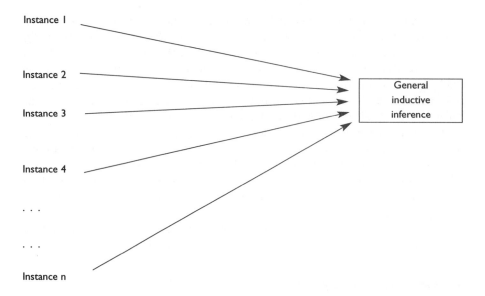

Figure 4.1   Inductive reasoning – from the specific to the general

to come to these conclusions: we base our reasoning on the strength of induction. From the experience of specific cases, we come to make inferences about things *in general*. This reasoning from specific cases to the general is characteristic of our attempts to understand the psychological world too. We might have two or three eventually unhappy relationships with partners who had different personalities to ourselves and come to the general conclusion that dissimilarity precludes happiness in relationships. Similarly, in the context of understanding other people, we might have noticed on one or two occasions at meetings that when faced with a consensus all around them some individuals go along with opinions they suspect are false. We might conclude that people *in general* conform when confronted with others in solid agreement.

Of course, these inductive conclusions could well be erroneous. There might be (and in fact are) plenty of people who have perfectly delightful relationships with partners who have completely different personalities. At work you might just be attending meetings populated by particularly spineless individuals. This is the problem with induction: there is always the possibility that we do not have all the evidence. However, if we did not think inductively, then every situation, every event, every encounter would have to be treated as a new, individual case – the processing load would be huge. However, every induction we make limits our capacity to give unusual and unexpected cases the full attention they deserve.

How does induction relate to the research process in psychology? If we look at any published psychology research journal article, we will find that the author begins her research report with a review of previous relevant work in the area such as earlier experiments and case studies. Such reviews are intended to convey the rationale for the new study being reported by demonstrating what general conclusions the researcher had arrived at inductively prior to carrying out her own research and how the new study helps to test some inferences about that previous work. Some review articles in *Psychological Review* or *Annual Review of Psychology* are essentially exercises in inductive reasoning, in which the authors try to identify general trends or principles on the basis of specific studies. In both cases, induction can be messy, with the researcher not trying to find a general statement that covers all instances perfectly but rather trying to cover as many cases as possible given the balance of the evidence for and against the conclusion. But, the researcher is still trying to move towards making inferences about psychological processes and behaviour *in general* based on *specific* relevant instances. The specific instances that the researcher draws upon will principally be particular previous studies.

Induction then is a summary statement based on all known previous instances but which goes beyond the information given. Conclusions based on inductive reasoning cannot be held to be definitively true, since there is always the possibility of new evidence coming to light. Nevertheless, we should seek to assess whether the conclusions drawn are the most reasonable ones.

Assessing inductive arguments

It is helpful if we organise our assessment of inductive arguments around eight key questions. These questions and the issues they address do overlap, but it is useful to keep the questions distinct as they will help us to think clearly about induction when we come across it.

Eight key questions for evaluating inductive arguments

1. Are the premises and conclusion clearly identified?

2. Are the premises true?

3. Does the conclusion follow from the premises?

4. How does the author deal with conflicting evidence?

5. Has the author taken into account all the relevant evidence?

6. Is the conclusion supported?

7. Is there a more appropriate conclusion to be drawn?

8. Has the author acknowledged that inductive inferences are only provisional and never definitive?

Are the premises and conclusion clearly identified?

Inductive arguments in the psychological literature are very rarely presented as a formal argument. Indeed, the conclusion and premises are unlikely to be set out in any immediately obvious way at all. It is quite possible that the word 'conclusion' or 'it can be concluded' will be found in the text but this is not always the case and, even in research articles, hypotheses are not always formally declared as

---

Conclusion spotting

Often when a conclusion is not explicitly identified as such we can still spot it by looking out for particular key phrases which are used to convey the inductive inference. Some of these include:

- 'the research evidence would clearly seem to suggest that...'
- '...therefore it can be seen that...'
- '...thus X seems to be an important influence on Y'
- 'It is clear then that...'

It should be noted that conclusions can be extremely tentative in the psychological literature, indeed some are so tentative as to border on the apologetic:

- 'Thus it is possible that under some conditions X may have a small effect on Y...'
- 'It is perhaps conceivable that...'
- 'It might be expected then that...'

---

such. In literature reviews there may be several conclusions drawn about several different aspects of a topic, with the same piece of evidence (for example a particular study) sometimes being used to support more than one conclusion.

Another key aspect of identifying the premises and conclusions of inductive reasoning is the *sequence* of their presentation. Unlike formal syllogisms in philosophy books, in psychology literature reviews the 'conclusion' is sometimes presented *before* the supporting evidence. This is not because the author has made her mind up in advance of the evidence, but is merely a presentational device to help the reader to know where the argument will lead. In general terms this is good practice. If the conclusion is pulled out of the hat right at the very end, the reader needs to go back and check that each piece of evidence does in fact support the conclusion. In some cases, however, authors deliberately hold back their inductive inference for dramatic effect when the conclusion is surprising or controversial – but this is the exception rather than the rule.

Are the premises true?

In the case of a review article or research report, this question amounts to asking whether or not the studies being cited are themselves trustworthy. It is extremely time consuming to go back to the articles reporting the original studies (unless you have *already* read the studies referred to) but ultimately this is the only way to check the relevance and strength of the evidence. Usually some significant details are reported in the literature review such as the variables and sample used, and the author's judgements about the usefulness of certain studies used in the evidence can be challenged on the basis of these details. Often this issue is not so much 'are the premises true', but rather 'are the results of the studies reported convincing?'

Does the conclusion follow from the premises?

We should remember that two things must be true for an inductive argument to be sound. First, the premises must be true and second, the conclusion must *follow* from the premises. Here for example, is a sound piece of reasoning:

Premise 1:   *Ninety per cent of deaf children are born to hearing parents*

Premise 2:   *Most hearing parents of deaf children cannot use sign language*

Conclusion: *Many deaf children will not learn sign language by copying their parents*

It is no good, however, having true premises and a true conclusion if the conclusion does not *follow*. Here is a poor piece of reasoning:

Premise 1:   *Ninety per cent of deaf children are born to hearing parents*

Premise 2:   *Deaf children of deaf parents usually do better on reading assessments than deaf children of hearing parents*

Conclusion: *Deaf children will benefit from specialised educational input*

Note that both premises are true (Bee, 1995: 429), *and* the conclusion is true, but as an inductive argument this is very weak, because the conclusion does not *follow* from the premises. That is to say, while it *is* the case that *Deaf children will benefit from specialised educational input,* the reason *why* this is true is not be found in the premises presented here (even though they are all true). This is a fairly obvious example but many more subtle cases are to be found in the published psychological literature. What this indicates is that critical thinking involves more than just rejecting statements that are not *true* but rejecting arguments that are not *well constructed.*

How does the author deal with conflicting evidence?

When the author is reviewing several studies, there is often evidence pointing in different directions. In other words, some of the premises support the conclusion, while other premises fail to support it and point instead to a different conclusion. You will find that authors deal with this in a number of ways.

The author might try to suggest that some or all of the studies which have given results inconsistent with the conclusion are flawed in some fundamental way and can be *dismissed.* Often the alleged flaw is a methodological one, where the author will suggest that inadequate experimental control, sampling or statistical analysis was carried out. Alternatively, the author can argue that the inconsistent evidence is not relevant to the argument and can be *ignored.* This can be the case if a study has used the same name for a different phenomenon (see Chapter 5 on theoretical constructs, conceptual definitions and concrete operationalisation). If the evidence cannot be dismissed or ignored, then the author can consider the 'balance' of evidence. That is, the author presents the conclusion (a claim or a hypothesis) as being *reasonable* given the overall quantity and quality of evidence available. We must think, however, about whether we agree with the assessment of the author about the evidence.

Has the author taken into account all the relevant evidence?

The *selection* of the premises of an inductive argument is very important. The author is claiming that all the studies included in the review are relevant (or are representative of all that are relevant) and all those that have not been included are not relevant. But the author could be wrong on both counts. Studies which are included may not in fact relate to the claim the author wants to put forward (or at least not in the way intended) and other studies are excluded which should have been included. The relevance of evidence can be a matter of significant dispute. Sometimes the relevance of whole areas of work to an issue can be controversial. Some psychologists argue, for example, that evidence from studies of animals in their natural habitat has no relevance to the study of human social behaviour, while others argue that it does. Similarly, some psychologists argue that computer programs are not relevant to understanding human thinking and memory. If a study is not included, it is usually because the author considers it irrelevant, but it might be because she does not know about it (although this is getting rarer nowadays with the accessibility of computerised databases of research reports).

In order to approach this issue critically, it is important to ask the question 'What kind of study and result would significantly change the support for this conclusion?' and then look out *specifically* for that kind of study, rather than just looking for more studies on the same topic. For example, a review might be making the claim that a 'hands-on' approach to teaching computing in schools is better than a traditional 'lecture' approach. If the author identifies six studies which show that a hands-on approach is better and none that show that it is not, there is no point in finding a seventh that similarly shows hands-on is better. What we want is a study that shows that hands-on is not better, because only that sort of result would change our assessment of the author's claim. (Astute readers will have no doubt noticed that this kind of thinking is a search for potential disconfirmation of the kind recommended by Popper, Chapter 2).

Is the conclusion supported?

The main question to be asked about inductive inference is whether or not the evidence presented does allow the stated conclusion to be drawn. The conclusion might be, or lead directly to, a hypothesis to be tested, or the conclusion might amount to a claim about the state of knowledge in the area of psychology being reviewed. However, even if the evidence does support the conclusion, our critical thinking is not complete – we must ask whether there is a *better* conclusion to be drawn.

Is there a more appropriate conclusion to be drawn?

Sometimes the evidence presented enables stronger or weaker claims to be drawn than that reflected in the conclusion put forward by the author. It is possible that the evidence is actually stronger than the author's claim requires. Thus the conclusion is *understated* in the sense that a stronger claim is justified, but not made. Since psychologists are not particularly known for their modesty or lack of ambition, it is rare for them not to make the strongest possible claim for their evidence – but it does happen. Much more common is the case where the claim goes further than the evidence really permits. In such circumstances we can say that the claim is *overstated*. This can happen when a claim is made which is presented as having a wide, indeed possibly universal, application, when in fact the available evidence suggests that the conclusion is true only under certain circumstances. You will see, as you read through the psychological research literature, that many claims and theories *begin* as universal claims, only to be whittled down by a thousand qualifications as more data are collected and other psychologists point out the limitations in the arguments being used. Whether a conclusion is assessed as being an overstatement or an understatement of the available evidence, it is important to consider the ways in which the claim can be reformulated to match the evidence more appropriately (see Chapter 3 on empirical support for theories).

Has the author acknowledged that inductive inferences are only provisional and never definitive?

No matter how many pieces of evidence have been taken into account as premises for a stated conclusion, that conclusion must be presented as subject to further revision since there is always the possibility of further evidence appearing. If the inductive process is presented as actually being carried out in order to derive a hypothesis for empirical testing, then obviously the provisional nature of the inductive generalisation is very clearly acknowledged. However, in such cases we need to assess whether the hypothesis is a good one.

Overall then there are many different kinds of question that need to be asked of inductive arguments. In different contexts in relation to different kinds of inductive arguments, these questions will be given more or less emphasis, but they do represent the kind of critical orientation to induction that every psychologist must have.

THINK IT THROUGH

Assessing the quality of our own inductive arguments

In this section we have largely been considering the evaluation of inductive arguments made by others. It is important, however, that we apply the evaluative questions identified above to our *own* reviews and the claims we make. We have to keep checking that we have a clear rationale for what evidence is relevant to our claim and that we have dealt with all that evidence. We need to make sure that our claim is the strongest possible which can be justified by the evidence. It is good academic practice to be explicit about the overall structure and rationale of your

---

THINK IT THROUGH (cont'd)

inductive arguments. You should clearly state what your criteria for relevance are and why. You could also state why you are rejecting stronger (or weaker) versions of your conclusion. In short you should state what can and cannot be inferred from the evidence you cite. Since research psychologists are aware of the kind of criticisms or counterarguments which can be thrown at any sort of inductive argument, they often raise potential objections within their review and then try to deal with them. You should do this too. Read your own inductive arguments from the point of view of a critical outsider – what objections will they raise? You can then start to *write into* your inductive review your defence against these possible objections (see Billig and rhetoric, Chapter 2).

As mentioned earlier, one of the most important aspects of induction is the way it provides a starting point for experimentation as part of hypothetico-deductive reasoning. We shall consider this application shortly but first we must examine the other main form of reasoning relevant to critical thinking in and about psychology – deduction.

Deduction

While induction is essentially about drawing general inferences *from* specific cases, **deduction** is the business of drawing inferences *about* a specific case on the basis of a general principle (Figure 4.2).

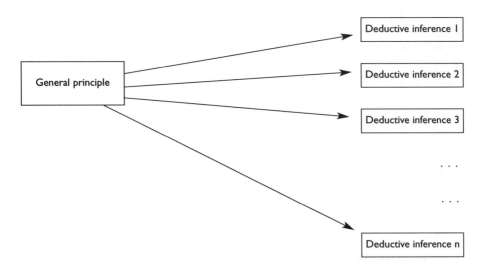

Figure 4.2   Deductive reasoning – from the general to the specific

Let us begin with two simple examples of deduction:

Example 1

Premise: *All dogs are animals (general principle)*

Premise: *Fido is a dog (specific case)*

Conclusion: Fido is an animal (deduction)

Example 2

Premise: *All children like ice cream (general principle)*

Premise: *Tommy is a child (specific case)*

Conclusion: Tommy will like ice cream (deduction)

The basic idea in deduction is that the conclusion follows from the premises as a *matter of logical necessity* and the conclusion will be valid as long as the premises are true. Unlike inductive reasoning, there is no additional information (premises) which can overturn the conclusion. If it turns out that we look at the world and find that our conclusion is not true, it must be because one of the premises is false. In Example 2, we might find Tommy graciously refuses the offer of ice cream. The only things that can be wrong here are either Tommy is not a child or all children do not like ice cream (or both). Since Tommy seems to display all the characteristics of being a child (wails, looks cute periodically and so on), we are left with the first premise which we must now consider to be false (which indeed it is).

This ice cream example is an important one because a version of it underpins the rationale for most experimental research in psychology (and other sciences, for that matter). Let us see why this is with a psychological example.

Let us suppose we have reviewed the research literature and come up (inductively) with the conclusion that social skills training helps violent offenders recently released from prison to reintegrate into the community. We can apply deductive reasoning as a framework to test our inductive claim by treating it as a hypothesis about the way the world is:

Premise 1:   *Social skills training helps the rehabilitation of offenders into the community (general principle – in this case derived by induction from review of the relevant literature)*

Premise 2:   *Twenty ex-offenders have received social skills training (specific case – here a specific empirical study)*

Conclusion: *The ex-offenders' rehabilitation will be improved compared to a similar group who do not receive training (deduction)*

We then run the study. If the rehabilitation of the offenders *is* improved, then we have evidence to support our original inductive claim. If, however, the offenders do not improve, we have only one option – we have to reject Premise 1.

A good experiment is one in which if the conclusion implied by the deductive argument is not found to be the case then we have no alternative but to reject one of the initial premises.

All this induction, deduction and premises business in a nutshell

The general idea is that we structure our inductive inferences from previous research and our deductive inferences from theories in such a way that they correspond to the format of a deductive syllogism we *already* know to be valid. The prediction plays the role of the conclusion. This means that whether the prediction turns out to be supported or unsupported by data we know exactly what the implications of the result are for our theory because of the tight logical structure in which we have placed our reasoning.

It is worth going into deductive reasoning just a little more because a little understanding of this kind of reasoning goes a long way in psychology. Consider the fact that the basic form of many deductive claims in psychology is based on an IF–THEN structure:

IF social skills training is given to ex-offenders THEN their rehabilitation improves

IF Prozac is given to a depressed patient THEN he will feel less depressed

IF information is presented in a structured way THEN it is remembered better.

When we run an experiment we are effectively manipulating the 'if' side of the claim to see whether the 'then' part really does happen. In formal deductive reasoning, the 'if' part is known as the **antecedent** and the 'then' part is known as the **consequent**. If we look at the examples, we can see that the antecedent corresponds with the kind of experimental *manipulation* we might perform, while the consequent corresponds to the *prediction* we might make about that manipulation.

Thus the general form of an experiment in deductive terms can be expressed as:

IF the experimental manipulation is carried out (antecedent) THEN the predicted outcome will occur (consequent).

Experiments are designed in such a way that their structure corresponds to the structure of these logical arguments. Specifically, experiments are structured so that if the results do not confirm the prediction, the only explanation will be that Premise 1 is false. Let us look at one further informal example.

Supposing we review the literature and come, inductively, to the tentative conclusion that relaxing music improves retention of information. We formulate this as a hypothesis and design an experiment to test the validity of this conjecture. In our experiment two groups read an extract from a book – one group listening

---

Modus ponens versus modus tollens

We know from formal logic that two particular arguments are relevant to experimental design. The first is known as **modus ponens** and has the general form:

Premise 1:   If X happens then Y happens

Premise 2:   X happened

Conclusion: Therefore Y happened

The second is known as **modus tollens** and has the general form:

Premise 1:   If X happens then Y happens

Premise 2:   Y did not happen

Conclusion: Therefore X did not happen

If we do run our experiment and do not see our predicted outcome (for example offenders do not improve) then we apply modus tollens to show that Premise 1 must be untrue (since we know that the overall modus tollens argument is valid).

---

to relaxing music, the other group listening to stirring music. We administer a test of recall one hour later.

Let us assume first of all that the 'relaxed' group do *not*, however, perform better in the test. In that case, we can consider Premise 2 in modus ponens and consider the possibility that 'Not X', that is, that the manipulation did not happen (in which case modus tollens could be ignored). But the fact is that the manipulation *did* happen, so something else has to give. The awful truth of course is that it is Premise 1, our cherished hypothesis, which must be false. In other words because we know that modus tollens is a completely valid argument, we have to accept the inevitable deduction that one of the premises is false, namely, the hypothesis (that is, Premise 1). Modus tollens tells us that if we really *do* have a true IF–THEN assertion (that is, if our hypothesis really is true), then the *only* logical circumstances under which a consequent is not observed is when the antecedent is missing too. And that is why every experiment that has ever been conducted is about making absolutely sure that the antecedent *is* present, so that if the consequent is not observed we know it is not because of a missing antecedent. To put it one final way – experiments are constructed so that ultimately the results are a reflection of the validity of the hypothesis and nothing else.

Hypothetico-deductive reasoning – bringing induction and deduction together

Hypotheses can be derived purely from inductive reasoning about previous studies. However, science requires more than a summary of previous cases. It has to offer an explanation of why those previous cases are the way they are. In the light of the inductive summary, the psychologist will offer a theoretical model of *why* the data collected so far look the way they do. For that reason theories have to be produced and tested. To do this we have to bring inductive and deductive reasoning together. For example, Storms (1973) noted inductively that there are many instances of individuals explaining *other* people's behaviour in terms of the characteristics of that person but explaining their *own* behaviour in terms of the influence of the situation. For example, we might see someone trip and think 'what a clumsy person he is', whereas if *we* were to trip we would think 'what poor quality flooring'. Storms could have just said on the basis of his induction that 'people explain others' behaviour in terms of personality, and their own behaviour in terms of situations'. However, Storms went further and put forward a *theory* as to why this was the case. Specifically, he suggested that when we are trying to explain others' behaviour (that is, we are the observers) the main focus of our visual attention is the other person, whereas when we are considering our own behaviour (we are the 'actor' of the behaviour) the main focus of visual attention is the situation around us (we cannot really see ourselves very well). Storms *deductively* derived from this theory the fact that *if* the differences in visual attention were the cause of attribution differences and *if* the visual perspective differences were removed *then* the differences in explanations should disappear. To test the hypothesis that differences in attribution are caused by differences in visual perspective, Storms set up an experiment where subjects explained examples of their own behaviour and the behaviour of others that had both been recorded on *film*. Since viewing our own behaviour on film is very similar in visual terms to viewing the behaviour of others, the difference in visual perspective was removed. As predicted, the removal of differing visual perspective did lead to the eradication of differences in attribution.

The hypothetico-deductive argument in this case might look something like this:

Premise 1:   *Many studies (and everyday experiences) indicate that observers attribute behaviour to stable internal factors such as personality, while actors attribute behaviour to the external situation*

Premise 2:   *Actors and observers differ in terms of their visual perspective on behaviour*

Premise 3:   *Differences in attributions between actors and observers are caused by differences in visual perspective*

Conclusion: *Removing the difference in visual perspective erases differences in attribution*

Note that Premises 1 and 2 are *inductive* premises (they are drawn directly from previous empirical observations) while Premise 3 and the Conclusion are based on a *deductive* inference. The overall syllogism is also an exercise in deductive logic. Premise 3 is phrased in the past tense to emphasise that the syllogism is designed to be *the argument the psychologist wants to be able to be in a position to present after the experiment has been carried out*. Thus we can see the contribution of both inductive and deductive reasoning to research and theory, and the role of the experiment to the overall argument.

================================ **SUMMARY** ================================

Inductive reasoning involves drawing a tentative general inference from a set of individual cases. Deductive reasoning involves drawing sound conclusions about specific cases on the basis of general principles. Inductive argument is both common and important in psychology, as researchers are often motivated to carry out research on the basis of an inductive review of specific prior studies which suggest a general principle to be tested. Deductive reasoning in psychology is reflected in the structure of experimental design, in which the researcher seeks to set up a controlled observation in such a way that, given specific data being found, she can deductively conclude that the manipulated factor was the cause of the observed change or difference in the phenomenon, and not something else. The inductive review leading to a possible general hypothesis, deductive inferences from theory and the logical structure of experiments which test that hypothesis is what is meant by the hypothetico-deductive method.

KEY TERMS

Antecedent ■ Conclusion ■ Consequent ■ Deduction ■ Deductive
Hypothetico-deductive ■ Inductive ■ Modus ponens
Modus tollens ■ Premises ■ Syllogism

================================ **FURTHER READING** ================================

Garnham, A and Oakhill, J (1994) *Thinking and Reasoning* (Oxford: Blackwell) provides a clear and authoritative account of experimental research on thinking.

A comprehensive review of how humans reason deductively, where they go wrong and some ideas about why they go wrong is to be found in the article by Johnson-Laird, P N (1999) Deductive reasoning. *Annual Review of Psychology*, **50**, 109–35.

================================ **USEFUL WEBSITES** ================================

Critical Thinking Glossary
http://www.kcmetro.cc.mo.us/longview/ctac/glossary.htm
A first rate resource for learning about the structure of arguments and their analysis.

University of Northern Colorado – Guide to Arguments and their Evaluation

http://www.unco.edu/philosophy/arg.html

A more systematic site than the Glossary above, and with the unique added feature of an invitation to send in your arguments for assessment by philosophy lecturers and students at UNC. Possibly too much time on their hands. Still, an excellent site with a light touch.

Writing a Review Article for *Psychological Bulletin*

http://www.geron.uga.edu/convention/bem.writing.html

A wonderful page outlining the main skills involved in writing review articles. For our purposes, this article can be read as a clear practical guide to writing inductively in psychology, since the main thrust of the piece is how to present *specific* pieces of evidence from a wide range of sources to present a clear *general* conclusion.

Thinking Critically
about Experiments

5

CHAPTER OVERVIEW

In previous chapters we considered the nature of theories and how we should assess them. Central to any such assessment is the quality of support a theory receives when tested through empirical enquiry. In this chapter we shall look in detail at experimental research in psychology and try to bring out what really needs thinking about. We shall briefly review the different types of variables associated with experimental research and different types of experimental designs. We will see that an experiment must be designed in such a way as to permit inferences to be drawn about the causal influence of one variable on another. In this context, the important idea of internal validity of an experiment will be introduced and various ways of dealing with threats to internal validity identified. We will also see that an experiment should be externally valid and ideally permit inferences to be drawn about a wide range of situations in the real world and not just in the artificial confines of the laboratory. The important area of ethics with human subjects is considered and relevant issues which need critical thinking in relation to any experiment are identified. Finally, the relationship between theory and experimentation is revisited to highlight the idea of 'operationalisation' of theoretical constructs.

LEARNING OBJECTIVES

By the end of this chapter you should be able to:

- Define what is meant by 'independent', 'dependent' and 'control' variables and the relationships between them
- Define what is meant by 'internal validity' and outline how to deal with the main threats to it
- Define 'external validity' and give examples of how it can be improved

---

> **LEARNING OBJECTIVES (cont'd)**
>
> ■ Outline the main features of the codes of ethics of the British Psychological Society (BPS) and of the American Psychological Association (APA) and state briefly how they differ
>
> ■ Explain the relationship between theoretical constructs, conceptual definitions and concrete operationalisations and their relationship to 'operational narrowing'

Variables, hypotheses and experiments – a brief refresher

It is essential to develop a good grasp of the main principles and terminology of experimental research. We do not have the space to offer that in detail here so what follows is only a taster (if you have not studied the area before) or a refresher (if you have).

Psychologists want to know how psychological *responses* (such as recall, motivation, depression, conformity, visual recognition and so on) are influenced by *stimuli* (for example particular social settings, instructions, presented words, colours and so on). When stimuli and responses can be measured along various dimensions, we refer to these as **variables**. Psychologists study phenomena by manipulating (that is, increasing or decreasing) the level of one or more of these variables to see how it affects other variables.

Table 5.1 summarises the main concepts in experimental design and illustrates them with an example from a (hypothetical) study of the effect of alcohol on dream imagery. In this study, a psychologist would give different amounts of alcohol to different groups of volunteers. Some volunteers would get more alcohol to drink than others, and some would get none at all. Each morning the volunteers would record the extent to which their dreams contained vivid imagery.

Key issues in thinking about experiments

If we are to think critically about experiments, there are two key questions we must ask about the way an experiment has been designed and carried out. First, does the experiment actually test what it claims it is testing? Second, are the results relevant to the real world? Both these questions relate to what is termed 'validity'.

Validity

A study is valid to the extent that it actually does permit deductions about the hypothesis being evaluated to be made. In order for a study to be valid, it must not be open to criticism that some explanation of the results other than that indicated in the hypothesis is possible. Note that a study can be a valid test of a hypothesis but that hypothesis does not receive any support from the data. Validity is about the adequacy of the test, not the outcome. In the hypothetical example given above, the

Table 5.1 Key concepts in experimental design for behavioural research

Key concept	Meaning	Example in drink and imagery experiment
Independent variable	The variable the psychologist manipulates. The participants are pre-assigned by the researcher and this is *independent* of what the participant does	The number of units of alcohol given to the participant
Levels of an independent variable	The different *amounts* of treatment or *degree* of exposure to the treatment received by the participant. Each level amounts to a condition in the experiment	For example: 0 units, 4 units, 8 units of alcohol. Each participant would be allocated to groups which would receive one of these levels of 'treatment' which would create an experimental 'condition'. Thus the giving of 8 units might be labelled the 'high alcohol' condition
Dependent variable	The variable the psychologist measures. So called because the 'reading' *depends* on the participant	The total number of references to vivid imagery in dream diary
Hypothesis	The prediction the psychologist has made about the psychological phenomenon. The way the dependent variable responds (or not) to the independent variable will tell the psychologist whether the hypothesis should be rejected or not	'Higher levels of alcohol will lead to higher levels of vivid imagery in subsequent dreams'
Control variable	The variable(s) the psychologist tries to keep the same for all participants to ensure that like is being compared with like	Number of vivid dreams the participant normally has; number of units of alcohol normally drunk and so on
Experimental group	The group of participants who are given the main 'treatment' of the experiment (could be several such subgroups, each getting a different amount of 'treatment')	The participants who are randomly allocated to the subgroup(s) who will receive alcohol
Control group	The group of participants who do not receive the treatment. This group is used as a baseline for comparison with the experimental group	The group of participants given no alcohol at all. Their level of reported vivid imagery would be used as a baseline for comparison

(cont'd)

Table 5.1 Key concepts in experimental design for behavioural research (cont'd)

Key concept	Meaning	Example in drink and imagery experiment
Placebo	A dummy treatment given to the control group so that they don't know they are in a control group	Participants in a control group would be given tasteless liquid and told that it is alcoholic spirit
Double-blind	An experiment where not only do the participants not know whether they are getting the real treatment or the placebo but the researcher or technician running the experiment does not know either (in order to stop them unintentionally treating control and experimental groups differently)	The technician administering the drinks or rating the diaries would not know which subjects had received alcohol
Randomisation	The allocation of participants to the control or experimental group on a random basis. This makes sure there are no systematic differences between the two groups	As each participant turns up for the experiment, the researcher flips a coin to determine whether the participant goes into the experimental group or the control group. Or, if a double-blind is being used, the researcher flips a coin to determine which numbered set of glasses of liquid is given to the subject
Between-subjects design	An experimental design where participants are put in either an experimental or control group but not both. The comparisons are thus between (groups of) participants (that is, Participant one at level one with Participant two at level two)	A between-subject design version of this experiment would involve participants being allocated to one and only one of the 0 units, 4 units or 8 units groups.
Within-subjects design	An experimental design where participants are allocated to both experimental and control conditions at different times. Comparisons are within subject (that is, Participant one at level one with Participant one at level two and so on)	A within-subjects design version of this experiment would possibly involve participants being allocated to one of the levels on day one and then one of the other two levels on day two and the third level on day three

study would be valid to the extent that it actually did provide a good *test* of the claim that levels of alcohol affected the vividness of dream imagery. Whether the results turn out to support the hypothesis is irrelevant to the validity of the experiment.

A study is valid if and only if it tests what it *sets out* to test. An experiment that is actually a good test of the effect of caffeine on talkativeness is low on validity if it was originally designed to be a test of the effect of relaxation on interpersonal attractiveness. It is worth mentioning this because some research papers have all the superficial features of intensive research (several variables, multiple levels, large number of subjects and so on) but are rather vague in the introduction section about what the hypotheses are. We cannot tell from reading the report on the work done in a laboratory if the experiment was a valid one or not – we need to know what the experiment was *intended* to test. In general terms, it is important that an experiment is not just a logical and internally consistent test, it must also be a test that has some broader applicability across a range of contexts and external to the laboratory. In other words, all experiments should be able to demonstrate both **internal** and **external validity**. In practice, these forms of validity are treated very differently.

Internal validity

Internal validity is the extent to which the study actually does assess the relationship between the variables which it sets out to assess. A questionnaire study might just test a correlation between two variables so it would be internally valid if it achieves that aim. However, since experiments are designed to test *causal* relationships between variables, an experiment is valid to the extent that it allows inferences about causality to be drawn. In order to achieve this, the experimenter must adhere to the basic design principles of randomisation and experimental control. The researcher must design the study to show that any differences between the experimental condition and the control condition on the dependent measure are attributable only to the different levels of the independent variable *and not something else*. The experimenter must also show that as actually executed the experiment did not succumb to various potential threats to the aim of demonstrating the effect of the independent variable on the dependent variable.

When comparing two or more groups, there is always the danger of **contamination** between conditions. That is to say, the treatment intended for only one group leaks out and affects some other group as well. For example, if you are testing the effect of rock versus classical music on study effectiveness, you do not want your rock subjects distracted by Mozart or your classical participants distracted by Meatloaf as it wafts/pounds from an adjacent cubicle. Similarly, if you are comparing two types of rehearsal strategy in a memory experiment, you do not want subjects swapping notes with each other at the break about what technique seems to work better. The thing that is most likely to leak in human research is information. You do not want your subjects discussing the experiment with each other beforehand. Thus dealing with the threat of contamination means controlling not just the acoustic environment, but the information flow. As far as possible, keep your participants as far apart in space and time while maintaining identical all other aspects of their experience.

A further possibility is that participants will realise that they are in a control group and seek to prove a point by performing better than anticipated. If students in a learning experiment are allocated to a group which involves just reading a book chapter 'in the way you normally do when studying', they may get a vague sense that they are just there to provide a baseline for the other subjects next door who are going to be doing all the interesting stuff. All of this underlines the fact that experiments are social transactions involving complex interaction, group dynamics and personal pride. We turn now to considering how this social dimension can threaten even a well-designed experiment, in which variables are well defined, subjects are randomly allocated to two or more groups and the behaviour of interest is carefully measured.

The experiment as social interaction

Imagine you are invited to participate in a laboratory experiment. You walk into the laboratory at the appointed hour and the experimenter gives you a piece of card with the following instructions on it:

Experimental instructions

University Department of Psychology

1. This is a study designed to assess job applicants' capacity to handle stress in face-to-face situations.

2. You will be interviewing an unemployed person who is here as part of a real job selection procedure. If the applicant does in fact do well on the test, he will be recommended for employment. If the applicant does not do well, he will not be recommended for employment.

3. Your task is to read out a set of questions to the job applicant and then give critical responses irrespective of the accuracy of the applicant's response.

4. After the applicant has answered the first eight questions you should respond as scripted on the accompanying sheet. What you should say is listed under 'stress remarks'.

The applicant comes in and appears well qualified and experienced for the job. You read out the first eight questions and the answers you are given are intelligent, lucid and to the point. You remember the experimenter's instructions and you look at the first stress remark:

'This job is much too difficult for you according to the test.' (Please state irrespective of applicant's answer.)

What would you do next?

To help you to think about what you believe you would do, consider the responses of the following five people and ask which is nearest to *your* likely response in this situation.

1. *John* looked at the highly professional instruction cards and the expensive video recording equipment and decided this was a test of management skills. So he attempted to stay calm and read out the questions in a controlled, professional manner in order to show the experimenter that he was made of stern stuff and competent at handling difficult interpersonal situations. However, he was so nervous about doing the task well that he mixed up the order of questions and read them out too quickly.

2. *Jane* remembered the mix of male and female participants in the waiting area and noted the fact that the researcher was male. She decided that the experimenter has predicted that female participants will be less likely to make the stress remarks and so she simply ignored them and said 'Well done, you are doing well, aren't you!' in order to help the researcher's project.

3. *Su* remembered the mix of male and female participants in the waiting area and noted the fact that the researcher was male. She also decided that the experimenter has predicted that female subjects will be less likely to make the stress remarks and made a point of not only making the stress remarks, but of saying them in an aggressive manner – in order to disabuse the researcher of his possible gender stereotyping.

4. *Tom* looked at the nervous applicant and the door to the room where the researcher was taping the experiment and decided that he didn't really want to make the stress remarks. However, he could not face walking out and leaving the candidate confused and the experimenter embarrassed, so he read the stress remarks out as best he could.

These are all different possible reactions to the unusual circumstances of a psychological study. They all represent specific reactions to the challenges of being in the role of participant in a psychology experiment. In fact this scenario is taken from Meeus and Raaijmaker (1995), who were interested in studying the processes of obedience in bureaucratic contexts.

John is displaying a version of what is commonly known as **evaluation apprehension,** that is, the tendency to construe a study (especially an experiment or questionnaire) as a form of *test* where intellectual, social or other competence is being assessed. Subjects respond by trying to avoid 'failing' the test, or not doing worse than other subjects or worse than the experimenter expects. Of course many questionnaires and a small number of experiments *are* tests of competence but most are not. Even in these cases, the psychologist has no scientific interest in an individual's performance as such but rather the spread of the competence and the factors which might affect performance. It remains true that many participants do treat experiments as tests and respond in unexpected ways. This kind of behaviour is usually thought of as being motivated only by a fear of failure (hence the term evaluation *apprehension*) but it is probably true that many participants welcome the (perceived) competitive element in experimental tasks and respond accordingly. Some such subjects enjoy the testing per se, but of those who do welcome it, most welcome it because they expect to do well. Thus as well as evaluation apprehension, there is **evaluation confidence**. 'Apprehension' and 'confidence' are, however, just two of many reactions to perceived evaluation and maybe it is more useful to think in terms of an **evaluation orientation**.

Jane is apparently motivated to be a 'good subject'. She wants to 'help' the experimenter by acting as she thinks he will have predicted. She has been influenced by the features of the experiment which seem to her to convey what behaviour is expected or appropriate. These features are usually referred to as **demand characteristics** and are a major threat to the internal validity of the experiment. If subjects are behaving in ways which reflect their beliefs about what they think they should do rather than behaving 'naturally', then we will not be able to claim that any observed differences in the dependent variable are due to the independent variable. Here Jane is demonstrating subject compliance and not her 'real' behaviour when faced with an instruction to make stress-inducing remarks to an innocent job applicant. The role adopted by Jane here has been described as the **good-subject role** (Weber and Cook, 1972: 283 – an article embodying excellent inductive reasoning).

Su also appears to be sensitive to the demand characteristics of the experiment but she responds to those characteristics in a very different way. She resents the stereotyping as she sees it and behaves accordingly. Su acted the way she did because she does not accept male assumptions about female behaviour. However, some participants will react against the perceived experimenter expectations just to assert their individuality. This is a common response in everyday life and experiments and the term **subject reactance** is often used to describe how people in general and psychology subjects in particular resent being pigeon-holed. This should not be confused with the less admirable disposition of some other subjects who attempt to subvert the experiment for fun and adopt a **negativistic-subject role** (Weber and Cook, 1972).

Tom is not so much concerned with helping the experimenter as avoiding looking a fool. He has private doubts but is primarily concerned about how he will look *to others*. He displays a version of what is known as **self-presentation**, a tendency to consider how a particular course of action will look to others and what it says about oneself.

These dynamics at work in the psychology experiment often occur together of course. Although some individuals are preoccupied with the idea of doing well in tests but are not concerned about whether others know or not, most people want to do well on tests (or perceived tests), *and be seen by other subjects and the experimenter* to be doing well. Thus evaluation apprehension and self-presentation can go hand in hand. Similarly, reactance and self-presentation can go together, with participants concerned to make sure that they not only act as individuals but let the experimenter *see* them expressing their individuality.

What these forms of **reactivity** have in common is that they are all examples of participants who are behaving differently because they are being observed as part of an experiment. It is sometimes claimed that it is true of all branches of science that the action of observing a natural phenomenon and trying to record it will inevitably change the very phenomenon being observed. The Heisenberg uncertainty principle states that we cannot measure perfectly both the position and momentum of an object at the same time, so how can we measure behaviour without affecting it? We always need to bear in mind as we read about psychology experiments the simple questions: How did it look to the participant? What did they think was expected of them? What impression did they want to give? All of these 'subject roles', and the general problem of reactivity, mean that participants' behaviour is not always a response to the independent variable as we defined it, but as they perceive it to be on the basis of their interpretation of the environment around them and the interactions they have with the experimenters and other participants. Although this is a particular problem in social psychology, it affects all areas in one way or another.

All these dynamics are threats to both the internal and external validity of the experiment. If subjects are reacting to what they are interpreting the variables to be, then we cannot draw inferences about how the independent variable is affecting the dependent variable as we defined it, and consequently internal validity is low. If subjects are acting in some special way because it is an experiment, with all its evaluative connotations, then their behaviour in the experiment may not be true of their behaviour outside the experimental laboratory and the external validity would be low.

Search for meaning
The subject's search for meaning is role-motivated – if they are adopting a good-subject role, they will seek information in order to conform to the experimenter's expectations. If they are adopting a negativistic-subject role, they are looking for information to provide clues as to the simplest way of sabotaging the experiment.

THINK IT THROUGH

'Subject 29 failed to complete the assigned task'

The stereotype of the negativistic-subject role is taken for granted in most discussions of subject behaviour in experiments. He (and somehow it is always assumed to be a 'he') is presented as churlish, ignorant and destructive. Masling (1966: 96) even refers to this behaviour as the 'screw-you effect'. But is it really as simple as that? There are many reasons for subversion and resentment, not all of them misconceived and few of them irrational. It might be the case that the negativistic subject is indeed also a 'negativistic' father, student and fisherman too, visiting brooding resentment on children, lecturers and fish in equal measure, but I don't think that is always necessarily the case. Maybe the negativistic subject is coping with evaluation apprehension, or perhaps has been compelled to take part for that most debased of currencies, course credit. Perhaps he had a bad day, or the experiment is not what he thought it was going to be about. Maybe the negativistic subject is just a good subject asked to fill in one questionnaire too many.

In everyday life people are, variously, helpful, suspicious, nosey, proud, vain and vulnerable. When people enter the psychology laboratory and become 'participants' or 'subjects', they do not leave their personalities at the door. When people walk alone into a job interview, new workplace, examination hall or party, they are typically self-conscious and actively search for cues on how to act from others around them. When people walk into a laboratory it is much the same. Subjects are always actively searching to work out what is going on, what is expected of them, what judgements are being made about them and how the experimenter will interpret their behaviour (both formally in recording the behaviour and informally as another human being). Individuals do not necessarily passively accept what they are told and then respond automatically to the stimuli presented to them.

Alternatively, subjects are happy to go through the motions without trying to work out anything in particular about the interests of the experimenter. After all, one reaction time or group discussion experiment is very much like another, as long as the experiment fits the script then the subject can sail through on automatic pilot. However, when something goes wrong or there is a surprising twist to a study, then the subjects start to process information about the situation more closely. In the Meeus and Raaijmaker study above, what appeared to be an agreeable little role-play suddenly becomes an uncomfortable social dilemma, pitting one fundamental social rule (obey legitimate authority) against another (do not hurt others).

Reactivity then is when subjects act like real people rather than like subjects. Within the context of the hypothetico-deductive method, reactivity is a problem because subjects are not responding to the different levels of the independent variables as the psychologists have defined them. Instead, subjects are constructing and projecting their *own* meanings onto the experimental instructions and stimuli which means (i) the hypothesis is not being tested at all and (ii) there may be systematic differences in the effects of the independent variables on the subjects' behaviours.

'Psychologists are all perverts, you know'

Some subjects come to the laboratory with a particular view about psychology and its experiments *in general* and perceive all instructions and arrangements within that perspective. This is particularly true of some members of the general public who invariably see psychologists as a nightmare hybrid of sociobiologist and psychoanalyst, leading to the wholly unfounded suspicion that every psychology experiment is ultimately a sordid exercise in deducing bizarre sexual fantasies on the basis of unguarded arm movements. Lacking even the most rudimentary understanding of research protocol, some naïve subjects further expect that an experiment's sole purpose is to *confront* subjects with such revelations. Little wonder that researchers often rely upon student samples.

Institutional threats to validity

Most psychological research is carried out in the psychology departments of universities by research assistants on behalf of lecturers and professors. Research projects are normally funded over three years by external organisations such as research councils, charitable organisations or government departments. Over that period of time, several studies will be run by researchers in the same department using largely the same equipment, rooms or questionnaire following a well-defined **paradigm**. Naturally professors talk about their own research in their lectures and direct students to read articles which they have written, and understandably so. New posts get advertised within departments attached to existing or renewed research grants. Over a period of time, the theoretical, practical and empirical aspects of the research programme become common knowledge among staff and students alike, discussed at coffee breaks and in the lifts as much as in the lecture theatre and seminar room. In this context, there is always the possibility that the 'cover story' of any research procedure can be 'blown' and it becomes increasingly difficult to find 'naïve' subjects.

Similarly, when new researchers or research students join an existing team, the expectations to find significant results can be powerful. If the new researcher does not deliver the expected finding, the researcher can be perceived as incompetent or an outsider. Outright fraud is probably extremely rare in psychological research but the *subtle* pressures to conform and contribute to a team research project located in an institution can lead to corners being cut and ambiguity resolved in favourable directions. Possibly the most common occurrence is the quiet putting aside of non-significant results but shouting about significant results from the rooftops.

File-drawer statistic in meta-analysis

A recent development in statistical analysis is that of meta-analysis, whereby the results of a whole series of studies from around the world over several years, relating to the same hypothesis, are analysed together to determine whether the studies *taken as a whole* offer support for the hypothesis. One intriguing aspect of this procedure is the identification of what is sometimes known as the 'file-drawer statistic'. This figure is an estimate of the number of studies which would need to have been carried out which failed to support the hypothesis *but which were thrown into a bottom drawer of a notional filing cabinet somewhere* rather than being submitted for publication. In other words, meta-analysis indicates the overall probability of the hypothesis being due to something other than chance – and then states that there would have to be, say, 67 'unsuccessful' studies in file drawers of researchers around the world before the conclusion from the main part of the meta-analysis would have to be revised. The very *existence* of the file-drawer statistic confirms the extent of erroneous disregard for non-significant results by scientists. A non-significant result may be useful for science, but it is not useful for careers.

Taken together, the institutional culture of grants and publication provides a pervasive setting in which subjects, researchers and technicians can find themselves unintentionally undermining the validity of individual studies or a series of studies. These *institutional threats to validity* are rarely discussed in methodology textbooks but probably bear further examination.

Let us return to the interview experiment. Of course *we* all believe that *we* would not read out the stress remarks, lying to and hurting the applicant, and almost certainly undermining his chances of getting the job. In fact the above outline of instructions to subjects is again taken from Meeus and Raaijmaker's (1995) research on what they call 'administrative obedience', a modern-day version of the classic Milgram studies which involved subjects obeying instructions to give electric shocks to recalcitrant learners (see Chapter 7). Meuss and Raaijmaker's studies found that 91 per cent of managers did read out *all* the stress remarks. But of course *we* are all different from those subjects and would never do such a thing to a fellow subject just because we had been told to by the experimenter.

Would we?

External validity

External validity is the extent to which the results of a study can be applied to circumstances outside the specific research setting in which a particular study was carried out. In other words, the extent to which the results can be applied to what is known as 'the real world'. For example, a researcher interested in the effects of noisy working environments on the accuracy of readings made from machine instrumentation might set up a laboratory task involving single pitch noises being played while participants read numbers from dials and counters. The experimenter would be able to control the volume and duration and even location of the sound in relation to the subject. But the noise in *real* factories is normally many different sounds at different pitches and volumes and so the results of the study would be seen as being low in external validity.

The problem here is one of trading off experimental control for external applicability. It is difficult to reproduce in a laboratory setting the complex stimuli and circumstances of the real world, but psychologists try to get the balance right in a way that reflects the major aims of their research. If the research is interested in human information processing, then the study would use well-defined, controllable stimuli. On the other hand, if the focus is on the application of research to specific settings then more 'messy' but realistic situations will be used. Of course rather than trying to *reproduce* complex sensory and social environments in the laboratory, it is easier to actually *go* out into the real world itself and carry out the research 'in the field' using the situations we find there. However, such field research is expensive and difficult to do well.

There is generally a trade-off between internal validity and external validity in all psychology research. A study which makes tight experimental control over a narrow set of circumstances and a homogeneous set of participants a priority is unlikely to find results that are widely applicable to a large number of other settings or relevant to a more diverse range of human beings. Conversely, a study that tries to capture the unpredictability, uncertainty, diversity and ambiguity of real-world settings is unlikely to find results that are immune from criticisms about poor internal validity.

Stanley Milgram's experiments on obedience to authority in the 1970s were criticised on the grounds of low external validity. Many of his critics argued that as interesting as it was, being ordered to give electric shocks to poor learners did not involve the same psychological processes as say those which affected German prison guards in concentration camps. Milgram did not accept this criticism, however, arguing that although superficially the circumstances were less severe, the psychological processes were *sufficiently* similar to allow inferences to be drawn from the laboratory and applied to real life. Milgram argued that in both cases individuals stopped acting as autonomous individuals and adopted an 'agentic state', that is, acting merely as the agent of another.

> While the coloring and details of obedience differ in other circumstances, the basic processes remain the same, much as the basic process of combustion is the same for both a burning match and a forest fire. The problem of generalising from one to the other does not consist of point-for-point comparison between one and the other (the match is small, the forest is extensive etc.) but depends entirely on whether one has reached a correct theoretical understanding of the relevant process. In the case of combustion, we understand the process of rapid oxidation under conditions of electron excitation, and in obedience, the restructuring of internal mental processes in the agentic state. (Milgram, 1974: 174)

THINK IT THROUGH

Milgram's analogy of combustion processes as justification for the external validity of laboratory research is one of the most famous in social psychology. But do *you* find it convincing? What natural science processes are *different* in the laboratory and in the field? How do we know whether Milgram's combustion analogy is an appropriate analogy? Consider our discussion of analogies in Chapter 2.

Improving external validity

It is much easier to reconstruct some psychological phenomena in the laboratory than others. For example, obedience to authority in the real world is a complex and multifaceted phenomenon involving powerful forces and subtle interpersonal transactions. On the other hand, colour vision in a psychology laboratory is much the same as it is in a submarine or at the top of Mount Everest, during a wedding ceremony or during a jailbreak. When we review social psychology, developmental psychology and cognitive psychology in later chapters, we shall see that external validity is an issue for all areas of psychology, albeit in different ways.

For that reason there is no simple formula for improving the quality of external validity in psychological research. Different types of researcher have different ideas on how best to achieve better external validity, since they each have different ideas about what is significant for psychology about the 'real world'. Additionally, for mainstream positivist researchers, the main goal is to establish linear cause and effect relationships between variables which are robust enough to be demonstrable across a range of real-world contexts. For more qualitatively minded researchers, external validity relates to modelling the subtle, reciprocal and evolving relationships between people and the structures which produce action since both, they argue, have a complexity which cannot be easily captured in the laboratory (see Chapter 6).

Generally speaking, external validity is improved whenever naturally occurring rather than artificial stimuli are used, whenever participants have to confront subjectively real situations rather than artificial simulations, whenever the situation is representative rather than atypical of the range of situations of that type, and whenever stimuli are presented in context rather than in an artificial setting. One final way of improving external validity is to ensure that the group of people who take part are representative of the population of interest. This brings us on to consideration of how we select the people who are going to take part in our research – the people who are going to make up the sample.

Samples

Since the subject matter of psychology is the study of human behaviour and experience, at some point there is no alternative but to recruit participants to your study. Generally speaking, the aim of a psychological study is to make conclusions about people in general and not just a narrow subset of them. This is inherent in the positivist approach to psychology typically emphasised by experimental psychologists. Given that we cannot test *all* the people that our hypothesis might relate to (the 'population'), there has to be some attempt to make sure that the people who *do* take part (the 'sample') are in some way representative of that larger group. Ideally, the sample should be *randomly* selected from the population of interest. If we are to have a hypothesis which predicts that counselling is more effective than drugs in treating postnatal depression, then clearly the relevant population is all women who have ever had postnatal depression. The *sample* is all those women who agree to take part in our study and actually finish up doing so.

It should be clear that the sample is not going to be *completely* randomly drawn from the population. Even after setting aside the logistics of travel and availability, our sample will not be random as many women do not want to take part in studies of any kind and, more trivially, some may never receive the postal invitation to take part because they move house. The best we can hope to do is to make the sample as representative as possible by including as wide a range of different types of women as we can. At the very least we must be aware of the ways in which our sample is different from the population in question. If we find that the majority of our sample are aged between 19 and 24, and that all of them are white, we need to make sure we limit our conclusions from the study to that age and ethnic group.

When reading through psychological studies, you will find that the vast majority are carried out on undergraduate psychology students, especially first-year or 'sophomore' students. This is defended on the grounds that the processes being studied are generally the same in undergraduates as they are in the rest of the population. Often the content of the task reflects students' concerns. So for example in a study of persuasion, attitudes to the legalisation of cannabis might be used. No one is suggesting that students' attitudes towards marijuana are representative of the general population's attitude, but rather the *processes* of attitude change for relevant issues for students regarding drug law reform are representative of the processes involved generally when people change their views on issues that are relevant to them. Thus the content is not representative but the processes are, and in that sense student samples are treated as acceptable.

But is this distinction between content and process enough to justify student samples? Sears (1986) found that 72 per cent of studies reported in the main social psychology journals used American undergraduate students aged between 17 and 19. He argues that even the processes of attitude change of this group are not representative of the attitude processes overall. Students, he argued, may still be developing their political and social attitudes and these attitudes are therefore more likely to change than those of the average person. Such 17–19-year-olds, largely from middle-class backgrounds, are already known from other research to be more egocentric, obedient to authority and dependent on the approval of peers but less empathetic and with a less stable circles of friends. Social psychology's model of people being conformist and malleable might be a direct result of relying so heavily on an undergraduate student sample.

Reliability

The **reliability** of a measure is the extent to which it provides consistent information every time we use it. A ruler is a very reliable instrument since every time we measure the same object it gives as the same 'reading'. Psychological measures tend to be much less consistent. We want to use instruments (including questionnaires and rating scales) which will give us the same assessment every time we apply it to the same behaviour. The issue of reliability is particularly crucial in the study of personality where personality and ability tests are the most common form of methodology.

Ethics

It is of the utmost importance that psychological research is carried out to the highest possible ethical standards. The role of research psychologists puts the individual in a position of authority that is open to abuse. We do not need to be familiar with the experiments by Milgram on obedience to realise that participants in experiments are vulnerable to the instructions of the researcher. The key principles of ethics for research on human subjects are normally taken to be:

1. Doing no harm
2. Informed consent
3. Avoiding deception
4. Freedom to withdraw

5. Confidentiality
6. Adequate debriefing
7. Reporting research accurately

Doing no harm, informed consent, freedom to withdraw and confidentiality are the main principles identified by the British Psychological Society in its ethical code of conduct (BPS, 1996). American ethical codes tend to be more extensive and also include such issues as plans for data security, reporting of results, publication credit, avoiding plagiarism and sharing data (APA, 1992).

THINK IT THROUGH

What would you identify as the most difficult ethical principle for psychologists to adhere to? Write your answer down along with your justification. After you have read this section, return to your answer and consider whether you want to change it.

Doing no harm

Research should not involve participants being exposed to risks which are outside the range of risks to which they would normally expose themselves. Participants should not be subjected to painful experiences either physically or emotionally. The assessment of potential harm has been a key issue in some classic social psychology experiments, such as the obedience to authority experiments of Milgram (1974) and the studies of Zimbardo (1971) on the effects of role on behaviour. Assessing potential psychological harm is much more difficult than assessing potential physical harm. During psychological experiments participants can experience feelings of hurt pride, anxiety and embarrassment. This might possibly be no more than might be expected in the everyday course of events but sometimes it is to a more extreme level, as was the case in the Milgram experiments where participants experienced significant distress at the perceived pain of another. Participants can also feel bad *after* a study when they realise how they treated another human being, or how foolish they were to have been so easily taken in during some procedure.

   Even when participants have been reassured that what they have been exposed to is not what they thought and that their reactions, although surprising, are similar to those of many others, participants can still harbour residual feelings of annoyance, low self-esteem and confusion. Of course participation in psychological research can also be positive. Participants can find some experiments fun, informative and even offering insights into their own behaviour and that of others. Exceptionally, participation can lead to a radical rethinking of direction in life as was reportedly the case by some of the participants in Zimbardo's role-play studies. In truth, though, the vast majority of psychology experiments are just plain *boring* for the participant, since often the same behaviour such as pressing a button on a keyboard has to be repeated sometimes hundreds of times. Similarly, social psychology research often involves completion of lengthy questionnaires or workbooks. Most researchers justify their studies in terms of costs outweighing benefits. However, such calculations can be problematic (as we shall see in Chapter 7 when we discuss Milgram in more detail).

Informed consent

No one should be coerced to take part in a study. Participants must be told what is going to happen to them, they must understand what they are told and they must give consent on that basis and on that basis alone. If the research extends over a period of time then consent must be sought on several occasions. The emphasis here is on *informed* consent. If a subject agrees to take part in a study, that agreement can only be to that which he, as an intelligent adult, understands his participation in the study to involve. It is just not on, for example, to ask someone to take part in a study using a 'PPG' – unless you also explain to them very, very clearly that a PPG is a penile plethysmograph designed to record the strength of erections. (If anyone is mug enough to agree to participate in your study, there should, however, be no excuse for any further ethical malpractice, since there is a whole section on the use of this bizarre equipment in the BPS ethics guidelines. The interested reader is referred to page 45 of the BPS (1996) Guidelines). Those guidelines also helpfully point out that PPG assessment 'should only be carried out in appropriate physical conditions with due regard to the standards of safety, privacy, comfort and current hygiene recommendations'. And I don't think any of us would argue with that.

Avoiding deception

Sometimes psychological research requires that the participant is not aware of all the features of an experiment. Sometimes the deception is trivial, as when a researcher asks everyone in the room to complete 'the' questionnaire in front of them, clearly implying that there is only one definitive questionnaire, when in fact there are four different versions around the room each with subtle differences in the instructions. More usually, however, deception in the past has involved, for example, telling a subject that she has performed poorly on a test of intelligence in order to observe the nature of her subsequent contributions to a decision-making group to test the impact of low self-esteem on social confidence.

If we tell subjects everything about a study, the study will be pointless since they will alter their behaviour. If we tell them nothing, then they will occasionally and understandably complain that we have deceived them. Where do we draw the line? The general rule is that *deception should not be used* unless:

1. subjects are not likely to object once they are told about how they were deceived
2. the prospective scientific, educational, or applied value justifies the deception
3. there are no alternatives.

Although psychologists are urged by both the BPS and the APA to consult with disinterested and independent advisors, the application of these principles is the responsibility of the individual researcher. Students should always consult their tutor or supervisor about any worries they may have on ethical matters. Just how one is to judge in advance whether subjects would object if they had been told, whether the costs outweigh the benefits or who decides whether there are any alternatives is spelt out much less clearly.

Freedom to withdraw

If the experiment turns out to be different from that which the subject antici-pated, or the subject has second thoughts about participation, she should be free to leave the experiment without penalty. This applies whether or not the subject has been paid to take part (although there is no guidance on whether such subjects should return the payments). This right to withdraw can be applied *retrospectively* by the subject. For example, a subject might take part in an experi-ment which seemed fine at the time, only to discover later that the experiment was full of inappropriate deception and abuse. Even though the subject has taken part, he can tell the investigator that he now wishes to withdraw and that all his data should be destroyed (BPS, 1996, S6.2: 9).

THINK IT THROUGH

Rethinking ethics

Recently Laura Brown (1997) has advocated a movement towards a radical new approach to ethics in psychology termed **liberatory ethics**, which tries to redress what she sees as some of the limitations of traditional ethics codes such as the BPS and APA guidelines. Drawing on experience in feminist therapy, Brown argues that traditional ethics codes:

■ regulate only the process and not the content or consequences of psychological research

■ enable psychologists to split the private from the professional, enabling them to avoid responsibility for certain actions

■ set too high a set of thresholds for what constitutes unprofessional behaviour.

More generally, Brown argues that current codes of ethics tend to protect the status quo and the professional and legal interests of psychologists rather than the real needs of the 'subjects' of the research. Brown advocates an explicitly feminist code of ethics that blurs the distinctions between subjects/clients and researchers and avoids a hierarchical regulatory force behind the code. Illustrative of the very different model of ethics advanced by Brown and her colleagues is the fact that a commitment to anti-racism and anti-racist projects is identified as an ethical prerequisite for all psychologists.

What do you think of Brown's idea? Could it be the outline of a new system of profes-sional ethics or should it just be an appendix to an established system? Is it compro-mising professional liberty or a recipe for giving psychology back to the people?

Confidentiality

All information gained about a participant during an experiment is confidential unless explicitly agreed in advance with individual subjects. Thus subjects must never be named or otherwise made identifiable from any written report on the study. Legal considerations might overrule this in terms of the Data Protection Act 1998 or court order. Psychologists do not enjoy the same kind of privileged relationship with their subjects as doctors do with their patients or lawyers with their clients. Subjects are often reassured to be told that results will only ever be presented as aggregates with no individual data being identified. A distinction must be drawn between anonymity and confidentiality. 'Anonymity' means that the subject cannot be identified subsequently, even by the researcher, while 'confidentiality' implies that, although the subject is in principle identifiable, no identification will in fact be made. It is important when running your own experiments not to promise anonymity when what you mean is confidentiality.

Adequate debriefing

When the subject's participation is concluded, the psychologist is required where possible to complete the subject's understanding of the research study by providing a clear account of the purposes of the experiment. This might amount to no more than a limited elaboration of the hypothesis in some experiments, but it might involve a more extended discussion in complex studies. It is also necessary to make sure that the subject has adequate opportunity to inform the researcher of any negative experiences they have had during their participation, or make complaints or observations about any aspect of the conduct of the study. For this reason, the common practice of preprinted debriefing sheets which are distributed to subjects after their participation is, on its own, probably inadequate. Most subjects are more likely to bring problems to the researcher's attention if they get the opportunity to engage in a conversation.

The fact that subjects are going to be debriefed does not of course provide an excuse for subjecting them to all sorts of deceptions and torments simply because they can be told the truth and calmed down later. Subjects exposed to procedures which lower their self-esteem are not brought to their original level of self-confidence simply by being debriefed and told that the feedback they received on their IQ or whatever was a deception. Therefore, where deception or emotional manipulation of subjects has been carried out, debriefing is a necessary but not sufficient corrective procedure for ensuring the subject's well being.

Reporting research accurately

Once the data has been collected, analysed and is ready for publication (be it in a journal or student project report), the ethical responsibilities of the psychologist have not finished. In terms of publishing research, psychologists must not plagiarise (that is, present others' work as their own) and must not publish the same data twice (as though it were two different experiments, for example). Copies of data must be kept available for other researchers to scrutinise in order to check claims made about results.

THINK IT THROUGH

Go back to your answer to the question I posed earlier about which of the principles of ethical behaviour is most difficult to adhere to. Are you still happy with your original answer? Give your reason for changing or not as the case may be.

Thinking about theories and experiments together

In Chapter 3 we discussed how we can think about the extent to which any given psychological *theory* is likely to be useful. So far in this chapter we have discussed how we can think about the extent to which any given psychological *experiment* is likely to be scientifically effective, externally applicable and ethically sound. What we need to do now is think about how theories and experiments are *connected*.

The reason why we do experiments is to test theories. More precisely, we deductively derive hypotheses from theories, which are then put to empirical test. You will remember from Chapter 3 that theories are made up of theoretical constructs (for example 'frustration' and 'aggression') and relational propositions (for example 'causes') which describe the relationship between these theoretical constructs. Thus, we can derive specific hypotheses from theories such as 'everything else being equal, increases in frustration will lead to increases in aggression'.

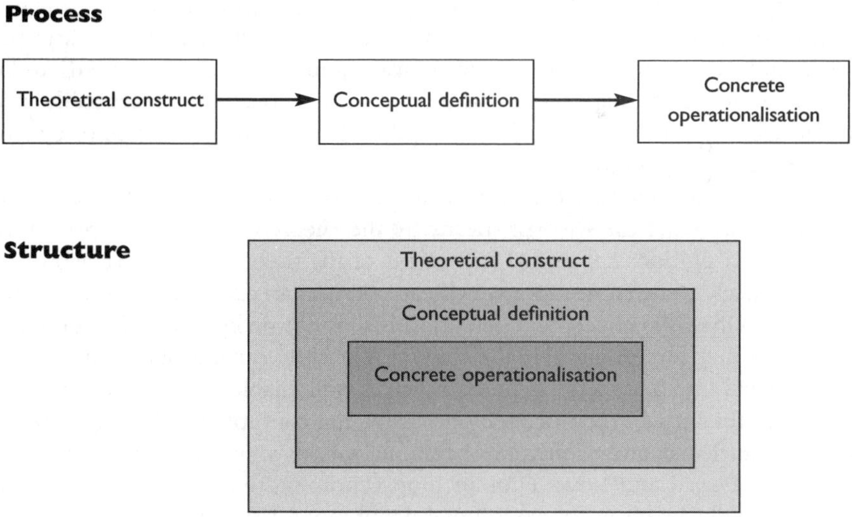

Process

Structure

Figure 5.1   Process and structure of operationalisation

However, theories and hypotheses are not in themselves specific enough to be directly testable. We need to transform these rather abstract statements into something more practical if we are to do any real research rather than just talk about it. What is required is a translation of the theoretical construct first of all into a **conceptual definition** that defines the theoretical construct more narrowly for the purposes of the experiment. Although the conceptual definition should be a simple *definition* which defines the theoretical construct for all experiments, in practice in psychology conceptual definitions are usually *examples* of the theoretical construct. Finally, we need a **concrete operationalisation** which identifies the practical means by which the conceptual definition (and hence by implication the theoretical construct) will be measured. The process and structure of operationalisation is presented in Figure 5.1.

Some examples will make things clearer here. In a social psychology experiment involving the hypothesis that perceived similarity leads to attraction, the conceptual definition of 'similarity' might be 'perceived similarity of attitudes' but the concrete operationalisation might be 'the number of questions on a social issues questionnaire which the other person is presented as having answered in the same way as the subject', and so on. Table 5.2 gives some examples across different areas of psychology (the example for developmental psychology will be looked at in more detail in Chapter 9).

Generally, psychologists often talk about this entire translation process from theoretical construct/relational propositions to conceptual definitions and concrete operationalisations as *operationalising* an hypothesis. One of the challenges of reviewing the research literature in an area is the wide range of conceptual definitions and operationalisations that is used. Thus the inductive process of moving from a wide range of specific cases to a general (tentative) conclusion is made difficult because of the use of many different operationalisations of the same theoretical constructs. Of course if a theory can be conceptualised and operationalised in different ways and is not disconfirmed (in the Popper sense), then that theory can be said to be robust, and is probably more useful than a theory which has been tested with only a narrow range of conceptualisations and operationalisations.

The theoretical construct is turned into a more specific conceptual definition which clarifies what the theorist means by the theoretical construct. Sometimes conceptual definitions are formal statements of the theoretical construct but they are more likely to be an instance which can count as an example of the theoretical construct. Often the conceptual definition is simply a definition of the theoretical construct which is meaningful in the context. The conceptual definition has still got to be turned into a something practical which will enable measurement of a real variable in the actual experiment. By necessity, the conceptual definition is turned into the much narrower concrete operationalisation which specifies exactly what will be measured and how. Thus in biopsychology, the theoretical construct, 'arousal', might be given the conceptual definition, for the purposes of an experiment, of 'increases in nervous system activity', which is further specified for practical measurement purposes as 'average of 10 readings on a heart rate monitor'.

Thus, there is a progressively greater specificity of definition as we go from the theoretical construct to conceptual definition and concrete operationalisation.

Table 5.2 Examples of conceptualisation and operationalisation in five areas of psychology

	Social psychology	Developmental psychology	Cognitive psychology	Personality and individual differences	Biopsychology
Theoretical constructs	Perceived similarity	Social interaction	Recall	Extraversion	Arousal
Conceptual definitions	Perceived similarity in terms of attitudes on social issues	Discussing task with peers	Recall of words following category cue	Sociability, impulsiveness activity, liveliness, excitability	Increased activity in the autonomic and central nervous system
Concrete operationalisations	Perceiving other to have 75% or more similar answers on a social attitudes questionnaire	Receiving clues about task from two other children while sitting at a small table with the experimenter	Numbers of words legibly written down in two minutes, three minutes after exposure to three groups of 10 related words	Score on extraversion subscale of Eysenck personality questionnaire	Average of 10 readings on a heart rate monitor

However, specificity is bought at a cost – the more precise we try to be about what we mean and how we want to measure it the narrower our focus, a process we can refer to as **operational narrowing**. We need to be alert to the consequences of excessive operational narrowing, since it will limit the kind of inferences we can subsequently draw from the study. In some cases, we may finish up with a concrete operationalisation which only covers a very narrow aspect of the theoretical construct from which it is derived. In terms of a specific study, we might find that claims about 'social interaction' are tested by the measurement of a very specific type of social interaction which may or may not be representative of social interaction in general. While it might be the case that children sitting round a table counts as 'social interaction', what happens around that table might not be true of social interaction *in general*. Thus an operational definition might be *consistent* with a theoretical construct but it might not necessarily be *representative* of it. In extreme cases, the concrete operationalisation might not even be consistent with the theoretical construct, as might be the case if we defined 'social interaction' in terms of some irrelevant feature such as 'words recalled'. Usually the extent of 'operational slippage' is a matter of dispute and is not as clear cut as this.

Reports of psychological research are not always explicit about whether the theoretical construct, conceptual definition or operationalisation is being referred to at different points in the text and some amount of detective work can be involved. We will explore this further in our analysis of operationalisation in Chapter 9.

SUMMARY

The central aim of an experiment is to set up controlled observations which will allow the experimenter to test the claim that the manipulation of the independent variable, rather than anything else, was the cause of any observed changes or group differences in the dependent variable. This aim can be pursued through laboratory or field experiments but the former, being easier to control, are perceived as more effective in this respect. The internal validity of an experiment is the extent to which hypothesised causal links can be inferred from the experiment as designed and executed. Various threats to internal validity can be addressed by running comparable groups and randomising subjects between those groups. External validity is the extent to which the design and execution of an experiment is such that the results of the experiment are applicable to a range of real-world settings outside the laboratory. Ethical codes provide guidance on protecting the physical, psychological and social well being of participants but some feminist writers have suggested that they do not address all the relevant issues around morality and psychological practice and have proposed alternatives. Returning to the relationship between theory and research, it can be seen that translating an abstract theoretical construct into a workable practical research activity often requires compromises and narrowing of the original theoretical definition. While not necessarily damaging to the validity of the experiment, operationalisation does require us to think carefully about what exactly an experiment is testing in the final analysis.

KEY TERMS

Conceptual definition ■ Concrete operationalisation
Contamination ■ Demand characteristics
Evaluation apprehension ■ Evaluation confidence
Evaluation orientation ■ Good-subject role
Internal/external validity ■ Liberatory ethics
Negativistic-subject role ■ Operational narrowing
Paradigm ■ Reactivity ■ Reliability ■ Self-presentation
Subject reactance ■ Variables

FURTHER READING

There are many texts which cover experimental design and statistics in readable and accessible ways. Among the better more recent ones are Haslam, S A and McGarty, C (1998) *Doing Psychology: An Introduction To Research Methodology and Statistics* (London: Sage) and McQueen, R A and Knussen, C (1999) *Research Methods in Psychology: A Practical Introduction* (Hemel Hempstead: Prentice Hall).

USEFUL WEBSITES

Bill Trochim's Centre for Social Research Methods
http://trochim.human.cornell.edu/kb/index.htm
A breathtaking hypertext guide to all things methodological. A quantitative bias but very comprehensive and authoritative. The Knowledge Base is an electronic textbook on research methods in the social science which continues to expand.

American Psychological Association (APA) Ethics
http://www.apa.org/ethics/
APA Ethics Guidelines.

Australian Psychological Society (APS) Ethics
http://www.psychsociety.com.au/about/fr_about.htm
Australian Psychological Society's code of ethics.

Canadian Psychological Association Code of Ethics
http://www.cpa.ca/ethics.html

Spanish Psychological Association Ethics/ Colegio Oficial de Psicólogos
http://www.cop.es/English/docs/code.htm
The English version of COP's code of ethics.

Thinking Critically about Qualitative Research in Psychology

6

CHAPTER OVERVIEW

As discussed in the previous chapter, the dominant approach to contemporary psychology research is the laboratory experiment. However, there have always been concerns that such research is missing something important about human behaviour and experience. It has been argued that the subtleties and nuances of everyday life do not always lend themselves to arrangement into the variables and statistical tests characteristic of experimental research carried out within the framework of logical positivism. Traditionally, alternative methods which involved the direct observation of, or even participation in, various real-world social groups, practices and institutions were looked upon as suspect by mainstream researchers. Recently, however, there has been a resurgence of interest in qualitative methods, fuelled in part since the 1970s by renewed awareness of philosophical and cultural issues in psychology. Nevertheless, many mainstream researchers remain sceptical of all qualitative research, claiming that such approaches are sometimes not even worthy of the name 'psychology'. This chapter will explore some of these issues and provide a basis for assessing qualitative work. Issues around evidence and validity will be reviewed and consideration given to the distinctive value base of qualitative research.

LEARNING OBJECTIVES

By the end of this chapter you should be able to:

- Identify the main differences between qualitative and other forms of research in psychology
- Articulate the main features of the value base of qualitative research
- Think critically about the role of traditional conceptions of validity as they apply to qualitative research

Both Angela and Tom are interested in finding out more about the psychology of bullying at work of workers by managers. Angela believes that the best way to do this is to set up an experiment in which bosses are randomly allocated to a 'pressure' or 'no pressure' condition. In the 'pressure' condition, the manager has to make a rapid series of complex judgements on the basis of detailed calculations against the clock and simultaneously supervise the work of another subject. In the 'no pressure' condition, the manager simply has to circle all the vowels on a page while supervising the subject. Angela will compare the number of intimidating remarks made by the managers to their 'supervisees' in both conditions using statistical tests.

Tom, on the other hand, decides to interview a range of managers and victims of bullying in the workplace. He is interested in the interpretations each side makes of the other's behaviour. He will record these interviews and transcribe them. Later he will interpret the meaning of the comments, possibly analysing the main themes, metaphors, contrasts and categories used.

Angela is taking a broadly logical positivist approach to the study of bullying. She will be using operational definitions of 'pressure' and 'intimidating remarks', and she will be using statistics and deductive reasoning to determine if the former *causes* the latter. Tom, on the other hand, is interested in the way managers and workers talk about and interpret the *meanings* of pressure, intimidation and bullying.

THINK IT THROUGH

Which of these two approaches appeals to you? What are the advantages and limitations of each? Which approach is the more likely to lead to reliable conclusions? Which one is more likely to yield useful information in order to reduce bullying?

Overview of qualitative approaches

A small but increasing number of psychologists feel that the positivist approach alone cannot provide the answers to the questions that psychologists are posing. Indeed some psychologists feel that the scientific approach, with its emphasis on quantification and controlled experiments, is *hindering* attempts to understand human beings and should be abandoned immediately. As an alternative to the quantitative approach of mainstream experimental psychology based around the hypothetico-deductive model, some psychologists advocate a range of qualitative methods that are designed to explore the more subtle and fluid aspects of human experience.

These qualitative methods, however, are in turn criticised by mainstream researchers as subjective, loose and leading to results that cannot be **replicated**. Many scientific psychologists consider most qualitative approaches to be little better than impressionistic journalism and have no place in psychology. They might argue, for example, that, although Angela's work may be seen to be narrow, her conclusions will be more easily traced back to the evidence than Tom's.

Relativist and realist qualitative methods

At the outset we need to note that there are two kinds of qualitative research in psychology. Although most qualitative researchers adopt a relativist position, others adoption a realist position. Relativist qualitative researchers (sometimes referred to as doing qualitative research with a capital 'Q') completely reject the epistemology of positivism and subscribe instead to relativism and social constructionism. Realist qualitative researchers (sometimes referred to as doing qualitative research with a small 'q') by contrast broadly accept the realist and **essentialist** assumptions of logical positivism but argue that experiments are not the only means to draw strong inferences from data.

Interviewing as a technique is used by both relativist and realist camps, but the interpretation of participants' responses betrays their very different epistemologies. The replies an interviewee gives in a realist interview are seen as potential indicators of a real underlying psychological belief, attitude or emotion (for example Marcia's (1980) analyses of young people's stages of identity development). For that reason interviewers often seek to follow detailed protocols which ensure consistency with different interviewees and different researchers. This can be contrasted with the kinds of interview used as part of relativistic qualitative research, in which the words, phrasing, forms of argument and justification the interviewee uses are themselves the main source of interest (see, for example, Potter and Wetherell, 1987). The relativist position is explored in more detail in Chapter 8 but for now we will look at relativist research as an alternative to traditional scientific research in psychology.

Relativist qualitative research and logical positivism compared

We shall return to realist qualitative research later but we must first consider the important differences between relativist qualitative research and traditional 'scientific' logical positivism as they apply to psychology. We should recognise immediately that the dispute between relativist qualitative researchers and quantitative (logical positivist) researchers is not simply about methods. It is not the case that both sides agree on the nature of human psychological life and why we should be studying it but simply disagree on the best investigative technique. The dispute runs much deeper than that, and any attempt to think clearly and critically about qualitative approaches must begin by recognising the extended battle lines between these two camps.

The disagreement is first and foremost about what we can *know* about human behaviour and experience. For positivists, human behaviour such as happiness, jealously and memory – if they can be studied at all – can only be treated as any other kind of *natural* phenomena such as combustion, gravity or photosynthesis. For relativist qualitative psychologists, human activity, however, is not a given within the natural world but *constructed* – partly by the individuals themselves, partly by the culture they live in and, in the event of empirical inquiry, by the research process itself. Thus, the dispute is fundamentally about the kind of knowing that is possible about behaviour and experience, that is, the dispute is primarily about epistemology. It is essential to keep this in mind when making sense of relativist qualitative research in psychology, particularly in relation to issues concerning the validity and value of such studies.

A useful way of establishing an initial orientation to the difference between these two camps is to recognise that while quantitative research is concerned with understanding the *causes* of a phenomenon, relativist qualitative research is concerned with understanding the *meaning* of a phenomenon. Thus while the positivist might ask 'What factors cause jealousy to occur?', the qualitative researcher might instead ask 'Under what conditions is it meaningful to my participants for them to say that someone *is* jealous?' or, 'What do they mean by using the term "jealous"'. In order to understand the cause, the positivist will seek to test whether the phenomenon can be produced under certain controlled conditions (usually in a laboratory), while in order to understand the meaning, a qualitative researcher will seek to interpret the processes and structures which give cultural and social significance to the phenomenon (usually in real-world settings). It is often pointed out that quantitative research is generally focused on *prediction* while qualitative research is generally focused on *description*. Some quantitative researchers grudgingly accept that there is a role for qualitative research as a first step in getting a basic picture of a phenomenon. However, qualitative researchers usually reject the idea that qualitative research is merely some kind of preamble to the 'real' business of proper (positivistic) research.

For relativist qualitative researchers, the idea that psychology should search for systematic, universal (nomothetic) general rules of behaviour is naïve. Human behaviour is too messy and too much a part of immediate contexts to lend itself to general equations. Qualitative researchers are sceptical of any kind of strong causal claims but do seek to interpret their findings with reference to both local organisational and community features (such as subcultural practices or institutional procedures) or more general structural features (such as poverty or racism).

The research technique known as 'participant observation' illustrates some of the issues relevant to relativist qualitative research in general. Participant observation involves the researcher engaging in a role (or seemingly engaging in a role) similar to, or connected to, the roles of those being studied. For example, Marsh et al. (1977) stood on the terraces at football matches to better understand 'hooliganism's. Participant observation has its roots practically and intellectually in the work of anthropologists who would live among agricultural communities as part of their study of social organisation. The importing of the anthropological method to more bureaucratic and technologically complex urban societies is often referred to as 'ethnography' or the 'comparative, descriptive analysis of the everyday, of what is taken for granted' (Toren, 1996: 102). Participant observation can be overt (where the researcher tells at least some of the participants that she is a researcher) or covert (where no one is told). The advantages and disadvantages of each are fairly clear. Covert research in principle means that 'participants' (they do not know they are participating in anything of course) act as they normally would. On the other hand, there is a serious ethical issue in not revealing to others that you are observing them for the purposes of social science. By contrast, overt ethnography, while arguably more ethically defensible, leads to the possibility that participants' behaviour will change precisely because they are being observed (a form of reactivity). Experienced ethnographers claim that after the first few hours or days of a period of observation participants 'forget' the researcher is there, or at least become less concerned about their presence and act more 'naturally'. Similarly, over longer time scales, participants as informants develop trust in the participant-researcher and will talk freely about their organisation, gang, lifestyle or whatever. A crucial dynamic in participant observation is the fact that an important source of data is often not the observations of the *participants* at all, but rather the experience of the *researcher* and her insights into the practices of the group she is studying as a lived experience (a form of reflexivity; see below).

The relativist qualitative researcher Steve Woolgar (1988, cited in Johnson, 1999) has argued that the logical positivist enterprise is doomed to failure because its aim of a universal, objective, value free science of social behaviour (or anything else) is undermined by the problems of *indexicality, inconcludability* and *reflexivity*. Paradoxically, however, relativist researchers celebrate these features and explicitly incorporate them into their research as important issues intrinsic to any analysis of human conduct. By 'indexicality', Woolgar means the fact that accounts of a research activity and the object of the study are produced in the here and now in particular local circumstances that can never be replicated. In this view, *reliability* is impossible (and so scientists tear their hair out). But for relativists, indexicality is interesting precisely because it emphasises local accounts of unique social interactions, rules, roles and relationships. 'Inconcludibility' means that there is never going to be a definitive judgement on the meaning of an observation or experimental result because there is always more research that can be done, and there are an infinite number of facts and assumptions that underpin any given experiment (because all research is inductive in part). In this view, *validity* is impossible. While this might drive scientists to distraction, relativist qualitative researchers positively promote the fact that everyone can offer their own accounts of an event or process, often building imaginatively on prior interpretations by others. Finally, argues Woolgar, 'reflexivity', that is, the tendency of the research process to bend back on itself, means that claims to objectivity and detachment are spurious. The researcher approaches the research enquiry with preconceptions about the phenomenon under study which shape how that phenomenon is studied and reported. This also undermines validity but spuriously improves reliability (because the preconceptions are recycled by others). While scientists attempt to resist reflexivity, relativists embrace it believing that the concepts and analyses applied to the *focus* of research should be applied also to the *process* of research.

The emphasis on the importance of indexicality, inconcludability and reflexivity is closely allied to the relativists' strong commitment to the interpretation of the functions and structure of *language* as a key element in understanding human conduct and experience. The analysis of language in the real world as a legitimate form of enquiry in psychology is one of the most rapidly developing and controversial areas in the discipline. There is a clear shift away from the idea of language simply being a means to an end, seeing it instead as a substantive phenomenon in its own right. The way in which language creates objects and performs functions in the social world, rather than merely describing that world, is increasingly seen as central. Of particular interest recently have been (i) the way in which users of language deploy particular *rhetorical* devices to ensure they come across credibly and (ii) the way in which language generally maintains an *oppressive* divide between the have and the have-nots in society. Both these functions of language are evident in new developments. *Discourse analysis* involves the careful interpretation of transcripts to identify how speakers rhetorically accomplish social actions such as blaming, justifying and expressing attitudes through language (Potter and Wetherell, 1987). Discourse analysts are interested in how speakers deploy so-called 'interpretative repertoires' (that is, ways of speaking about specific social practices such as 'researching', 'partying' or 'studying'). Thus discourse analysts ask 'What is the speaker *doing* when he says such and such at this point in the conversation?'. But discourses analysts would not be satisfied to answer such a question with 'he's asking a question' or 'he's giving a description'. The things which can be done in a conversation depend upon the forms of social life in which that encounter occurs. To discourse analysts the things which can be done in a conversation depend upon the cultural, institutional, situational and role relationships which serve as contexts for that conversation. Thus by asking a question a subordinate may be 'challenging the authority' of his listener, if he is not expected to ask questions, given his role.

An alternative form of discourse analysis which focuses on the oppressive function of language is the *critical psychology* approach (for example Parker, 1997). This involves a detailed analysis of language to find what it tells us about the forms of meanings that are possible within a culture. In this approach there is less emphasis on how *specific* speakers are constrained or empowered by the linguistic options, instead there is a strong emphasis on the role of language in maintaining forms of social practice, as might be observed perhaps in the discriminatory treatment of women, the 'mentally ill', 'disabled' and ethnic minorities. For some qualitative researchers, all psychology is political. Thus, 'we help to determine what the human condition will be, rather than just passively describing it. The researcher's role as a moral and political agent is not avoidable; those who are not aware of it still play such a role, but unwittingly' (Sapsford, 1997: 151).

Overall then, relativist qualitative researchers differ from the scientific mainstream by arguing that the 'problems' of positivistic research are in fact the most interesting aspects of the discipline, and advocating the analysis of language in all its forms in order to make sense of human psychology.

Values of relativist qualitative research

Thus there are a number of basic principles or values of relativist qualitative research which set it apart from other areas of the discipline. Three of these which we will discuss in more detail are *participant collaboration, rejection of value-neutrality* and *inconcludability.*

Participant collaboration

Qualitative researchers seek to work *with* groups of participants rather than carry out research *on* them. This extends in some forms of qualitative research to actively discussing with participants what the aims of the research might be. Similarly, in some forms of qualitative research such as discourse analysis, participants are invited to comment on whether or not the researcher's interpretations of the participants' experience are accurate and meaningful. This can lead to difficulties when the participants are unhappy with the researcher's account, if, for example, it portrays the participants as *victims* of broader social and cultural forces. It can be seen here how the collaborative value comes into conflict with the analytic principle of 'false consciousness', highlighted originally by Marx, which argues that sometimes victims (of capitalism) delude themselves into thinking that their condition is better than it 'really is'.

Rejection of value-neutrality

To a large extent, qualitative research rejects the idea that research is, can be, or should be, a wholly dispassionate and disinterested activity. Qualitative researchers argue that *all* research is biased in one way or another and that traditional psychologists simply fail to realise or acknowledge this adequately (see the quote from Sapsford above). Qualitative researchers often seek to document the ways in which specific groups of people are oppressed by institutional structures such as psychiatric services, educational establishments, welfare systems, criminal justice systems and the institution of marriage and the family. Qualitative researchers are very clear that there is nothing inherently problematic about sympathising with those whose lives are constrained and defined by such institutions. Qualitative researchers often seek to use the research processes and outcomes as leverage against the state or other agencies in order to effect improvements in participants' lives, arguing that research should be driven by a search for *justice* as much as by a search for truth. Central to much of the work carried out by feminist psychologists using qualitative methods, for example, is the aim of giving a voice to those women who have been silenced by institutions, and enabling some form of empowerment to emerge from the research activity itself.

Inconcludability

Qualitative researchers are suspicious of the idea of carving everyday life into tidy segments to be analysed by experiments, which define, manipulate and measure such segments in a mechanistic fashion, which then yield a definitive end result.

Even to the extent that human activity could be definitively segmented, there could be no definitive interpretation of what that segment meant, given the multiple contexts in which the behaviour occurs. Woolgar (1988) has pointed out that this 'inconcludability' of social life means that scientific research can never make strong claims about validity. Many qualitative researchers consider social life generally to be open ended, in the sense that there are rarely any natural breaks in the continual flow of interpersonal communication, relationships or social structures. Qualitative researchers often consider social life to be like a *text*, which lends itself to multiple interpretations or 'readings' much as other texts such as a novel or movie might. Everyday behaviour for qualitative researchers demonstrates various features of 'textuality' such as narrative, character, agency, reference to other stories, irony, conflict, enactment and so on. As a text, social life can be segmented and interpreted in so many different ways that there can be no final definitive account of 'what really happened' in any specific circumstances. Any interpretation given by a researcher of an incident must always be recognised as a partial and provisional account open to further reworkings and amendments by future researchers. Indeed the account offered by a researcher, presented in a book or article for example, itself becomes another text to be interpreted by other researchers. Kidder and Fine (1997: 48) for example, suggest that researchers should be offering 'ever partial, temporary and kaleidoscopic interpretations(s) to readers, inviting them to generate their own'.

Thinking critically about relativist qualitative research

How are we to think critically about relativist qualitative research if the criteria for experimental research do not apply? To answer this question we have to consider alternative criteria put forward for assessing the validity of claims made by relativist qualitative researchers.

Qualitative research is often criticised for failing to produce valid or reliable observations. The empirical observations and interpretations of qualitative work are seen to fail the validity test because they are inherently subjective. For example, the researcher carrying out a participant observation might see a street gang go into a shop frequented by an opposing gang and then shouting abuse at the shopkeeper. This might be recorded by the researcher as 'symbolic aggression' (an interpretation which, with some rephrasing, the gang members themselves might even confirm). But can we trust this judgement to be valid? Maybe the gang was trying to test the commitment of new member, or perhaps the aggression was displaced rather than symbolic, or maybe something else entirely was going on. And there is no way of deciding between these alternatives. The data on which the researcher made her observations are not available (unless she videotaped the whole event on a camcorder, which seems on the whole unlikely and even that is a partial picture) nor is it possible to reconstruct the situation. There are rarely any kind of explicit criteria established in advance for what would count as a certain type of behaviour. So it is not simply the case that criteria for 'symbolic aggression' existed but it is impossible to say whether they were met, there just would not have been any such criteria in the first place. Observations of this kind therefore cannot be *reliable* in any traditional sense, since any other researcher investigating the same phenomenon would not have criteria available to apply to a new setting. Even if such criteria were available, it is unlikely that different researchers would agree on whether certain behaviour could or could not be described in the same way. Relativistic qualitative researchers do not worry too much about this because they accept the principle of inconcludability.

Nevertheless, relativist qualitative researchers are concerned that these studies are, and are seen to be, rigorous, but recognise the difficulties of demonstrating such rigour, given that they have thrown traditional procedures of scientific enquiry out the window. Potter (1996) suggests that there are four main considerations that need to be borne in mind when trying to ensure the validity of a piece of qualitative research. The first consideration is that of *deviant case analysis*. Here the analyst seeks to find cases which are counterexamples to the overall pattern she is claiming to find in the data. Rather than illustrating the limitations of the claim about the general case, however, these anomalies can show why the majority of cases are the way they are by showing *how* the exceptions are different. Second, argues Potter, one way of confirming the interpretations of the researcher is to check whether the *participants agree* that the interpretation is a meaningful one. A third way is to consider the *coherence of a collection of studies* rather than just considering single studies in isolation. A study that illustrates something useful about social interaction is likely to be built upon by future studies. Finally, argues Potter, an important feature of discourse analytic work is the *further interpretations* of the transcripts which readers of published articles can make for themselves (an example of capitalising on inconcludability).

Thus overall validity and reliability in qualitative studies are very different from that of quantitative laboratory studies which draw upon logical positivism. The very concepts of 'validity' and 'reliability' are called into question and replaced by a broader conception of how the quality of interpretation can be secured and improved.

However, this qualitative approach to validity does have its problems. For example, 'deviant case analysis' is a sensible way of interpreting patterns in data but it is not clear what happens to the general claim if the deviant case *cannot* be construed as an illustration of why the general pattern is the way it is. Similarly, participants' agreements on interpretation is often advanced as a radical way of confirming the claims to meaningfulness of qualitative research. However, it is not clear just how influential participants' comments are in practice. Indeed it is not clear how influential these comments should be. Participants might state that the researcher's interpretation is not valid but do so for all kinds of reasons unconnected to their view of whether the account really is valid. And of course simply because the participants say that an account *is* valid does not mean that it is. A participant's account about the accuracy of a researcher's interpretation is just another text to be interpreted. Such an account might be interesting but it does not provide the researcher with any external point of reference for the validity of her interpretation.

The aim of including participants in making judgements is principally to avoid white, middle-class researchers making fatuous and oppressive interpretations of those whom they study. This is particularly relevant when those they study might be from a different social background and, crucially, when those judgements might in some way contribute to the ongoing oppression of those people. This aim is laudable but is not equivalent to guaranteeing the accuracy and quality of interpretations. Similarly, subsequent studies can demonstrate the usefulness of earlier analyses but they might also just be reinforcing a cliché. Just because some researchers use an idea subsequently does not *in itself* mean that the idea is better or worse than some other idea that is not being used. There are many reasons why some ideas are built on more than others and many of these reasons have nothing to do with the *quality* of the idea itself. Historical, ideological and cultural pressures all play a part, as do the vagaries of academic publishing and the academic social networks. More radical accounts of what validity can and should mean in qualitative research are emerging, such as the idea of 'analytic realism' (Altheide and Johnson, 1994), which seeks to combine the reflexive stance of the researcher with the tacit knowledge that participants bring to a research interview and which provides the context for answers they give to questions.

Qualitative researchers argue that their colleagues working with numbers in the laboratory are wasting their time trying to establish irreproachable levels of validity and reliability in their methods. These attempts are pointless, they say, since complete validity and reliability can never be achieved. They argue that it follows from this that criticising qualitative researchers for measures that fail the scientific tests of validity and reliability is pointless, for those tests can never in fact be met by anyone. Many quantitative researchers hotly reject this argument, however. Quantitative researchers often suspect qualitative researchers of hiding behind this fig leaf of unattainability of complete objectivity and truth in order to carry out looser, easier and, ultimately, politically motivated research. The quantitative researcher's argument is that, even if *completely* objective reliability and validity are not achievable, it is still worth striving for the most valid and reliable studies that are achievable.

Thinking critically about realist qualitative research

Realist qualitative research is primarily concerned with using more flexible methods, such as interviews and direct observations rather than the traditional experiments and questionnaires, while still subscribing to the basic positivist world view. Such methods are used in order to explore aspects of a real psychological world, possibly even including a search for causal links within that world. Even so, we cannot apply quantitative criteria to realist qualitative work but, as we shall see, there are suggestions for alternative criteria for assessing such research.

Some qualitative researchers, who subscribe to realist rather than relativist epistemologies, have recently tried to develop their own versions of validity, reliability and generalisability which amount to an attempt to structure judgements of the 'trustworthiness' of qualitative research (Henwood and Pidgeon, 1992; Johnson, 1999). In this framework, validity is replaced by 'credibility', reliability by 'dependability' and generalisability by 'transferability' (Robson, 1993). Table 6.1 lays out the main features of the relationships between quantitative and realist qualitative criteria for judging research results and the claims made for them. Credibility can be achieved, for example, through triangulating evidence from two or more sources and providing as much detail as

Table 6.1 Origins, meanings and problems of alternative criteria for judging realist qualitative research

Quantitative criteria for judging results	Meaning	Criticism by relativist qualitative researchers	Meaning	Alternative criteria from 'realist' qualitative researchers	Meaning	Possible problem with alternative criteria
Validity	The extent to which the result is accurate	Inconcludibility	Every result is open to further and further reinterpretation. 'Accuracy' can never ultimately be resolved	Credibility	Ensuring the result is based on a range of convergent evidence (triangulation)	Triangulation is still vulnerable to the inconcludibility 'problem'
Reliability	The extent to which the result can be repeated	Reflexivity	The researcher has preconceptions and these affect approach and account. Similar findings emerge from similar preconceptions	Dependability	The result/finding would be found again in *similar* settings by using systematic and well-documented data collection	This still requires additional criteria for what counts as 'systematic'. Some qualitative data cannot be collected systematically or be well documented
Generalisabilty (external validity)	The extent to which the result can be applied to other settings	Indexicality	Each finding, and claims based on those findings, is a product of a unique time and place. The findings cannot be applied to other settings	Transferability	The application of a finding from one setting to another is considered on a case-by-case basis	There is no way of resolving disputes about what counts as a 'similar setting'

possible on the circumstances under which it was collected. (This might even involve the sort of techniques advocated by Potter (1996) discussed above.) The notion of dependability involves systematicity in data collection in order that there is every reason to believe that the evidence is a function of the setting rather than the researcher. Transferability is achieved by providing extensive details about the circumstances in which the findings and the interpretation of them were produced. Transferability is different from generalisability. Generalisability implies that a result could almost be taken automatically to be applicable to a range of settings, because of the way the original study was conducted. Transferability requires that each potential application of the original result is thought through and assessed on a case-by-case basis (Robson, 1993).

It is too early to assess the usefulness of the credibility/dependability/transferability framework, however, some preliminary observations are possible. Robson (1993) notes that because achieving 'transferability' depends on providing extensive descriptions of the context in which the research was carried out, it is not easy to separate the actual data collected from such 'contextualising descriptions'. In fact the very idea of relying upon 'a description which specifies everything that a reader may need to know to understand the findings' in order to assess 'transferability' Robson finds 'suspiciously circular' (1993: 405). We might also ask: How do we trust (or transfer) the *contextualising description*? Do we need that contextualised too? This is always the problem in justifying qualitative research – every time the researcher points to some separate, external justification, someone always asks how we know *that* is reliable.

THINK IT THROUGH

Is (the process of thinking about) transferability the key?

Perhaps the most important of the three alternative criteria is still 'transferability', as it offers an interesting middle ground between two extreme views about generalising research results. The traditional scientific idea is that all laboratory research is automatically generalisable to all other settings (because supposedly fundamental process are examined in the laboratory – the external validity principle). By contrast, the relativist qualitative view is that research findings cannot be applied to *any* other setting (because every setting is socially and linguistically unique – the indexicality principle). Transferability demands that each potential application of the findings from one setting to another requires detailed examination of the circumstances under which the findings were made in the first instance and of the setting in which they are to be applied. However, it is not clear how disputes about transferability are to be resolved. How similar do two settings have to be before transferability is justified? How is such similarity to be measured? To some extent, the *process* of thinking through whether transferability is 'high' or 'low' is more important than the conclusion we come to. Find some examples of qualitative studies and assess their 'transferability'. Even if you come to no definitive answer, does thinking about transferability help your understanding of the topic of the study?

=============================== **SUMMARY** ===============================

Qualitative research differs from quantitative research in terms of the methods used to investigate psychological phenomena. Differences between *relativist* qualitative and quantitative approaches in methodology reflect deeper differences regarding epistemology, about what can be *known* about human behaviour and experience. *Realist* qualitative approaches, however, accept much of the positivist epistemology. All the qualitative approaches have been criticised by mainstream quantitative psychologists on the grounds that the interpretations made by qualitative researchers of their seemingly unsystematic observations are subjective and cannot be replicated. In response, qualitative researchers argue that the nature of everyday life is such that attempts to establish complete objectivity and reliability of measurement are misplaced. Relativist qualitative researchers often see behaviour as a text to be analysed and that the analysis itself should become the subject of further analyses by other researchers. Qualitative research has long been perceived in psychology as suitable only for preliminary investigations into phenomena in order to get a better perspective on what kinds of experiment could be carried out. However, qualitative researchers are no longer prepared to take on this limited support role and seek to establish the qualitative approach to psychology as a legitimate form of enquiry in its own right. It would seem, however, that there are still several issues around the quality of analyses that remain to be resolved.

KEY TERMS

Essentialist ■ Replicated

=============================== **FURTHER READING** ===============================

A number of texts try to combine the theoretical and practical aspects of qualitative research. The most accessible and effective of these is Richardson, J T E (ed.) (1996) *Handbook of Qualitative Research Methods for Psychology and the Social Sciences* (Leicester: BPS) which provides one chapter of theory and one chapter on practicalities for each of a wide range of qualitative methods.

Smith, J, Harré, R and van Langenhove, L (1995) *Rethinking Methods in Psychology* (London: Sage) and Hayes, N (ed.) (1997) *Doing Qualitative Analysis in Psychology* (London: Psychology Press) cover much the same ground as Richardson but integrate theoretical and practical aspects as they go along.

Banister, P, Burman, E, Parker, I, Taylor, M and Tindall, C (eds) (1994) *Qualitative Methods in Psychology: A Research Guide* (Buckingham: Open University Press) provides very accessible coverage of all the main methods in the context of debates about validity and reliability of qualitative analyses.

Denzin, N and Lincoln, Y (eds) (1994) *Handbook of Qualitative Research* (London: Sage) is more heavyweight but worth reading selectively.

And finally, an interesting article covering the distinctive aspects of the challenges facing student qualitative research in psychology: Burman, E (1998) Disciplinary apprentices: 'qualitative methods' in student psychological research, *International Journal of Social Research Methodology*, I: 25–45.

USEFUL WEBSITES

Qualpage – Qualitative Research Resources
http://www.ualberta.ca/~jrnorris/qual.html

A Directory of Qualitative Resources on the Web
http://www.nova.edu/ssss/QR/web.html
Two sites that are regularly updated and cover conferences, books, research projects and prepublications on qualitative research.

Narrative Psychology Page
http://web.lemoyne.edu/~hevern/narpsych.html
An excellent site dealing with narrative psychology – interpreting human life as a structured text particularly the storied nature of human conduct.

Review of Part I

Toolkit for critical thinking about psychological research and theory

We have now reached the end of Part I (Principles). We have covered quite a lot of ground and dealt with some complex ideas and concepts in the process. These ideas and concepts will be applied in Part II (Applications) to a wide range of psychological theory and research, so it is useful if we now review what we have put in our conceptual toolkit.

We have considered the way psychologists have studied thinking and how their ideas can help us to think critically about psychology. We have reviewed the ideas of some of the philosophers of science such as Ayer, Popper, Kuhn and Feyerabend, which have given us an insight into the nature of evidence, disconfirmation, scientific revolution and even epistemological anarchy in psychology. We have considered what criteria we need to apply to psychological theories in order to assess their usefulness and we have looked at many imaginative techniques for generating new hypotheses to test. By considering the structure of inductive and deductive arguments, we have put ourselves in a good position to understand experiments and what can undermine them. We have considered also the perspective of qualitative researchers, who reject experiments in favour of a greater focus on the meanings rather than the causes of human behaviour.

Along the way we have discussed many issues and pointers to effective analytic and synthetic thinking in psychology, in other words, not only the formal evaluative reasoning we should apply to check that studies and theories are up to scratch, but also the imaginative and creative thinking we need to engage in if we are to generate new ideas in the first place.

In this Review we bring together the key questions that we need to guide our thinking as we consider research and theory. Whether we are reading the work of another psychologist or designing our own study or theoretical model, the following questions should be informing our critical thinking at all times. Indeed, we will use elements of this list to guide our analysis of specific areas of psychology which we will cover in Part II.

The list divides into four sections covering both analytic and synthetic thinking about research and about theory (and provides references to the relevant sections in Part I). It almost goes without saying that these categories are not mutually exclusive. Analytic thinking leads to synthetic thinking and research should be motivated to test theories. Nevertheless, this arrangement of questions provides us with a useful toolkit with which to approach thinking about traditional and contemporary psychology in the rest of the book.

Thinking analytically about research

Thinking about a study in general

Is the study quantitative or qualitative and what is its methodology? (Chapters 5 and 6)

What epistemology does the methodology reflect? (Chapter 2, Table 2.3)

Consider the study in its own terms

What is the hypothesis and how is it derived from previous research (induction) and from specific theories? (induction and deduction, Chapter 4)

Does the study as designed and executed actually test the hypothesis?

Are the theoretical constructs adequately represented in the conceptual definitions?

Is there any 'operational slippage'? (Chapter 5)

Do the concrete operationalisations fall within the definition of the theoretical construct? (Chapter 5)

Are the concrete operationalisations a fair example of the theoretical constructs?

Have all potentially confounding variables been controlled for? (Chapter 5, Table 5.1)

Is it possible in principle for the theory to be disconfirmed by the study? (Popper, Chapter 2)

Generally, does the study demonstrate *internal validity*? (Chapter 5)

Generally, does the study demonstrate *external validity*? (Chapter 5)

What evaluation of the study is appropriate?

Does the outcome of the study support the hypothesis fully, partially or not at all?

Is there a specific study which could be done to remedy some specific flaw in the study?

Is the study acceptable in terms of ethics? (Chapter 5)

Is the principle of *do no harm* adhered to?

Is the principle of *informed consent* adhered to?

Is the principle of *avoiding deception* adhered to?

Is the principle of *freedom to withdraw* adhered to?

Is the principle of *confidentiality* adhered to?

Were any *special ethical aspects* adequately addressed (such as the use of children or the psychologically vulnerable)?

Thinking synthetically about research

Creative thinking about research results (see McGuire, Chapter 3, Table 3.3)

How can the result be applied to real-world problems?

Do anomalies in the results suggest new ways of looking at the problem?

Do the results suggest interesting links to other studies?

Is there a trend in the data which bears further analysis?

Is there a pattern among some but not all of the subjects which suggests individual differences at work?

With respect to what circumstances is the study externally valid?

Does the claim cover all exemplars of the popular 'common-sense' category?

What next steps does the study suggest, or lend itself to?

Imaginative thinking about ethics

Could the study have been improved in terms of ethics?

Could the experience of the participants have been made more positive?

Could the participants have been given more advance information without undermining the experiment?

Could the participants have been given more confidence, support and reassurance about their right to withdraw and the consequences of withdrawal?

Could the participants have been given more information of how the results will be used?

Consider the study in other terms

What is the historical context for the claim and the evidence?

What is the cultural context for the claim and the evidence?

What is the argument not addressing? What is missing, ignored, or excluded?

What does the study take for granted? What are its assumptions?

What *philosophy of science* is most useful in assessing the study? Is the study an example of 'normal science' or 'revolutionary science'? (Kuhn, Chapter 2)

Can the study (especially if a piece of applied research) be treated as an exercise in problem solving? How well does it fare in terms of *Sternberg's seven steps in successful problem solving*?: problem recognition, definition of problem, strategy construction, representation of information about the problem, resource allocation, monitoring and evaluation (Chapter 2, Table 2.1)

Thinking analytically about theories, hypotheses and claims

Are we looking at a *theory* (a structured explanation), a *hypothesis* (a prediction deduced from a theory) or an *inductive claim* (a general summary statement of previous findings)?

If it is a theory, how does it rate against the *criteria for assessing theories:* comprehensiveness, parsimony, clarity of constructs, internal consistency, testability, empirical support and heuristic value? (Chapter 3, Table 3.2)

If it is a hypothesis, is it clearly and logically derived from a theory? (Chapter 4)

If it is a claim, what evidence is presented to support it? Is the *inductive reasoning* sound? (Chapter 4)

What *level of explanation* is the theory, hypothesis or claim pitched at? (Chapter 3, Table 3.1)

Thinking synthetically about theories, hypotheses and claims

Can the theory be *improved* against the *criteria for assessing theories* by increasing the degree of comprehensiveness, parsimony, clarity of constructs, internal consistency, testability, empirical support and heuristic value? (Chapter 3, Table 3.2)

Can the theory be *transformed* by improving the quality of one of these features even at the expense of another feature?

What are the limitations of any *analogy* being used and is there a better one with which to illuminate the behaviour being explained? (Chapter 2)

Can a new hypothesis be derived from an existing theory and the results through the application of one of *McGuire's heuristics*? (Chapter 3, Table 3.3)

If it is a hypothesis, can it be improved by broadening or narrowing its scope or, in other words, by revising the *conceptualisation*? (Chapter 5, Table 5.2)

Part II

Applications

Thinking about Experimental Social Psychology

7

CHAPTER OVERVIEW

In this chapter we will highlight some of the distinctive issues of social psychology and the implications of the 'scientific' approach to researching social behaviour. We will analyse some classic studies in the area of attitude change (Hovland) and obedience (Milgram) to illustrate some of the problems related to assessing the validity and ethical acceptability of social psychological research. We will also identify the ways in which the assumptions of reductionism, determinism and individualism are used in experimental social psychology. We will review the criteria for assessing the quality of theories as they apply to social psychological theories, with particular reference to process models which social psychologists are increasingly taking from cognitive psychology. The implications of the logical positivist approach to understanding social behaviour will be assessed.

LEARNING OBJECTIVES

By the end of this chapter you should be able to:

- Identify the main features of experimental social psychology that distinguish it from other areas of psychology
- Specify the three main assumptions of experimental social psychology
- Think critically about the problems involved in establishing whether or not a social psychology experiment has internal validity
- Think critically about claims regarding the external validity of social psychology experiments
- Recognise the difficulties in assessing whether a social psychology experiment is ethically sound
- Assess the quality of a theory in social psychology
- Outline the main justifications and criticisms of experimental social psychology

What is social psychology?

Social psychology has been defined as 'an attempt to understand how the thought, feeling, and behaviour of individuals are influenced by the actual, imagined or implied presence of others' (Allport, 1985: 3). Aronson has suggested that social psychology should be defined in terms of 'the influences that people have upon the beliefs or behaviours of others' (Aronson, 1995: 6). Alternatively, social psychology can be defined as 'the scientific study of the effects of social and cognitive processes on the way individuals perceive, influence, and relate to others' (Smith and Mackie, 2000: 3).

If you only read American textbooks, you would get the very strong impression that *all* social psychology is experimental social psychology. In fact, contemporary social psychology is made up of several different historical strands, sometimes complementing each other, sometimes contradicting each other. For the moment, we need to note that social psychology is split into two opposing camps: the *experimental* and the *constructionist*.

The experimental approach grows out of the logical positivist tradition, which emphasises scientific rigour, quantification and objectivity. It is sometimes also referred to as the **nomothetic** tradition, as one of its main aims is to develop *general laws* of social psychology (from the Greek *nomos* meaning 'law'). By contrast, the social constructionist approach grows out of the **hermeneutic** tradition emphasising interpretational rigour, qualitative analysis and subjectivity. Each of these traditions defines social psychology in a different way, has its own methodologies and its own criteria for assessing useful research (see Chapter 6). We shall return to the details of the constructionist approach and how it differs from the experimental approach in the next chapter, but for now we will concentrate on the assumptions, principles, history – and problems – of the experimental approach to social psychology.

Assumptions of the experimental approach to social psychology

Experimental social psychology seeks to establish general laws of cause and effect for human social behaviour using the experimental method. These laws generally have the form 'everything else being equal, increases in variable X will lead to increases in variable Y'. Even though researchers might not always talk explicitly about 'laws' in any strict technical sense, it is law-like descriptions of psychological phenomena to which their studies and theories aspire. The experimental method is used as only it provides the control required to test hypotheses about causes and effects. So, for example, a nomothetic social psychologist might be interested in establishing a causal 'law' about attitude change and might hypothesise that 'everything else being equal, increases in speaker credibility will lead to increases in audience's attitude change'. The researcher would then go on to design an experiment in which the credibility of a speaker would be manipulated, while other variables (for example strength of arguments in the message) would be held constant and the effect on attitude measured. Experimental social psychology, in drawing upon the logical positivist model of science, assumes that social behaviour is objectively measurable, is caused by identifiable factors and that general principles or laws can be specified which describe the link between these factors and the social behaviour in question.

Since positivism deals with objective, discrete, causally determined events, the experimental approach has to make some assumptions about social behaviour in order to apply a logical positivist approach to it. Understanding these assumptions is central to any attempt to think about social psychology and in this chapter we will look at them in some detail. The main assumptions involved here are **reductionism, determinism** and **individualism**. We shall think through whether these assumptions are *good* ones or not later – for now we will describe them.

Experimental social psychology first of all breaks down the behaviour under study into its *constituent components*. Thus 'persuasion' might be reduced to the characteristics of the speaker, the message and the audience, while 'aggression' might be broken down into the characteristics of the perpetrator, the victim and the setting. Similarly, interpersonal 'attraction' might be broken down into the physical, personality and social characteristics of the couple along with the communication skills of each partner. In addition, experimental social psychologists would look in their theorising for *underlying mechanisms* such as the thought processes, motivations and personality dispositions which produce and maintain the social behaviour observed. This strategy of reducing the complexity of observed social phenomena to its key components and underlying mechanisms is typical of experimental psychology generally and is usually referred to as reductionism.

Experimental social psychologists, again like psychologists generally, believe that psychological phenomena could in principle be explained and predicted through law-like statements. There is a general assumption that social behaviour is, to a very large extent, determined by antecedent (that is, pre-existing) factors. Experimental social psychologists believe that even if we never discover *all* the antecedent factors that affect any specific attitude change, aggressive act or attraction, we might be able to identify some of the *key* factors which typically have a substantial influence on those processes. This assumption that social behaviour is at least in part substantially influenced by (and hence predictable from) antecedent factors is known as a commitment to determinism.

One less obvious, but nevertheless pervasive, assumption of experimental social psychology is its belief that researchers should focus on the ways in which situations, groups, relationships and social episodes generally affect *individuals*. This is clear in the definitions of social psychology given at the start of this chapter. In the area of attitude research, for example, even if an attitude is common throughout a society and is discussed across a whole range of institutions and subcultures, the experimental social psychological emphasis would be on the *individual's* attitude in that context. Indeed some experimental social psychologists go so far as to say that it is precisely this emphasis on the individual which makes social psychology psychology, rather than say sociology or social policy. This assumption of individualism is clear both in the experimental methods used (where the individual subject is the focus of investigation) and in theoretical models (where the underlying processes of the individual are described).

The science of persuasion

The logical positivist philosophy of science evident in the experimental approach of social psychology is exemplified in the work of Carl Hovland at Yale University in the 1950s (Hovland, Janis and Kelley, 1953). Hovland attempted to establish a set of law-like principles to predict the conditions under which attitudes change in the face of persuasive messages. The main elements of persuasion, according to the Yale team, were the *source* (for example the speaker), the *message*, the *audience* and the *setting* and hypotheses about each of these were tested over a 10-year period in an extensive research programme still cited in textbooks today. More importantly, the experimental methods used by Hovland are still central to contemporary experimental social psychology.

Let us consider the nature of experimental social psychology as exemplified by Hovland's work. In order to construct a model of the persuasion process, he reduced the socially complex occasion of a persuasive encounter to its psychologically significant components: source, message, audience and setting – for Hovland everything else was essentially irrelevant. It would have been conceivable to analyse persuasion by keeping all the parts of a persuasive encounter together. For example, Hovland, in principle, might have looked at political or religious rallies and considered *how* all the elements had a part to play in the ceremony and drama of a mass gathering. However, Hovland, by virtue of adopting a positivistic approach with its implicit commitment to *reductionism*, sought to construct laws about individual elements of the phenomenon of persuasion. The experimental procedure adopted by Hovland usually involved intense 15-minute lectures directed at randomly constructed groups of American GIs or students. While this arrangement may seem artificial, it was necessary in order to establish the kind of scientific control required by Hovland's positivism.

We can also see how in Hovland's work the assumption that the aim of social psychology should be the construction of general laws (the nomothetic assumption) is clearly evident. Hovland made several predictions of the form, 'everything else being equal, increases in variable X will lead to increases in variable Y', where 'variable Y' was usually 'attitude change towards the position advocated by the speaker'. Sometimes, however, these hypotheses, although generally supported, needed further qualification and caveats (Billig, 1987). For example, as hypothesised, messages about the feasibility of nuclear submarines were more influential when presented as originating from high-credibility sources (that is, American scientists) than when presented as coming from low-credibility sources (that is, Russian news agencies). However, when attitudes towards the feasibility of nuclear submarines were measured *three weeks* after exposure to the message, rather than immediately, it was found that there was little or no difference

Table 7.1   Main variables in the Yale model of the attitude change

Source variables	Message variables	Audience variables
Speaker credibility	Strength of arguments	Audience's prior attitude
Speaker expertise	One- versus two-sided arguments	Audience's prior anxiety level
Speaker trustworthiness	Appeal to fear versus appeal to gain	Audience's prior knowledge level

between the high-credibility and low-credibility conditions. Hovland argued that this was due to subjects 'dissociating' the source of information from the message itself, dissolving the credibility gap between them. Subsequent studies found that, as predicted from this interpretation, when subjects were *reminded* of the identity of the supposed sources of the information, the credibility gap re-emerged and the two groups differed again on the perceived feasibility of nuclear submarines. This 'sleeper' effect, as Hovland called it, was genuinely unexpected and illustrated how a well-designed experiment can be informative especially when the main experimental hypothesis is not confirmed. The sleeper effect attracted much subsequent research right up to the late 1980s and cast light on how messages are processed as a function of who we think they are from. It was found, for example, that the sleeper effect is much more likely to occur if subjects are told the source of the message *after* hearing that message (Gruder *et al.*, 1978).

THINK IT THROUGH

Just how universal are 'universal' social psychological laws?

The 'sleeper' effect illustrates how an initial nomothetic 'law' that 'everything else being equal, increases in source credibility will lead to increases in attitude change' required subsequent qualification to 'everything else being equal, increases in source credibility will lead to increases in attitude change *for as long as the source is associated with the message*'. Indeed, still further modification was required to 'everything else being equal, increases in source credibility will lead to increases in attitude change for as long as the source is associated with the message *always providing the source is identified before the message is presented*'. Nomothetic researchers would point to this as an example of how well-formulated hypotheses generate meaningful experiments which in turn allow useful fine-tuning of the original laws. Critics of nomothetic social psychology would point out, however, that there might be no end to the number of qualifications that have to be made to these supposedly universal laws, rendering them practically useless. The laws only relate to the rather circumscribed conditions which they were originally meant to explain and can only be presented as having wider applicability for as long as the diversity and complexity of social life is suppressed. In particular, critics have pointed out how social psychological 'laws' derived from experimental laboratory research are rarely applicable beyond their original national and historical settings. Think through how these debates are linked to Woolgar's considerations of 'indexicality' and 'inconcludability' (Chapter 6) and to Billig's ideas about contradiction (Chapter 2).

Within its *own* terms, Hovland's research programme was immensely successful, generating scores of law-like statements about the factors influencing attitude change. A series of theoretical models, which tried to synthesise the findings, was produced and other researchers were attracted to applying or challenging the details of the models.

However, we can also see how Hovland's research programme illustrates some of underlying assumptions of experimental social psychology mentioned above:

- *Objective measurement assumption: social behaviour can be described and measured objectively.* Hovland used measurement scales to record attitudes before and after exposure to messages. What Hovland as an individual subjectively thought of those attitudes was irrelevant and certainly did not influence how they were measured.

- *Reductionism: observed social behaviour can and should be broken down into component parts.* Hovland identified source, message, audience and setting as the key elements which together made up the persuasion context.

- *Determinism: social behaviour does not just happen spontaneously, randomly, chaotically or mysteriously but is caused by a range of factors internal and external to the individual.* Hovland predicted that persuasion depended on source credibility and expertise and the strength of arguments in the message. He believed that by manipulating features of the source the observed attitudes would change.

- *Nomothetic assumption: internal and external factors are linked to these social behaviours in ways that are regular and lawful.* Hovland predicted that 'everything else being equal, increases in variable X will lead to increases in variable Y'.

Thinking about ethics and external validity in experimental social psychology – Milgram's studies of destructive obedience

Stanley Milgram (1974) was interested in exploring the factors that influence a person's decision to obey an order to do something they would not otherwise do. Milgram suspected that the tendency to 'obey orders' and perform antisocial acts was not restricted to war criminals but was a feature of certain kinds of situation. As such, performing violent acts on others is something which any of us might do, given the 'right' circumstances. In a series of classic studies, Milgram assessed the extent to which individuals would obey instructions to hurt another individual in a 'standard' setting and then explored the factors which would increase or decrease that baseline level of obedience.

In the basic experiment, Milgram and his researchers instructed subjects to give increasing levels of electric shock to a 'learner' next door who consistently made mistakes as part of an experiment on 'learning'. No shocks were in fact being delivered to the learner (who was a confederate of the experimenter) but the subjects believed there were. If any subjects indicated they wanted to stop, the experimenters would deliver verbal 'prods' to the subjects to instruct them to continue. In spite of the clearly visible warning notices on the equipment (labelled 'shock generator') and the sounds of pain coming from the cubicle next door, *all* subjects were prepared to deliver a significant number of apparently painful electric shocks before refusing. In fact, 65 per cent of subjects were prepared to continue *right to the very end*, administering the highest possible levels of shock, undeterred by the 'XXX' labelling on the dial.

> **Study Tip**
>
> At this point you might want to read any social psychology textbook account of Stanley Milgram's experiments on obedience. Better still, read Milgram's own account in *Obedience to Authority* (1974, New York: Harper & Row).

These studies are probably the most famous, most disturbing, most discussed, most criticised and most notorious in the history of psychology. It raised and continues to raise questions about laboratory research, ethics, external validity, and for that matter the nature of humanity and inhumanity. It bears further examination. We cannot say that we have thought about social psychology unless we have thought thoroughly about what Stanley Milgram and his colleagues began on that early August day at Yale University in 1961.

Thinking about ethics in social psychology experiments

Milgram's experiments and the controversy which followed them illustrate many general principles relevant to understanding the nature of ethics in social psychological research. However, we need to begin by noting, when considering Milgram's research in terms of ethics, that most of the principles of 'doing no harm', 'obtaining informed consent', 'avoiding deception unless necessary', and 'freedom to withdraw' were less clearly documented and enforced then than they are now. Indeed, to some extent contemporary ethics codes are a direct consequence of the public and academic debates that followed Milgram's research. Nevertheless, in the Milgram experiments subjects were exposed to high levels of stress, did not have full informed consent (they were not told that they would be required to administer dangerous electric shocks) and subjects were certainly deceived – deceived about the 'learner', about the shocks and about the motivation of the laboratory-coated experimenter. Far from having freedom to withdraw, subjects were left in no doubt that they were required to continue. It would seem that ethically the studies were flawed to say the least.

However, it could be argued that only through deception, stress and insistence on completion (it was an experiment on obedience, after all) could this phenomenon be studied. That might well be the case, but it does not follow from this that the experiment is justified. Maybe there just are some psychological phenomena that cannot be studied because the only rigorous and valid way of doing so would entail some form of irredeemably unethical behaviour on the part of the researcher. Milgram and others took the view, however, that the experiment taken as a whole was justified, that the benefits outweighed the costs. For example, as a consequence of Milgram's experiments we might have a fuller understanding of the ease with which individuals obeying orders can act destructively, which in turn might lead to reforms of the army, the prison service and so on. We shall now examine not so much whether that claim is justified but rather the issues involved in thinking about such a claim.

Making *moral* judgements about social psychological research on human subjects is complex and challenging. We need to consider the issues that are relevant to individual subjects, psychology as a discipline and society as a whole. It is probably impossible to have a general rule-based moral code for behavioural research which lays down what is and is not acceptable since:

1. these rules need to be based upon some prior assessment of what is 'right' and what is 'wrong'
2. each study will be different and may or may not be covered by the rules in any straightforward way.

Ultimately, we need to decide whether each study is morally justified or not on a case-by-case basis. This will involve a careful weighing up of the costs and benefits of each particular instance. However, this weighing up is an extremely difficult task for a range of different reasons.

Weighing up the costs and benefits is not straightforward as both the costs and benefits are multiple and subjective. Some of the costs and benefits are *immediate* (the distress of subjects during the experiment and the direct observation of experience of real stress), and others are *longer term* (the possibility of unscrupulous tyrants using the findings to encourage more obedience and the possibility of helping individuals to defy illegitimate authority). Ultimately, attempts to resolve disputes over the ethics of Milgram's studies considered in terms of costs and benefits fail for the same reason that most ethical debates on costs and benefits fail: the costs and the benefits are fundamentally different in kind. How can we weigh up the very real suffering of a Yale student in 1961 with the possibility of designing a less oppressive prison regime in the 1990s? Or the opportunity to observe and understand the non-verbal gestures of an increasingly confident and defiant rebel with the damage to psychology's reputation among the general population?

In thinking about cost–benefit approaches to ethics in social psychology in general, it is necessary to think clearly about the difficulties of 'adding up' costs and benefits. These difficulties relate to what we can call: *multiplicity*, *subjectivity*, *potentiality*, *participation* and *retrospection* in ethical judgements.

- *Multiplicity*. We need to remind ourselves at the outset that costs and benefits are multiple. Every psychology experiment (just like any complex social activity) has a large number of different outcomes. It is difficult if not impossible to *identify* them all, let alone assess them. And, even if the costs and benefits can be assessed individually, they have to be *aggregated* in some way because we are being asked to make a decision on an experiment as an overall package, and not just on some parts of it. Aggregation of different types of costs and benefits is not easy – how can we, for example, assess how much 'deception' is worth how much 'new data' and so on? And yet psychologists one way or another make these judgements every day.

- *Subjectivity*. Ultimately, costs and benefits can only be subjectively assessed. Each individual values different kinds of experiences, be they gains or losses, differently. For one individual in the Milgram study, for example, having to live with the knowledge that one had administered an electric shock to another human being might be a minor (if rather surprising) moral misdemeanour, no more. For another it might be a devastating blow to one's self-esteem to which one is never truly reconciled. Indeed, what is a benefit from one point of view might be a cost to another. It might be the case, for example, that Milgram's work could lead to new limits on the power of officers in armies. But making armies less brutal and authoritarian might be considered a *cost,* not a benefit, to someone who believes army discipline to be too 'soft'. We might find this perspective in itself 'immoral' and discount the view – but *that* assessment would require us to make moral judgements about other people's moral systems, reducing us to infinite regress.

- *Potentiality*. In theory-driven research such as Milgram's, as opposed to applied research, costs tend to be real while benefits tend to be potential. Milgram's studies, like much psychological research and indeed research in general, require us to make comparative assessments about *real* costs versus *potential* benefits. The distress to the participants in Milgram's studies is real but the prospect of reducing the possibility of another Auschwitz is remote – even if extraordinarily desirable.

- *Participation*. Although the benefits of a study may outweigh the costs, overall, we should remember that for the *subjects* it is mostly all costs. Time, effort, stress and occasionally humiliation and deception are all borne by the study's participants. If there are practical tangible benefits, they are unlikely to be for them. It is a difficult judgement to assess whether one person's costs are worthwhile because of the benefits to another. Similarly, the costs are linked to specific people while the identity of the beneficiaries is less specific.

- *Retrospection*. We need to make decisions *before* a study takes place about whether or not it should be carried out. However, very often the full range and extent of costs and benefits will only become apparent *retrospectively*. When Milgram defended his studies in the face of his critics, he drew upon various pieces of information which could only be known in retrospect. The question that can be asked is: What would Milgram have invoked to justify his studies if the subjects had not behaved the way they had?

Since all these considerations are themselves likely to be the sources of dispute, we have a 'meta-ethical' issue (that is, a moral dilemma *about* a moral dilemma). Specifically, who should have the right to *decide* whether the benefits outweigh the costs? The researcher? The subject? The state? The university?

Thinking about external validity in social psychology experiments

External validity is the extent to which the findings of a study can be applied to 'real-world' examples of the phenomenon in question. The Milgram experiment might be seen as an extreme and atypical case but it does serve to throw into relief more dramatically issues which are relevant to most social psychological studies. What is true of the destructive obedience studies is not necessarily true of other experimental social psychological studies or of social psychology in general, but the *ways of thinking about external validity* which are illuminated by the analysis of Milgram's study certainly are.

In the Milgram case, real-world examples of the behavioural processes observed in the laboratory are on the face of it not difficult to find. Milgram himself drew a link between his own research and the Holocaust of the Second World War, when six million Jews were killed in the Nazi concentration camps by soldiers who were 'only obeying orders'. Milgram's findings, that destructive obedience could be elicited from otherwise ordinary people, reinforced observations by writers such as Hannah Arnedt, a reporter for *The New Yorker* magazine. Arnedt attended the trial in Jerusalem of Adolf Eichmann, one of the most notorious Nazi war criminals, and coined the phrase 'the banality of evil' to describe the 'normal' and unremarkable nature of evil as supposedly embodied in Eichmann and those like him.

Of course we cannot conclude that Milgram's studies are representative of real-world obedience simply because Milgram asserts that they are. We must consider the arguments put forward. Milgram claimed that the laboratory offered a means of examining the *underlying* processes of obedience, making an argument by analogy that 'While the coloring and details of obedience differ in other circumstances, the basic processes remain the same, much as the basic process of combustion is the same for both a burning match and a forest fire' (Milgram, 1974: 174). However, more recent commentators have argued that the Holocaust emerged not from authoritarian 'intentionalist' forces through a hierarchical chain of command, from Hitler downwards, but through 'functionalist' forces which emphasised 'bureaucratic developments and rivalries, improvisation, individual and group initiatives and other external conditions and forces' (Lutsky, 1995: 63). In other words, Milgram offers a model of destructive obedience to malevolent authority which mirrors *some* of the intentional actions of some people during the Holocaust. However, other psychological and social phenomena created, from the ground up rather than from the top down, the circumstances necessary to make mass killings of persecuted minorities possible. In this sense, Milgram's work offered a model of the Holocaust, which emphasised only one particular aspect which, while a real aspect, was not the only aspect that needed to be considered.

THINK IT THROUGH

In the light of Lutsky's claim, would you say that Milgram's destructive obedience was either necessary or sufficient for the Holocaust to have occurred? Have a look at the discussion on necessity and sufficiency in Chapter 3.

Nevertheless, the Holocaust is only one form of destructive obedience and we should not judge Milgram exclusively on the extent to which his research helps us understand it better. Destructive obedience in the real world takes on many different shapes and forms. Inevitably, Milgram's study reflects only some of these. Although he himself explicitly linked his work to the issue of the Holocaust, that linkage is problematic.

> Milgram's decision to frame the obedience project in the shadow of the Holocaust was of paramount significance because of the powerful emotions and intellectual controversies associated with efforts to understand the Holocaust itself. From their inception, the obedience experiments were seemingly endowed with an undeniably inflammatory, provocative essence, qualities that were, in an important sense, distracting in terms of Milgram's primary objectives. (Miller *et al.*, 1995: 3)

The external world is constantly in flux. The fabric of society and the cultural norms and roles within it, are constantly evolving. Since forms of authority have changed, the forms of obedience which were possible 100 years ago are not necessarily the same ones which are possible now or might be in the future. We need to have a fluid notion of external validity which is consistent with a 'real world' that is constantly in flux. So, ultimately, it would seem that we should not ask the question in social psychology 'Is this study externally valid?' and expect to find a definitive answer, but rather think through in what way and in what circumstances each particular study is likely to be externally valid. The external validity of a study is not a fact to be learnt, such as the number of subjects who took part, but is an exercise in critical thinking – a process, not an outcome.

THINK IT THROUGH

Consider the claims made by Milgram about external validity in relation to the discussion of 'transferability' in Chapter 6. To what extent is Milgram's work vulnerable to criticisms of 'indexicality'?

One example of research, which illustrates the challenges posed by trying to assess the external validity of studies which have been completed (such as Milgram's) and those which are at the design stage, is the area of destructive obedience in the workplace. This might seem a relatively mild and innocuous real-world reference point compared to the psychological and historical extremes of the Holocaust, but it is an area where issues of external validity are more relevantly addressed.

Recent research into obedience has tried to explore forms of destructive obedience in bureaucratic and organisation settings. Hamilton and Sanders (1995) have suggested that whatever the validity of emphasis on war as a context for destructive obedience, the world of work is a more commonplace context for malevolent authority:

> Most of the organized ways in which people do wrong happen when they go to work. It is part of Milgram's ... legacy that that psychologists realize that no question is more important for the next millennium than that of how human social organization can be made more humane. We need to learn, literally, who in the world really expects organizational actors to be autonomous moral beings. Perhaps then we may better understand when and why they are not. (Hamilton and Sanders, 1995: 85)

Another emerging approach to the understanding of obedience is to consider it not as a behaviour in itself but as a form of social interaction. Modigliani and Rochat (1995) analysed the tapes Milgram made of his subjects and came up with some fascinating findings. They found that subjects who challenged the authority of the experimenter at the early stages of the experiment were more likely to refuse in later stages to deliver all the levels of shock. Careful analysis of the exchanges between experimenter and subject reveals subtle patterns of refusal, negotiation and obedience, suggesting that obedience is not just an individual behavioural event but an interpersonal social *process*.

Thinking critically about theories in experimental social psychology

Models and explanations in experimental social psychology – the impact of cognitive psychology

With the victory of cognitive psychology over behaviourism in the 1960s, there have been extensive opportunities for incorporating thought processes and structures as explanatory terms in social psychological theorising. American social psychology had always had strong links with cognitive models through the work of German psychologists who had fled Nazi persecution in the mid-1930s, and through the work of American social theorists who were influenced by European social thinkers, such as George Herbert Mead. By the 1960s, however, cognitive explanations were seen as legitimate throughout the discipline. Increasingly, there were useful concepts emerging from cognitive psychology which provided a vocabulary for social psychologists discussing the role of thought and perception in social behaviour. Additionally, cognitive psychology was influential in presenting theories as process models (a kind of flow diagram of steps of thinking), and many experimental social psychologists saw this as a useful means of detailing their own theories about the underling thought processes that guide social behaviour.

Cognitive models of social perception

Many models in social psychology seek to explain the thinking processes that occur between social perception (input) and social judgement (output). Occasionally, the output side of the equation is a behaviour of some kind but this is the exception. This applies to the study of attitudes where the input might be the pros and cons of a certain point of view or course of action (for example legalising marijuana) and the output is the attitude expressed by the subject after hearing or reading the arguments. Similarly, in person perception studies, the input would be an observation of some 'target' individual or a list of personality characteristics or actions of that individual with the subject's output response being some kind of overall evaluation of the target. Thus given a list of person-ality adjectives (traits) such as 'calm', 'interesting' and 'intelligent', subjects would be required to rate a hypothetical person so described in terms of their overall attractiveness or effectiveness for example. Alternatively, in attribution research subjects are presented with a list of behaviours carried out by one or more hypothetical or real individuals and the subject would be asked to provide a judgement on the *cause* or *reason* of some specific behaviour.

An example of a complex model built on many experimental studies is the elaboration likelihood model of persuasion (Petty and Cacioppo, 1996) presented in Figure 7.1.

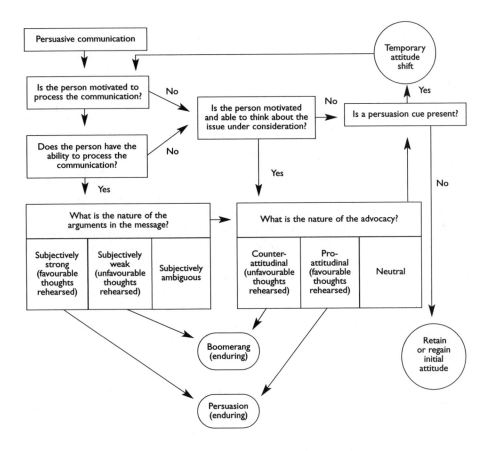

Figure 7.1   Elaboration likelihood model of persuasion
(Petty and Cacioppo, 1996: 264)

There are several features of the elaboration likelihood model (ELM) which are characteristic of cognitive models in social psychology generally which we should think through here. The arguments put forward to assess whether these features are *desirable* or not will be considered later.

First, the model is presented as a set of boxes and arrows, in which the boxes represent cognitive activity and the arrows the output of that piece of activity, hence where the control of processing 'flows' as a consequence. In other words, we have a **flow diagram**, embodying a process model of how people's attitudes change (and sometimes do not) when exposed to messages about an attitude topic. There are various *pathways* through the model reflecting the different kinds of cognitive activity that can occur given the various input arguments (pro, anti, neutral), various subject characteristics (motivation, processing ability) and various degrees of cogency of argument (strong, weak, ambiguous). Thus the model tries to explain the general *process* of attitude change by positing a set of smaller underlying *sub*processes which, it is claimed, subjects carry out. In this way, it is hoped that the diversity and complexity of all persuasion can be described in terms of a circumscribed set of mental tasks.

How do Petty and Cacioppo know that these activities occur? Their answer would be that each separate subprocess has been analysed by a specific set of experiments. Petty and Cacioppo and other psychologists have tested whether the subprocesses specified by the ELM really do happen, whether they happen in the sequence specified, whether there are subprocesses which happened but which are missing from the model and so on. In this way, it is claimed, the experimental nomothetic approach combines theory construction and empirical enquiry in a continuous cycle to develop new and better models. In this sense we can see that the model seeks to be *testable* and in principle can be *disconfirmed* by subsequent research (see Popper, Chapter 2). The model also seeks to present the underlying processes in as concise a manner as possible. Generally in the empirical sciences, the principle is that everything else being equal, the more concise an explanation or model is for a phenomenon, the more useful it is. Thus process models such as this meet the parsimony criterion for theories (see Chapter 3). This economy of expression is easy to achieve in process models, since a small number of subtasks can often be executed in many different combinations of sequences, giving a *combinatorial* complexity from a *simple* structure.

It can be seen how strongly influenced the ELM is by mainstream cognitive psychology. The model refers to 'rehearsal' (that is, reactivating a memory record of an item to keep it 'active' and accessible), 'central' and 'peripheral' processing, and 'cues' that trigger processing. Indeed, the model overall represents the ultimate in cognitive models of attitude change: attitude change is a function of the probability of thinking about the arguments and drawing out elaborative inferences from them. Or even more concisely – thinking causes attitude change.

A further feature of the model is that it describes the process of attitude change as occurring wholly within the mind of one individual. This individualism of the ELM is characteristic of cognitive social psychology in general. Experiments and theoretical models alike use the individual as the principal unit of analysis. The possibility that a couple, a family, a community, organisation or subculture could be *collectively* motivated and competent to *collaboratively* process and rehearse arguments in conversation publicly is not considered by this model.

Another striking feature of the model, and indeed of process models in social psychology generally, is that the process described is content free. In other words, the model seeks to describe the processes underlying attitude change *whatever the content of the attitude is*. According to the model, it does not matter whether the attitude is to do with politics, nuclear weapons, deforestation, space travel or the price of fish in Madrid – the general processes and subprocesses which occur are claimed to be the same. Much as the rules of addition and subtraction are held to be true for small, large, odd, even, whole numbers and fractions, the ELM is held to be true for all attitudes. If this claim is true, then such abstract models would indeed be very powerful, reducing the diversity of attitude psychology to a few simple rules specifying how argument and counter-arguments work without referring to any *particular* arguments. In this sense, the abstract cognitive rules of social judgement are seen to operate in the same way as the abstract rules of the grammar of a language specify how verbs, adjectives and nouns work, without actually needing to refer to any *particular* verbs, adjectives and nouns in the language itself.

Assessing theories in social psychology

The criteria identified in Chapter 3 for assessing theories in general can now be applied to experimental social psychological theories.

1. Does the theory display *comprehensiveness?*
2. Does the theory display *parsimony?*
3. Does the theory display *clarity of constructs?*
4. Does the theory display *internal consistency?*
5. Does the theory display *testability?*
6. Does the theory have *empirical support?*
7. Does the theory have *heuristic value?*

Theories in experimental social psychology are increasingly process models which specify the sequence of mental operations carried out by an individual on some input (for example a photograph) which result in some kind of output (for example an attractiveness judgement). The Petty and Cacioppo model of attitude change would be an example. The input of a message is transformed into a resultant attitude position. Models such as this tend to be strong on comprehensiveness, since they are content free. They are also parsimonious, since they capture a wide range of different specific *sequences* of processing from a small number of subprocesses. The constructs vary in clarity, but often a series of experiments leads to a refinement of the definition of those constructs. Internal consistency is generally high, as the specification of the theory as a processing model forces the theorist to be explicit about the links (relational propositions) between each component. Testability is usually strong, although some parts of the model are more testable than others. In the ELM for example, it is easier to manipulate the subject's motivation to process a message than their intellectual ability. As a result, there is much more empirical data on how increased motivation, rather than, say, degrees of expertise, affects the processing of persuasive messages. The heuristic value of process models in social psychology is generally low. Process models, precisely because they eliminate contradictions and ambiguities and express relationships in structured formal terms rather than florid metaphorical terms, leave little scope for the imagination. Another issue with process models is that they tend to be inductive. That is, they tend to seek to describe what the data from previous studies have already told us rather than boldly postulate new and hitherto undiscovered explanatory mechanisms. As a result, they rarely throw up any surprises. There are few new empirical implications because the model is only designed to account for what is already known. It might be argued, therefore, that whatever their other merits, process models in social psychology are largely conservative. Future studies tend to apply the models to new situations rather than rework the model itself. In that sense, process models in social psychology are what Kuhn called paradigms which lead to 'normal science' (see Chapter 2).

We noted earlier that experimental social psychology is strongly committed to the principle of determinism, that is, the idea that the next state of the world is determined by the previous state and that within the domain of psychology free will is just an illusion and an unhelpful one at that. Process models to some extent dilute this commitment to determinism, since they emphasise that at any one of a number of decision points the flow of control could go off in one of two or more directions. Thus in the ELM the individual may or may not be motivated to process the persuasive message. This does not amount to free will nor is the explanation in deterministic terms difficult, but the branching pathways through the various subprocesses reveal that experimental social psychology is addressing inherently *unpredictable*, as distinct from undetermined, processes. We should also note that theories in experimental social psychology, by relying on models of mental processes in the mind of one individual, are therefore reductionist theories, seeking specifically to explain interpersonal (between people) phenomena at the intrapersonal (within person) level. This idea that social behaviour can be explained by looking at its *constituents* is in marked contrast to social constructionist theorists who argue that social behaviour can only be explained by reference to its *contexts*.

Thinking critically about experimental social psychology

Experimental social psychology has been subject to many criticisms since the early 1960s and onwards (for example Armistead, 1974). Most of these criticisms are focused on the narrowness of the assumptions used and the implications for the kind of knowledge social psychology produces. We can consider first the kinds of objection that have been raised to the assumptions of experimental social psychology in relation to reductionism, determinism and individualism and then consider two further areas of critique: ethnocentricity and language.

The critique of reductionism

While reductionism is a principle which has served other disciplines well, most notably perhaps chemistry and physics, serious doubts have been raised about its appropriateness in psychology generally and social psychology in particular. Reductionism involves both:

1. analysing a phenomenon into its component parts

2. explaining those components in terms of some mechanism or process which exists at some 'lower' level of analysis.

The problem with this approach, it is argued, is that it misses the *contexts* in which those phenomena exist. In particular, a reductionist approach deflects attention away from the cultural, institutional, legal, historical and political dimensions of behaviour and experience. Consider again our example of explaining marital conflict in terms of the underlying differences in the beliefs each partner has about who is responsible for what. This approach would marginalise other features possibly relevant to understanding the nature of marital conflict, such as cultural values regarding the rights and obligations of husbands and wives, the institutional frameworks of social security systems that pay child benefit to the mother but unemployment benefit to the father, historical dimensions of women's changing role in society and political aspects of differing definitions of where the boundaries of physical abuse lie. Experimental social psychologists would typically claim that their research on individual (intrapersonal) beliefs is not at odds with these factors, but the research itself presents a picture of proximate, specific intrapersonal causes of conflict that lie outside any sociohistorical framework. The reductionism of experimental social psychology can lead to the analysis of social behaviour that takes it outside systems that 'host' and direct that behaviour.

The critique of determinism

Experimental social psychology adheres to a form of determinism, although as we noted with the ever closer links between cognitive psychology and social psychology, this determinism is being diluted. Critics of experimental social psychology and of positivism generally argue that determinism dehumanises individuals and provides the foundations for a model of individuals which deprives them of any capacity for autonomous action, particularly the capacity to resist oppressive forces in their individual lives or the lives of their community. Humanistic psychologists argue that many aspects of human life, such as creativity, personal growth, love and moral choice, have been ignored by experimental social psychology, as a consequence of its commitments to determinism. Experimental social psychologists react to this by stating that such areas of human life (assuming they exist in any meaningful way at all) cannot be defined in ways that lend themselves to systematic empirical enquiry. Again we see the strong links between ontology, epistemology and methodology. Another problem with the way in which determinism has constrained experimental social psychology is in the emphasis on **linear causality** at the expense of the consideration of **reciprocal causality**. That is, experimental social psychology looks at how factor X affects factor Y with little or no scope for looking at how factor Y also *simultaneously* affects factor X. Experimental social psychology takes a pragmatic approach to some aspects of determinism. It is useful to treat social behaviour *as if* it were determined, because by so doing we come to learn things about social behaviour that we would not know if we either used some other assumption, for example that people have free will, or agonised about the philosophical problem of whether or not people have free will.

The critique of individualism

Social psychology's commitment to individualism has been criticised largely for the same reasons that its commitment to reductionism has been criticised – it leads to psychology missing 'the big picture'. Focusing on the individual, it is argued, misses the way in which much social behaviour is carried out at the level of the relationship, group, community and culture. These contexts provide the means to perform certain behaviours, the rationale to perform others and the opportunities to collaborate to pursue still others. Believing, fighting, conforming, helping and achieving are all things which can be done by partners, groups and communities and not just by individuals. Indeed, even when individuals appear to be performing some piece of social behaviour in isolation, closer inspection often reveals the social interactions that underpin the behaviour. We saw this in the work of Modigliani and Rochat (1995), who showed that 'obedience' was less of a behaviour performed as a direct specific response to situational pressures, but was actually the culmination of an extended process of negotiation by the subject with the experimenter.

The critique of ethnocentricity

There have been many complaints that experimental social psychology is **ethnocentric**, that is to say, that it is preoccupied with the values, problems and experience of its host culture, specifically the culture of North America. Much of this ethnocentricity is subtle and possibly invisible to those who already take North American values for granted. In particular, the values of white middle-class America are seen as the primary frame of reference. Some subtle examples of this can be seen in American psychology textbooks, which typically begin chapters with examples taken from 'everyday life' which in fact reflect young, affluent, suburban, white lifestyles. It is too simplistic, however, to say that experimental social psychology has historically *reflected* American values of freedom, individualism and competitiveness. Rather, experimental social psychology (like Hollywood perhaps) has participated in a dialogue about American values and their fragility. It is possible to think speculatively about the political and cultural significance of social psychology in the US during and since the Second World War. The gullible listeners of Hovland, the supine conformists of Asch, the aggressive 'teachers' of Milgram and the 'blame everyone but me' attributers of Storms read like characters in a morality tale for modern America – 'look how fragile our free citizens are'. Democracy, and the individual liberalism which underpins it, is undermined by the gullible, the supine, the aggressive and the moral cowards. 'We should be concerned at how individualism is undermined so easily' it seems to be saying – 'a few minor changes to everyday situations and Americans lose their autonomy'. This kind of 'should we not be worried?' research illuminates the uneasy relationship between American society and social psychology. Liberalism depends on the rational exercise by each individual of uncompromised moral judgement and personal resolve. And yet social psychology, as Allport (1985: 3) defined it, is 'an attempt to understand how the thought, feeling, and behaviour of individuals are influenced by the actual, imagined or implied presence of others'. Experimental social psychology is almost by definition an investigation into everyday threats to liberalism and democracy.

The critique from language

Many of the critics of experimental social psychology gather around its impoverished conception of language. The questionnaires, experimental instructions and group discussions used in studies may all *use* language, but language itself, as an *explanation*, has traditionally been kept at arms' length within traditional experimental social psychology. The reasons why language is problematic for experimental social psychology should be clear to us by now. The very assumptions of experimental social psychology of reductionism, determinism and individuality are precisely the things that language resists. The interconnectedness of vocabulary and linguistic *structure* resists reductionism. The infinite variety and variability of language *production* undermines simplistic models of determinism, while the inherently social structure of *conversation* makes a mockery of individualism.

In social psychology, many terms for the phenomena being analysed are drawn from everyday natural language – 'conformity', 'aggression', 'attraction' and so on (unlike in cognitive or physiological psychology where phenomena are described more technically and formally). A consequence of this shared vocabulary is that the *theoretical* language of social psychology overlaps the *everyday* language used in domestic, educational, mass media and political contexts. This can mean that when a term such as, say, 'conformity' is used in a theoretical context, it can still have many of the connotations of the everyday usage. Disentangling what the researcher means from the myriad of possible everyday meanings is not always straightforward. Indeed it might be argued cynically that researchers sometimes need this ambiguity and fluidity to maintain the illusion that their constructs are all things to all behaviours in all settings. In this context, we need to check whether the researcher has a specific definition of their main theoretical terms, and then consider which of the many multiple connotations from everyday language are being excluded and ask what the implications are of excluding certain everyday meanings. Alternatively, if no formal definition of a construct is given and the researcher is relying to some extent on the general everyday meaning of the term, we need to check whether the researcher *in fact* is using one definition but is claiming a more general application of the findings of an experiment.

The arguments put forward by experimental social psychologists in favour of the continued use of the experimental method, and, broadly speaking, the logical positivist epistemology which goes with it, are largely pragmatic. As a methodology the experiment is not perfect, the argument goes, but it is the best we have and it forces us to think carefully about the relationships between definable variables.

====== **SUMMARY** ======

Experimental social psychology principally involves the systematic objective analyses of results of laboratory experiments. Social psychology employs the assumptions of reductionism, determinism and individualism in its theories and methods and seeks to establish general or 'nomothetic' laws of human social behaviour. Experiments in social psychology can be weak on internal validity, if the operational definition of a theoretical construct is not representative. The external validity can be weak, if the experiment does not capture in the laboratory the psychologically significant features of the phenomenon in the real world. Ethical considerations are central to the assessment of a social psychology experiment, but although it is often argued that the means justify the ends, it is difficult to weigh up the costs and benefits of any given study. Against general criteria, social psychological theories fare reasonably well but the use of computational process models taken from cognitive psychology may limit heuristic value. Experimental social psychology has attracted more than its fair share of criticism over the past 30 years and it is probably the case that its preference for narrow, if 'scientifically' reliable, investigations of social behaviour is no longer as convincing as it once was.

KEY TERMS

**Determinism ■ Ethnocentric ■ Flow diagram
Hermeneutic ■ Individualism ■ Linear causality
Nomothetic ■ Reciprocal causality ■ Reductionism**

====== **FURTHER READING** ======

One of the best North American introductions to experimental social psychology is Brewer, M B and Crano, W D (1994) *Social Psychology* (St Paul: West Publishing). There is nothing in there about the limitations of the nomothetic approach but plenty of examples of what that approach can achieve on a good day. There is a strong emphasis on clear exposition of theory rather than endless listing of studies, and sections on the applications of research to legal, educational and health contexts.

The links between society, social psychology and politics are well represented in Murphy, J, John, M and Brown, H (1984) *Dialogues and Debates in Social Psychology* (London: Lawrence Erlbaum). This is an invaluable collection of annotated extracts from key articles (often from difficult to get sources). A recurring theme is whether social psychology can or should define itself as an applied or theoretical endeavour, noting the ethical, political and moral dimensions of each possibility.

===== **USEFUL WEBSITES** =====

Social Psychology Network
http://www.socialpsychology.org/
Probably the most thorough and reliable source of information on social psychology on the web.

Social Cognition Paper Archive and Information Center
http://www.psych.purdue.edu/~esmith/scarch.html
A database of abstracts and articles in experimental social psychological approaches to cognition. Also contains links to other social psychology sites.

Stanley Milgram
http://muskingum.edu/~psychology/psycweb/history/milgram.htm
Biographical and bibliographic details on Stanley Milgram.

Analysing Social Interaction
http://php.indiana.edu/~heise/Download.html
An interactive site devoted to the detailed analysis of social behaviour. A good example of how reductionism in social psychology can be a helpful orientation.

Elaboration Likelihood Model of Persuasion and the World Wide Web
http://www.utexas.edu/coc/admedium/Ivory/CHOJCIRA/jcira.html
A fascinating article applying ELM to advertising on the World Wide Web. A must for any psychologist interested in the web.

Thinking about Social Constructionism in Psychology

8

CHAPTER OVERVIEW

Growing dissatisfaction with the theories, assumptions, methods and applications of experimental social psychology has led to the emergence of 'social constructionism' in psychology which seeks to present itself as a radical alternative to experimental approaches. Essentially, social constructionists argue that psychological phenomena are constructed by history, culture and language. This chapter reviews the social constructionist approach to psychology generally and to social psychology in particular, emphasising its very different assumptions and methods. Experimental and constructionist accounts of social life differ in many ways but one of the most important of these is the perspective of each on the fundamental issue of psychological reality. Experimentalists say that there *is* a single discoverable, objective reality on which to base psychological research, while constructionists say there is not. Debates *within* the constructionist camp are briefly reviewed including the debate between 'discursive psychology' and 'critical psychology'. The criticisms that are made of both these camps by positivist experimental psychology are considered.

LEARNING OBJECTIVES

By the end of this chapter you should be able to:

- Specify the assumptions underpinning social constructionism and contrast these with the assumptions of experimental social psychology

- Give examples of the topics addressed by social constructionists and the methods employed

- Identify and give examples of the main concepts of social constructionism

- Explain what is meant by the 'realism–relativism' debate and outline the positions adopted by social constructionism and experimental social psychology in that debate

> **LEARNING OBJECTIVES (cont'd)**
>
> ■ Describe the main features of discourse analysis and its rationale
> ■ Outline the differences and similarities between 'discursive psychology' and 'critical psychology'
> ■ Assess the limitations and possibilities of social constructionist accounts of social behaviour

So far we have considered the 'scientific' approach to psychology offered by logical positivism. That approach involves the use of controlled experiments in order to establish general ('nomothetic') causal laws. As we know, the experimental approach makes various assumptions about the subject matter (that is, the *nature* of human behaviour), the methodology (how human behaviour should be *investigated*) and the epistemology (the kinds of *knowledge* that are possible and desirable) of psychology.

But are these assumptions the only possible ones? We turn now to consideration of a radically different approach to psychology which has a very different set of assumptions about subject matter, methods and epistemology. That approach is known by several names and subsumes many strands of research and inquiry, however, consistent with recent practice, we shall refer to this alternative approach as social constructionism.

What is social constructionism?

Social constructionism is the idea that many of the things we take for granted in the world as being 'natural', 'real' or 'true' are in fact created by language, culture and history. Social constructionism involves some ideas that are very different to our everyday understanding of human action and experience. As a consequence, writings on social constructionism often use terminology that can take a bit of getting used to. It will be helpful if we start by considering some examples of how 'things' are constructed in our social world. Consider the following cases.

The social construction of witches – 'Now the following is their method of being transported. They take the unguent which, as we have said, they make at the devil's instruction from the limbs of children, particularly of those whom they have killed before baptism, and anoint with it a chair or a broomstick; whereupon they are immediately carried up into the air, either by day or by night, and either visibly or, if they wish, invisibly' (Malleus Maleficarum, 1486, quoted in Lumby, 1995).

The social construction of psychiatric cases – A perfectly ordinary man in his mid-twenties presents himself to a psychiatric hospital in a US state. His only symptom is that he had been hearing voices saying 'empty' and 'hollow'. Nothing else. He is immediately diagnosed as 'schizophrenic' and admitted to the hospital. As soon as he was admitted, he says he does not hear the voices any more. The label is almost impossible to shake off. The hospital keeps him in for seven weeks. His normal behaviour is construed as bizarre. When he is bored, he walks about the ward but the nursing staff take it to mean that he is 'anxious'. He feels that he has stopped being a person and is now only the label. His behaviour only has the meaning that the label 'schizophrenic' permits.

Both these stories illustrate how individuals can be constructed from the way others act towards them rather than simply from the features of the individuals themselves. These constructions are nevertheless influential in directing, shaping or limiting action. Social constructionists argue that many (and in some cases all) of the basic building blocks of our everyday lives are merely convenient fictions. Sometimes these fictions serve the function of making social life possible, at other times they permit the control and marginalisation of certain ideas or sections of society.

Note that in the examples above the constructed individuals were not separate from the activities that surrounded them. Accusations of witchcraft in the 15th century were part of the social practices of male exclusion of women from work and justice. Psychiatric nurses reacted to the diagnostic label as part of their administrative and clinical monitoring practices. It is a central idea in constructionist accounts that constructed objects are part of organised forms of life, social practices that emerge from, and reproduce, meanings.

The analysis of psychological disorder offered by labelling theorists is a dramatic example of social constructionism. They have argued that diagnostic categories of mental 'illness' are merely socially constructed categories ('labels') applied to individuals with whom society cannot cope. The label then structures lay and professional responses to the individual, reinforcing the idea of the difference, strangeness and 'otherness' of the 'schizophrenic', 'anorexic' or 'neurotic' (for constructionists all these terms are problematic). Social constructionists do not necessarily deny that some people suffer psychological distress – they just deny that diagnostic categories reflect some real internal essence or properties of that distress.

Rosenhan (1973) and his colleagues carried out a study which involved 'pseudopatients' (that is, healthy people feigning illness) having themselves admitted to psychiatric hospitals complaining only of hearing voices. Although they acted completely normally once they had been admitted, hospital staff continued to relate to them in terms of the original label.

Psychiatrists argue that there are distinctive genetic and biochemical abnormalities that underlie psychological disorders such as schizophrenia. By arguing that there are (in principle) knowable, objective, underlying real causes of schizophrenia, psychiatrists can be said to be rejecting constructionism and appealing to a form of essentialism. Essentialism is an underlying assumption of much positivist psychology that derives from and feeds back into everyday talk about mental descriptions. Constructionists claim that terms such as 'emotion', 'personality' or 'memory' – or for that matter the term 'mind' itself – are nothing more than objects created by discourse and associated social practices. Essentialism, by contrast, argues (or more often, takes for granted) the idea that these and similar terms really do have an underlying mentalistic or possibly biological *essence* which is not 'explained away' as linguistic artefact.

Causes of individual behaviour versus the social production of meanings

Positivistic psychology claims that the aim of behavioural science should be to determine the causes of individual behaviour. In Chapter 4 we saw that the assumption of individualism is central to experimental nomothetic social psychology. By contrast, however, one enduring and fundamental theme of social constructionism is that the very idea that psychology should focus on *individuals* is quite misconceived. The argument is that meaning is constructed between individuals through social interaction out of which the *appearance* of individual experience appears to emerge – rather than vice versa.

The fundamental premise then of social constructionism is that the basic subject matter of psychology should not be the causes of individual behaviour but rather *the productions of social meanings*. Everything else that social constructionism claims and assumes follows from this basic axiom. According to social constructionists, positivists are missing the point when they try to make sense of human affairs in terms of neutral, discrete, objective, measurable behaviours. Looking at the world that way, say constructionists, ignores the underlying structures and processes of human interactions. It is claimed that positivists have *forced* a particular kind of vocabulary onto behaviour in order that that behaviour *can* be studied in the laboratory.

Study Tip

Descriptions versus constructions

One way of keeping the differences between experimentalists and constructionists clear in your own mind is to remember the different roles they each accord to statements about the world in psychological theory and everyday talk. For experimental psychologists trained in logical positivism, descriptions of the psychological world are *hypotheses* which need to be tested against reality to see if they are accurate representations. By contrast, for social constructionists, descriptions of the psychological world typically *create* psychological reality for ourselves and others.

For social constructionists, everyday life is made up of objects from language ('discourse') which regulate, define, structure and generally organise our comprehension of the world and serve as a common frame of reference for our interactions with others. Social activities in turn continually *re*invent these meanings, producing and *re*producing ideas, stories, contrasts, categories and images through conversation and other dialogues. Examples of such objects might include 'patriotism', 'housewife', 'mate', 'cool', 'fair', 'professional', 'sexy', 'healthy', 'lover' and, for that matter, 'psychologist'. All these concepts are constructions but are treated as though they are parts of the natural world. Now, while most people would accept that 'cool' is culturally defined, social constructionists go further and say that concepts and labels that seem to be objective, such as 'intelligent', 'science', 'sane', 'old' and 'young', are also constructions.

Topics in social constructionism

If the construction of meanings is the core issue in this approach, what topics do social constructionists consider worth analysing? Among the most important and most common are:

- *Personal identity.* Where does the idea of 'personal identity' come from? What is its history in the culture? What do we mean by the concept of a 'person'? How do we use the idea in everyday conversation? How do conversational practices create our sense of self? How do we take our sense of maleness or femaleness from the culture we live in? Like the pseudopatients in Rosenhan's study – who is labelling us and with what consequences? How do we come to label *ourselves*?

- *Power.* How are meanings used to marginalise certain groups and certain kinds of experiences? Whose accounts of events are given priority in institutional settings? What kind of authority do scientists, including psychologists, take for themselves? *In whose interests* are the labellings carried out by psychiatry, education, the law and medicine? How are such labels resisted?

- *Narrative.* How do stories develop in a culture? How are stories used by people in their everyday dealings with each other to make sense and explain their actions? How are stories used to construct our sense of self over time within our biography (for example our career story, our love story, our 'personal growth' story and so on)? What linguistic devices do people use in their everyday lives to present their stories as *true*? What linguistic devices do *scientists* deploy to present their narratives as true? What stories are we expected to live out when we are labelled as 'schizophrenic', 'anorexic', 'menopausal' or 'lover'?

Social constructionism involves a self-consciously critical approach to psychology. It attempts to demonstrate that experimental and other forms of positivistic psychology (such as personality and intelligence measurement) are based upon an erroneous conception of human nature and a flawed epistemology. Potter (1996) has pointed out that constructionists do not fit easily within disciplinary boundaries, observing that 'constructionist researchers in psychology often have more in common with colleagues in the disciplines of linguistics or the sociology of science than they do with their colleagues who study ganglion sprouting or the ergonomics of car dashboards' (1996: 128). Social constructionism rejects the claim that positivist psychology can offer an unbiased, objective description and explanation of behaviour. Some social constructionists ('critical psychologists' – see below) are also unimpressed by what they see as psychology's complicity in the oppression of the powerless in society. This charge involves, among other things, the claim that psychology has failed to acknowledge the experience of women, minorities, the disabled and the poor. It is also claimed that psychology has become too dependent on funding from governments with applications to the world of business and institutions of social control. Some critical psychologists emphasise in particular the role of psychological technology and discourses in the control of the mentally ill, as exemplified most tangibly by the allegedly inappropriate use of electroconvulsive therapy (ECT) and sedative drugs ('the chemical truncheon') in psychiatric hospitals.

More generally, constructionist psychology accuses positivist psychology of subtly reinforcing certain values of society, despite its claim to scientific independence and value-neutrality. One of the most influential American constructionist psychologists, Kenneth Gergen, has argued that experimental research, despite its neutral veneer, is *inevitably* judgmental:

> the discipline of psychology not only stirs the pot of social meaning, but it is value saturated. That is, in spite of its attempt to be value-neutral, the interpretations of the discipline subtly lend themselves to certain kinds of action and discredit others. The tradition's most well-known research, for example, discredits conformity, obedience, and succumbing to attitude change and pressures. In this way the discipline subtly champions independence, autonomy, self-containment; cooperation, collaboration and empathic integration of the other are suppressed. So not only does the field operate to change (or sustain) interpretations it also functions unwittingly as a moral and political advocate. The hope of a value neutral science is deeply misguided. Gergen (1997a: 117)

Discursive psychology versus critical psychology

As noted by several constructionist psychologists including Burr (1995), there are two quite distinct strands of constructionist theorising in psychology. On the one hand is the model of **discursive psychology** which focuses on the accounts, rhetorical devices and interpretational repertoires generally which individuals deploy when justifying and explaining their actions and beliefs to others. On the other hand, **critical psychology** focuses on how selfhood, subjectivity and power are reflected in specific discursive practices. Discursive psychology focuses on how language works *in* social interactions, especially everyday conversations but also political speeches and television interviews. Critical psychology on the other hand, looks more broadly at the structure of the discourses in a culture, where those discourses come from and how they constrain people's lives. Critical psychology also considers how discourse constructs 'individuals' and 'speakers' in the first place.

Discourse analysis draws most closely upon conversation analysis, the sociology of scientific knowledge and the study of rhetoric. Critical psychology on the other hand is most heavily influenced by the French philosopher Michel Foucault (1926–84) and the French psychoanalyst Jacques Lacan (1901–81). Critical psychology is the more influenced by Marxist and contemporary feminist writings. Although both approaches express a generally *progressive* political orientation, critical psychology is the more explicit about the need for empowerment and emancipation of those who are oppressed by psychological and other discourses (see Table 8.1).

To oversimplify the distinction between discursive psychology and critical psychology: if a university was relaunching itself, a critical psychologist would probably analyse the language of the new prospectus, while a discourse analyst would analyse the transcript of an interview with the head of marketing trying to justify the money spent on it. This would be because a prospectus would reflect various rules, assumptions and subject positions ('Welcome to the University of

Table 8.1   Aspects of 'discursive psychology' and 'critical psychology' compared

	Discursive psychology	**Critical psychology**
Principal intellectual influences	Sacks, Schegloff	Foucault, Lacan
Method	Discourse analysis	'Textwork'
Emphasis on power	Limited	Central
Achilles heel?	Ignores power structures	Fails to analyse social interaction
Key analytic concepts	Rhetoric, accounts, interpretative repertoires, warranting	Ideology, subjectivity, power, psy-complex
What do they mean by 'discourse'?	Discourse is the *use* of various interpretative repertoires to accomplish situated demands of encounters	Discourse is a *system* of statements constructing objects and hence power
Why analyse talk?	To explore how interaction is achieved	To see examples of discourse systems

Newtown, you will find us open and supportive of you as a mature student...').
On the other hand, an interview transcript would reveal the metaphors, justifications, narratives and rhetoric reflecting interpretative repertoires about, for
example, 'access', 'reputation' 'education' and so on ('yes, we felt is was
important to present positive images of our mature graduates because they are
very important to what we do...').

Discursive psychology

Because meanings and their construction operate at many different levels and have
many different forms, there is no single methodology for social constructionism.
Within discursive psychology, however, the most common approach in the UK is
that known as discourse analysis as developed by Jonathan Potter and Margaret
Wetherell (Potter and Wetherell, 1987). This approach involves detailed analysis of
language such as the texts of interview transcripts, literary works and research
articles. Discourse analysis does not seek to develop causal models of behaviour
and therefore does not test hypotheses as such. The orientation of discourse
analysis is that the researcher offers an 'interpretative account' or 'reading' of the
text under scrutiny (an account which itself becomes a text for the next analyst).
Discourse analyses are never presented as being final or conclusive in any way, or as
supporting one hypothesis over another – a form of inconcludability (Woolgar,
1988, see Chapter 6). Similarly, discourse analysis does not try to sample from a
wider population or use any statistical techniques in order to be in a position to
make general claims about the world. Rather, discourse analysis is better thought
of as a *demonstrative* enterprise, illustrating how language legitimates, defines,
prescribes and constructs the *possibilities* of social interaction, rather than as an
investigative one, claiming to discover hitherto unknown facts.

Discursive psychology is one of the most active forms of social constructionism
and seeks to offer a radical *inter*personal alternative to positivistic individual

intrapersonal models of psychological phenomena. It emphasises the need to analyse how talk is conducted for what it can reveal about how interpersonal encounters are managed. The most common technique within the area of discourse analysis is a systematic focus on specific conversations and 'texts' to demonstrate the means by which they are constructed.

Discourse analysis draws on *conversational analysis* (which investigates the rules of turn-taking and coherence in everyday talk) and *ethnomethodology* (which investigates the fragility of the 'taken for granted' in social interaction). Discourse analysis has several aims:

1. to identify the interpretative repertoires of discourse
2. to investigate how specific rhetorical actions, such as blaming, justifying persuading or presenting as factual, are accomplished in talk
3. to demonstrate how traditional positivist psychological constructs, such as 'attitude', 'attribution' and 'memory', are in fact interpersonally accomplished.

Potter (1996) suggests that the identification of (i) constructions, (ii) actions and (iii) rhetoric is the basic task of discourse analysis. Asking questions about these features of talk and other texts helps to reveal the social organisation of the dynamic practices of everyday interaction. Discourse analysts have specific questions to ask in relation to each of these:

- *Construction.* What objects are constructed or taken for granted in this discourse? What interpretative repertoires are being drawn upon to accomplish this?
- *Actions.* What are speakers/authors doing with the words they use? What are the **performative** functions? What moves in the social game are being performed? How do the actions/moves alter the game that is being played?
- *Rhetoric.* What are the interests of the speakers here? What is at stake in this interaction? What persuasive and argumentative forms are the speakers/writers employing to achieve their aims?

Key concepts in discursive psychology

The following concepts, although sometimes used by all social constructionists, are most closely associated with discursive psychologists.

Interpretative repertoires

Potter has usefully defined interpretative repertoires as:

> systematically related sets of terms that are often used with stylistic and grammatical coherence and often organised around one or more central metaphors. They develop historically and make up an important part of the 'common sense' of a culture, though some are specific to certain institutional domains. (Potter, 1996: 131)

Within the constructionist movement, discursive psychologists such as Potter emphasise the importance of analysing how individuals deploy *existing* ideas and images in conversations. These 'interpretational repertories' exist in discourse as conversational resources for social practices such as explaining behaviour, justifying attitudes and presenting intellectual ideas. They exist beyond any particular conversation and their meaning derives from their extended prior use in a culture which both parties in a dialogue are familiar with. However, speakers draw upon different interpretative repertoires as the interaction demands, putting together possibly unique combinations of ideas from different repertoires. This leads to degrees of apparent 'inconsistency' across extended pieces of talk as speakers draw upon repertoires with different themes, images and metaphors – although speakers are rarely aware of this.

Although documenting the ways in which speakers draw upon interpretational repertoires for their interactional purposes has been the main focus of discourse analysis, constructionists argue that this is not a one-way process. Conversations themselves construct new ways of talking that feed back into the repertoires, albeit imperceptibly and over long periods of time.

An example of an interpretative repertoire in the area of higher education might be that of students being lazy, drink-sodden, drug-crazed, noon-rising, lefty, feckless and enjoying a round of loan-funded clubbing. Another interpretative repertoire in the same area might be that of the otherworldly, penniless, 'brainy' bookworms who are struggling to meet deadlines and pass tough exams. These two repertoires might be used by the same person trying to discuss the category of 'students'. Tabloid newspapers often present such repertoires in their most simplified form and the contradictions are often very conspicuous. In stories of political protest against education cuts, students are seen as lazy scroungers, while in stories of school standards, getting to university and becoming a student is seen as the epitome of parental and educational achievement.

Speech acts and the performative nature of language

We usually think of language as more or less accurately describing the world around us. The statement, 'There are three dogs in the garden', seems to be a description of a part of the world – which further examination will show to be true or false. This demonstrates the **representational** function of language. However, according to social constructionists, the most important role of language is its *performative* function. That is to say, the means by which we *do* things with language, most importantly the way we perform our social roles through it. Obvious examples of the performative role of language are when we make a promise, issue a command, ask a question, make an apology and so on. These statements are not describing the world as such but are meaningful *speech acts*.

However, there are other statements which, while having the superficial appearance of describing the world, are in fact actually speech acts which perform important interpersonal transactions. For example, when we say 'I love you' to someone, we are not describing an inner state but, among much else, inviting the other to a range of commitments, and accounting for our past and future transactions with the addressee in the social world. Even apparently describing an internal physical state by saying, for example, 'I have a sore throat' is a performative – performing perhaps the social act of *encouraging* some tender support from a loved one or serving to *excuse* the speaker from a press conference – according to the context. The world as we know it and, more importantly, as we are taken by others to know it, lends itself to an infinite number of descriptions. When we choose to make one of those descriptions rather than some other we are also acting performatively.

The key idea to think about here is that, even if a person who said 'I have a sore throat' could in some sense be said to be referring to a 'non-linguistic' and presumably anatomical referent, *it would not be that referent that would give the statement meaning*. For constructionists, the meaning of words is to do with the effect of words on people, an effect words achieve through pre-existing social practices, and not to do with the accuracy with which words refer to non-linguistic things. Further, constructionists contend that such a representational model is not only philosophically weak, but that any attempt to build a social science on the back of it is a very fragile enterprise indeed. The representational model of meaning is seen by constructionists to have been adopted by psychology, not through philosophical negligence but through a desire to be seen to be part of the natural sciences. Some indeed go further and argue that the representational model of meaning which underlies positivism survives in psychology *because* it reproduces the idea of psychological descriptions being merely dispassionately true or false, rather than politically or morally right or wrong.

Key concepts in critical psychology

The following concepts, although sometimes used by all social constructionists, are most closely associated with critical psychologists.

Discourse

This term is used to refer primarily to the forms of language that constitute culture and which are used by that culture. Discourse, however, can also refer to non-linguistic systems of meaning such as those involved in architecture, photography, cinema or advertising. Discourse at any given point in time will be made up of the residue of millions of previous conversations and texts in that culture. Thus discourse exists outside any particular individual's knowledge of the language. Forms of language and practice, it is claimed, construct objects, be they 'marriage', 'the current economic crisis', 'female sensitivity' or 'your depression', which in our everyday lives we might usually take to be natural and self-evident. In social constructionist accounts of discourse generally and critical psychology in particular, there is an emphasis on how discourse does not simply describe the world but also constrains it – shaping it, controlling it and creating key elements of it. Discourses, according to Foucault, are 'practices which systematically form the objects of which they speak' (1969: 49). Thus, for example, discourses about women with children who are not married form the object of the 'unmarried mother', an object which *then* appears in Hansard, TV debates and pub arguments.

Coming across constructionist claims for the first time, there is a temptation to respond 'but language doesn't create things – the things are really already there in the first place'. Let us consider what such claims do and do not mean in relation to the object of 'unmarried mother'. It does *not* mean that by talking about single women with children we make more people who are female, have given birth and who are not married. That would be ridiculous. What the claim means is that discourses about unmarried mothers construct an object in the culture, an object which is not *just* the basics of being a mother who is not married, but also, let us say, about being an 'immoral scrounger with inadequate parenting skills'. It is *this* object that is constructed. It is *this* object that politicians, tabloid newspapers and social policy makers engage with and formulate 'opinions' about. Thus while there really are women who are mothers and who are not married (and they most assuredly did not get pregnant because someone talked about them), the object 'single mothers' is an active construction accomplished through language's action on the world. The action in this case involving, among other things, the exploitation of enduring historical notions of 'innocence', 'family', 'motherhood' and 'responsibility', all themselves legacies of previous constructions.

Discourses are dynamic. Ongoing discussion and debate about unmarried mothers imperceptibly change that object, adding further properties to it which are possibly inconsistent with the original features. In this way, the discursive object can become full of contradictions and uncertainties. The way in which unmarried mothers are treated in legislation, by social workers and the media itself sustains the object that has been constructed. These practices serve to reproduce the category of single parent and provide the 'justification' for its continued use.

Voice

Social constructionists argue that psychology, as practised scientifically and professionally, excludes the alternative opinions (voices) of those who have less access to power. The constructed positions of discourse confer different kinds of rights to different kinds of individual. One of the major projects of feminist constructionist researchers in particular is to give oppressed and marginalised women a chance to communicate about their experience directly and not filtered through the categories of professional psychology.

Reflexivity

One of the things that language and other signifying systems refer to is themselves. For example, we can ask 'What does this word mean?' or we can take a photograph of a camera. Similarly, when we try to make sense of the world around us, and note that people create meanings with each other, we can reflect on the way in which our own observations and meaning-making activities *are themselves examples of meaning creation*. For example, if we carry out a research study on how people introduce themselves to strangers (to examine, say, the construction of identity in conversation), we could 'bend' our analysis back on itself and consider how *we* introduced *ourselves* as researchers to our participants. Social constructionists argue that we *should* do this and that positivist psychologists have been particularly negligent in failing to applying to themselves the 'insights' derived from the study of others. More generally, say constructionists, a commitment to reflexivity compels us to assess critically *all* our scholarly interpretations of human action, discourse and power. We should not make the mistake of assuming that because we are social scientists we stand outside the very meaning-making processes we seek to study (Woolgar, 1988).

Texts and textuality

To social constructionists, every spoken or written statement lends itself to a 'reading' which will, in principle, serve to illustrate the constructed rather than essentialist nature of representations. No genre of representation is excluded. Newspapers, soap operas, health and safety leaflets, legal contracts or instructions for a DIY bookcase are all in principle amenable to analysis for what they can illustrate about what is taken for granted in society and the kinds of reader 'positions' which are presupposed. More broadly still, all kinds of artefact, such as government buildings, formal gardens, road systems, airport seating arrangements and dances, lend themselves to constructionist interpretations of 'signifying systems' which represent and construct permitted opportunities of social practices and control. For social constructionists, all these representations, verbal and non-verbal, documentary and physical, are texts – instances of representation within meaning systems.

Subjectivity

Social constructionists emphasise the 'illusion of individuality' as presented by positivist psychologists and as perpetuated in everyday talk. For critical psychologists, discourse constructs images of particular types of individual which structure our subjectivity as a theory about the apparent coherence of our everyday experience. These internalised discourses include ideas about rights and duties in relation to others and to power. We have a *sense* of agency as we act out the expectations of such theories but in fact all that is happening is the discourse is being enacted by us. Thus **subjectivity** is the constructionist term which typically replaces 'individuality' or 'self' in the positivist vocabulary and which denies the essentialist assumptions of that vocabulary. Discourse provides 'subject positions' (for example 'single parent', 'patriot', 'psychologist' and so on) which, although messy and contradictory (because language is messy and contradictory), provide us with a way of thinking and communicating about ourselves.

> The person can be described by the sum total of the subject positions in discourse they currently occupy. The fact that some of these positions are fleeting or in a state of flux means that our identity is never fixed but always in process, always open to change. The subject positions that we occupy bring with them a structure of rights and obligations, they legislate for what 'that kind of person' may or may not reasonably do or say... Not only do our subject positions constrain and shape what we do, they are taken on as part of our psychology, so that they provide us also with our sense of self, the ideas and metaphors with which we think, and the self-narratives we use to talk and think about ourselves. (Burr, 1995: 152)

THINK IT THROUGH

'Subjectivity' is a tricky concept to get a clear fix on first time round, but these two exercises might help:

1. What kind of subjectivity might a single parent, clinical psychologist whose brother is currently serving in the army have? What kind of 'flux', 'rules and obligations' and 'narratives' might be involved here?

2. What are *your* 'subject positions'? What kind of 'flux', 'rules and obligations' and 'narratives' might be involved for you at this moment in time?

   (Your gender and student status might be two subject positions worth thinking about for starters.)

Subjectivity then is *not* a better theory of personality or attitude, it is a complete reworking of the very idea of a self-contained, autonomous individual which underlies any model of personality or attitude. The idea of fluid, contradictory and multiple selves as an alternative to traditional personality psychology is developed further in Chapter 12.

Psy-complex

In order to emphasise the overlapping and interconnected nature of 'scientific' and common-sense psychologies and the way in which both in fact draw upon similar assumptions, critical psychologists have coined the term **psy-complex** (Rose, 1985). This refers to the network of ideas that underpin both scientific and popular thinking about the mind. A useful definition is given by Parker:

> the network of theories and practices that comprise academic, professional and popular psychology, and it covers the different ways in which people in modern Western culture are categorized, observed and regulated by psychology, as well as the ways in which they live out psychological models in their own talk and experience. (Parker, 1997: 287)

Realism and relativism

One of the critical issues which divides positivist and constructionist psychologists is that of the nature of truth and reality in the study of human activity. This is essentially a question of the kind of *knowledge* that is possible in psychology and is therefore a debate about epistemology.

Let us tackle this head on. How do we know the real world exists? Our senses are imperfect at best. How then can we know the truth about the world? Different observers have different perspectives on the world. The child playing in a garden sees a 'pretty blue flower', the amateur gardener sees a 'Heavenly Blue' but the professor of botany sees *Ipomoea* and knows the seeds are poisonous. Which of their perceptions is true? They each see the plant *relative* to their own interests and knowledge – it *means* different things to each of them. The plant is not intrinsically any one of these things but *becomes* these things through the human *practices* of play, gardening and academic botany. Each of them makes sense through interpretations from prior knowledge structures. According to a relativistic argument, realities are constructed and multiple, and no form of interpretation can necessarily be given priority in any systematic or meaningful way over any other.

THINK IT THROUGH

Never mind 'pretty blue flowers'. How might a *psychology exam* be constructed through different perspectives? What social practices might encompass such an object? What about *getting arrested*? What about *going for a medical check-up*? What about *anger*?

As with plants, so with psychological experience. According to constructionists, our knowledge of the psychological world is doomed to be only ever relative to the perspective we bring to it. Does the psychological world as we commonly understand it exist independently of our engagements with it? Social constructionists argue that it does not. Even emotion – sometimes seen as the true essence of human beings – is characterised as a feature of social interaction and not an inner private experience to which we can refer.

> anger, love, fear, joy... let us view such terms as social constructions and not as indexing differentiated properties of the mind or cortex... we find that there are only certain actions that warrant anger as an intelligible response (for example insult, expressions of hostility). And once anger has been *performed*, the other is not free to act in any way; convention requires that one react, for example, with an apology, with an exonerating explanation, or with anger. (Gergen, 1997a: 124. emphasis added)

In order to understand meanings, claim constructionists, we have to recognise that meanings are determined by their historical and cultural context. Behaviour is only significant because of the meanings we attach to it. It follows that any given piece of behaviour can only be understood by reference to its historical and cultural context. Standing in front of a tank in Tiananmen Square is only significant because of the historical relationship between the army, the people and the government in Beijing, and because people aware of that relationship saw it happen. But more mundane behaviours such as holding hands in public can also only be described in relation to cultural practices.

Positivist psychology typically only addresses the local and immediate context of behaviour, if it addresses it at all. Experimental social psychology, as we saw in Chapter 4, is often defined in terms of the influence of the immediate 'social' environment on individuals. Wetherell (1996) contrasts the very different notions of social context used by positivists and constructionists:

The social context is a vague term and sometimes, particularly in laboratory experiments, it is taken to mean just the presence of an audience or one or more bystanders in the person's environment. It should mean much more than this, in my view. Social influences are pervasive and inescapable. The social context is structured by power inequalities; it is an *organized* way of life which includes the material environment, technology and modes of economic production as well as language, meanings, ideologies and culture. (Wetherell, 1996: 11)

An important aspect of relativism for social constructionists is the idea of psychological concepts and their interpretation being dependent on cultural and historical contexts. Gergen (for example 1973, 1985, 1997a) has argued that the theories of psychology in general and social psychology in particular are 'historically perishable', as behaviours carry no meaning in themselves, but depend for their meaning on interpretation. Since categories of interpretation come and go in the culture over time, perceptions of behaviours will vary over time. The constructionist argument would be that while, say, the properties of chemicals might be independent of history, the properties of social groups are not. Thus we can develop reliable universal equations for liquids (because, for example, water boils at the same temperature today as it did in the 14th century). But we cannot have universal equations for the conditions under which people fall out with each other at meetings (because the rules of etiquette and conversation are not what they were in the past and will change again in the future).

Thinking critically about social constructionism in psychology

Problems with relativism

Social constructionists are anxious to deal with several problems that present themselves in this relativism. First, there is criticism that relativism completely denies any kind of physicality or events in the world at all. Does this mean that the psychological world does not exist *at all*? For example, do people *feel* nothing when they are angry? According to social constructionists, the main thing to keep in focus is that any 'inner feeling' is irrelevant to the *meaning* of something such as anger. Constructionists emphasise that although 'naïve' realist ideas about the bricks and mortar world are easily shown to be based on a range of dubious taken-for-granted assumptions, we need not dispense with the idea of a real world entirely. In taking up this point, Wetherell and Still (1996) consider the idea of 'New Zealand' and 'hills' as constructed objects. On the one hand, there really is some land in the southern hemisphere given that name, but that should not blind us to the way in which our understanding and knowledge of it is *relative*:

> Social constructionists are not suggesting... that if someone thinks a piece of physical geography like New Zealand does not exist, it does not; not that all there is to the real world is ideas. New Zealand is no less real for being constituted through human constructions – you still die if your plane crashes into a hill whether you think that the hill is the product of volcanic eruption or the solidified form of a mythical whale, while if your reality construes the mountain as no more

than a gaseous phantom, its limitations will have been tragically exposed. However, the real world is no less constructed for being able get in the way of planes. How those deaths are understood and what is seen as causing them will be constituted through our systems of social constructions. (Wetherell and Still, 1996: 109)

The second common critique of constructionism is that in relativist psychology all forms of action and analyses are equally valuable. In short, that relativism leads to an *amoral* position where 'anything goes'. Racist, sexist and other oppressive interpretations of the social world would be as valuable as any 'inclusive' anti-oppressive discourse, since no account can be directly checked for truth against reality. The constructionist defence here comes in several forms, but the principal idea is that interpretations have to be assessed in terms of their actual or potential *consequences* rather than by the *correspondence* (or lack of it) with the way things are in the world.

Elective leftism

Given that all forms of constructionist psychology attack positivist psychology, it is worth considering the extent to which the criticisms have been answered. Abrams and Hogg (1990) have produced a counterattack on constructionism in general and its relativism in particular. Their main criticism is a version of the 'relativism means anything goes' argument applied to constructionism's progressive ideals. Abrams and Hogg argue that there is nothing in constructionism that justifies empowering *oppressed* groups – in principle, constructionists could make a commitment to helping, say, the extremist fascist organisations. In other words, they claim that, while constructionists *choose* to support oppressed groups from a left-wing perspective, it is not a necessary consequence of their analysis of culture and society. Burr (1995), while generally sympathetic of constructionism, concurs:

> It is fair to say that social constructionism as a theoretical approach seems to appeal particularly to those holding broadly liberal or left-wing views, and the reasons for this need to be examined, since there seems to be no particular reason why right-wing views could not equally well be served by social constructionism. (Burr, 1995: 173)

Leaving aside the taken-for-granted idea of 'broadly liberal' or 'left-wing' views in Burr's construction here, it *is* worth thinking about this kind of criticism carefully. Are constructionist ideas consistent with *every* political or moral code? Earlier we considered this notion in relation to Wetherell and Stills' resolution of the relativist ethical issue – a consequentialist ethics – that descriptions are neither right nor wrong but helpful or unhelpful. The issue here seems to be confused. Constructionist psychology, as a form of discursive analysis, especially of the critical psychology kind, does not have the *same* relationship to oppressed and fascist minorities. The dismantling of the representational approach to meaning is a blow against dominant discourses which then serves to support oppressed groups. While fascist minority groups might be circumscribed by liberal ideologies which contain constructed topics, they are not constrained in the same way. Fascist groups in developed capitalist societies essentially seek to rejuvenate rather than dismantle dominant discourses, to amplify and formalise oppressive categories. Oppressed groups seek to centralise marginal discourses. Thus, it can be argued that critical psychology stands in a different relation to all groups (minorities and the majority/ies) *as a function of the relations that those groups have to the dominant discourses*. If a group is oppressed by the dominant discourse then it will benefit when that discourse is subverted, if it depends upon it, then it will not.

Not 'scientific enough'

Constructionist approaches to psychology fare rather badly when matched against the standard criteria for assessing the adequacy of theories. As we noted in Chapter 6 they fare even worse when it comes to considering the internal and external validity of their empirical studies. Of course constructionism considers these criteria to be utterly irrelevant in assessing the quality of their contributions to understanding social behaviour. The traditional criteria for assessing theories are derived from those used in other natural sciences and, as far as social constructionists are concerned, are part of the problem with psychology, rather than independent yardsticks with which to measure the usefulness of a theory. Indeed, constructionism rarely has theories as such, only theoretical and analytical concepts. Individual studies demonstrate rather than discover the operation of these concepts in action. There is little or no attempt to test hypotheses or generalise from one study to another, so that issues of comprehensiveness, testability and empirical support are not at stake as they are in experimental social psychology. The heuristic value of constructionist accounts is, however, high since the analyses are often subtle, novel and imaginative, but the value is only to other constructionist researchers. Nevertheless, there is such a thing as poor constructionist/discourse analytic research, but it is much less easy to spell out why one study is better or worse than another, when the procedures for collecting and interpreting data and the criteria for assessing the outcomes are much less well codified than in positivistic research. Of course constructionist researchers would respond to this by saying that the positivistic criteria only look formal and tightly specified on paper, when in fact in practice they are applied, if applied at all, much more loosely. Constructionists continue to point out that not only are the criteria applied to quantitative research meaningful only to quantitative research, but that quantitative research itself often fails to live up to them. It remains to be seen whether the emergence of criteria for assessing qualitative psychology (see Chapter 6) will be brought to bear on social constructionism.

SUMMARY

In this chapter we have reviewed the perspective of social constructionism which offers itself as a more philosophically, historically and politically informed approach to the psychological analysis of the social world. Constructionism is highly critical of the 'scientific' approach to social psychology that seeks to use quantitative methods in order to be objective and detached from the topics of study. Social constructionism is based on the idea that social behaviour is constructed rather than objectively real. In that context the study of the social world should focus on the production of meanings rather than the efficient causes of behaviour. Constructionism rejects the reductionism, individualism, determinism, essentialism and realism of experimental social psychology in preference to a relativist account of knowledge. Constructionists focus on the role of discourses in everyday life and seek to empower those who are marginalised by such discourses. Discourse analysis is a form of constructionist methodology which involves the analysis of how people present themselves as rationale, credible and powerful in conversations. Critical psychologists argue that the adherence to the analysis of rhetoric only is insufficient for social constructionism, as it fails to take into account the power struggles waged with, and reflected in, language.

KEY TERMS

Critical psychology ■ **Discursive psychology** ■ **Performative Psy-complex** ■ **Representational** ■ **Subjectivity**

FURTHER READING

Burr, V (1995) *An Introduction to Social Constructionism* (London: Routledge). A highly readable guide to the origins and preoccupations of social constructionism. Effectively integrates European and American influences on both discourse analysis and critical psychology.

Stainton Rogers, R, Stenner, P, Gleeson, K and Stainton Rogers, W (1995) *Social Psychology: A Critical Agenda* (Cambridge: Polity Press). An introduction to critical psychology which plays around with many of the conventions of what a textbook should do. Although chatty and jokey in parts, this book presents complex ideas in an effective manner. Not to everyone's taste but probably the most imaginative social psychology textbook of the decade.

Billig, M (1987) *Arguing and Thinking: A Rhetorical Approach to Social Psychology* (Cambridge: Cambridge University Press). A distinctive contribution to the analysis of language, particularly rhetoric, in everyday life and in academic psychology. Billig's contention as discussed in Chapter 2 of this volume, is that argument and contradiction are characteristic not only of 'attitudes' but of thinking generally. In relation to social constructionism, the book gives some clear examples of how discourse can be analysed to reveal its performative (as opposed to the representational) function.

Fox, D and Prilleltensky, I (eds) (1997) *Critical Psychology: An Introduction* (London: Sage). A definitive guide to the emerging field of critical psychology, with contributions from some of the leading theorists in the US and the UK. A demanding read in many ways but certainly worth the extra effort.

Potter, J and Wetherell, M (1987) *Discourse Analysis and Social Psychology* (London: Sage). A text which led the way for discourse analysis. One key theme is that psychological phenomena such as attitudes are not located in the mind of an individual but are interactive practices performed in conversation. The task of discourse analysis is to examine the rhetorical devices people use in constructing these conversational attitudes. The text mixes theoretical review and practical guidelines with a wide range of texts and transcripts from the media and interviews.

Parker, I and the Bolton Discourse Network (1999) *Critical Textwork: An Introduction to the Varieties of Discourse and Analysis* (Buckingham: Open University Press). This volume provides examples of analyses of a broad range of texts ranging from advertisements, sign language, film, television and comic strips.

USEFUL WEBSITES

International Society for Theoretical Psychology
http://www.yorku.ca/dept/psych/orgs/istp/
'An international platform for theoretical and meta-theoretical analysis in psychology' with a special focus on critical psychology.

RadPSyNet
http://www.uis.edu/~radpsy/
Radical Psychology Network provides information on international aspects of research, teaching and policies relevant to critical psychology.

Bolton Institute Psychology Page
http://www.sar.bolton.ac.uk/Psych/default.htm
Includes links to the critical psychology information hosted by the Discourse Unit (also known as Centre for Qualitative and Theoretical Research on the Reproduction and Transformation of Language, Subjectivity and Practice).

The Virtual Faculty
http://www.massey.ac.nz/~ALock/virtual/welcome.htm
The 'Virtual Faculty' is an international group of psychologists, anthropologists and philosophers who share an interest in social constructionist ideas (particularly those relating to what we have termed 'discourse analysis' here).

Centre for Critical Psychology
http://www.nepean.uws.edu.au/histories/ccp/ccp.html
Contains among other things a useful introductory guide to critical psychology.

Thinking about Developmental Psychology

CHAPTER OVERVIEW

In previous chapters we have reviewed the methodological, conceptual and theoretical issues concerned with understanding social behaviour but we have not yet considered psychological research on how we *come to be* fully functioning adults in the first place. In this chapter we shall consider the ways psychologists have thought about how children develop, and consider how we should think about the claims they make on the basis of their theories and experiments. We shall assess when different methodologies do and do not enable us to make causal inferences about developmental processes. A particular feature of this chapter is the in-depth analysis of a recent experimental study of child development in order to illuminate some of the issues involved in turning an abstract idea into a practical experiment. This is particularly difficult in child psychology because of the communication, ethical and practical constraints of working with children, but the principles explored in this analysis are applicable to all types of psychological experiments.

LEARNING OBJECTIVES

By the end of this chapter you should be able to:

- Describe the main issues and topics which interest developmental psychologists

- Explain the relationship between child psychology and psychology generally

- State what can and cannot be inferred about causality from different research designs in child psychology

- Articulate the questions which need to be addressed in assessing the adequacy of theoretical formulations in developmental psychology

- Assess the claims of an empirical research report in relation to the extent to which the operational definitions used are consistent with the theoretical constructs investigated

What is developmental psychology?

Developmental psychology is the study of the changes in psychological functioning between conception and death. Until recently most research has been focused on childhood development but there has been a growing interest in what is known as 'lifespan psychology', which deals with the changes beyond adolescence through mid-life and into old age. Developmental psychologists are interested in how neurological, physical, motor, perceptual, cognitive, emotional, linguistic and social development take place across time. Although it is widely recognised that all these strands interact with each other, in practice they are often studied and theorised independently.

Issues in developmental psychology include:

- What are the relative contributions of innate biological mechanisms (nature) and the influence of socialisation (nurture) to development?
- How does children's thinking develop? Does it develop in distinct stages or is it a continuous process?
- How do parents interact with their children and how does this affect development?

Examples of specific *research questions* which emerge from consideration of these issues include:

- *At what age do newborn infants recognise their mother's face?* The earlier the child recognises the mother the less likely it is that experience is crucial and the more likely that biological disposition is important.
- *At what age do children understand that transferring a liquid from a shallow glass to a tall glass makes no difference to the amount of liquid?* Is it the same age as they understand that rearranging the layout of beads on a table does not change the number of beads? If the child seems to grasp both these *conservation* concepts at the same age rather than different ages, it suggests that there might be a special developmental stage for understanding conservation in general.
- *How do children react when their mother goes out of sight briefly?* Do children who seem distressed have a particular kind of attachment to their mother that is distinct from those children who seem undisturbed by a brief separation? If there are consistent differences, this suggests that the mother–child attachment might affect the development of social confidence.

Because child psychology deals with physical, motor, perceptual, cognitive and social development, it has implications for all areas of psychology. Similarly, because as an area developmental psychology draws upon both biological and social processes to explain development, it *takes* concepts and theories from many other parts of the discipline. Interestingly, developmental psychology is probably the most interdisciplinary area of psychology, in that it draws on ideas and data from genetic, paediatric, sociological and educational research. In this sense, developmental psychology is all of psychology in a microcosm. Developmental psychology is also distinctive in other important ways. The *ethical* issues raised by working with children are unlike any others. Additionally, good developmental research is also probably more resource intensive than any other kind of research. A full long-term study following a group of children as they grow older could take up to 20 years to complete and will involve scores of researchers.

The rationale for developmental psychology

Psychologists are interested in child development for its own sake – it really is interesting to investigate what is going on in those little heads behind those cute, if often rather messy, little faces. But developmental psychology is significant within psychology for other reasons too. The central goal of psychology in some respects is to understand why *adult* humans behave the way they do. Child psychology in that sense gives us a picture of the *origins* of the adult mind and behaviour. If we want, for example, to answer the question 'Why are some people extravert while others are shy?', one sensible place to look is childhood and early social experiences. There is a general assumption in child psychology that the younger the child is, the less his or her behaviour has been influenced by experience (nurture) and the more it is influenced by biology (nature). Thus a three-month-old's conception of movement is seen as being largely rooted in innate biological capacities, whereas a three-year-old's conception of the same phenomenon would be considered inevitably more of a combination of social and biological factors (nevertheless, we need to be wary of this – infants can experience a great deal in three months).

More generally, child psychology is an intellectual battleground between the biological and social views of human behaviour. It is fair to say that the prevailing point of view in child psychology comes generally to influence the whole of psychology. If children's shyness is explained in social terms, then we come to view adult shyness and adult personality in social terms also. If we view children's shyness as biologically influenced, then we tend to view adult personality in the same way. In the 1960s and 70s, social models of childhood development were in the ascendancy with a strong emphasis on parental and educational forces shaping the developing child. In the 1980s and 90s, by contrast, a more biological view, drawing on genetic evidence, has re-emerged. Fortunately, during the same period, more sophisticated models of how biology and environment *interact* have been developed, such that the new findings on behavioural genetics have not led to the wholesale rejection of the importance of nurture.

Try as we might, when we study children we do not approach them as though they were completely alien to us. Our *preconceptions* of what it is to be a child permeate all aspects of design, analysis and interpretation of research. Not necessarily personal views (although of course some research psychologists are parents too), but cultural views which influence things we 'take for granted' about children. Child research and theory has always reflected the social agenda of the society in which the research is carried out. The way in which children are viewed and socialised varies immensely across different historical periods and cultures, and the way in which psychological research is carried out varies too. It has been argued that the very category of 'child' as we currently understand it is a relatively recent cultural development (Aries, 1962). Before the 18th century, people were all treated as more or less old, and not divided into two separate categories of 'child' and 'adult'. Uncertainty over who children actually are is still reflected in legislation, with rights regarding marriage, criminal liability, consumer purchasing, military service and sexual behaviour linked to different age limits.

There has always been dispute about the fundamentals of child development as outlined below.

Hobbes, Locke and Rousseau – three enduring views on human nature

Thomas Hobbes (1588–1679) argued in his classic work *Leviathan* that humans formed organised society because they feared the inevitable savagery of humans in their natural state. He also argued that children were born with preformed innate ideas. By contrast, the English philosopher John Locke (1632–1704) argued that children were born as *tabula rasa* or blank slates onto which society writes its own values and knowledge. Thus Locke argued strongly in favour of *empiricism*. He argued against the idea popularised by Hobbes that children are born with specific innate ideas. Unlike Hobbes, Locke argued that the natural state of humankind was a happy one and characterised by reason and tolerance. Another influential writer on children and the 'natural state of man' outside society (that is, the influence of nature without nurture) was Jean Jacques Rousseau (1712–78), the French philosopher who argued that humans were born good and innocent but were corrupted by land ownership, education and trade. He maintained that education did not really tell the child anything new but simply drew out that which was already there. Thus for Hobbes the influence of nurture was benign on a savage nature, while for Locke and Rousseau the essential innocence and goodness of nature was distorted by nurture. These two opposing views of the effect of organised society on individuals continue to underpin much our interpretation of child and developmental psychology today. These early philosophical views continue to influence theorising, both directly through the social and philosophical models which psychology as a discipline inherits and indirectly through the circulation of versions of the ideas of Hobbes, Locke and Rousseau in political, cultural and educational ideologies.

Can you find examples of these points of view reflected in tabloid news stories about children? Can you find examples of these points of view reflected in psychology textbooks about children?

We can apply some of the ideas from Chapter 8 on social constructionism to these enduring views of childhood. It could be argued that many of the 'classical' views expressed by Hobbes, Locke and Rousseau are reflected in taken-for-granted ideas about children today. Children are seen as innocent and requiring protection from corrupting influences (Rousseau) – yet perceived as needing rules to civilise them (Hobbes). We should remember that what was at stake in much of this speculation about the innate state of children revolved around the frames of reference for *political* issues such as what kind of organized society was desirable and *epistemological* issues such as what it was possible to know directly about the world. From the point of view of social constructionism (Chapter 8), these views of childhood are sustained in discourses about children and might even contribute to 'subject positions' that some women might have as part of their subjectivity of being a 'mother'.

Fundamental to understanding much Western research on children are the concerns and challenges thrown up by the emergence of universal educational provision in Northern Europe and America particularly since the Second World War. This provided opportunities for mass testing and observation of children under controlled conditions. The growth of literacy which mass education created further enabled the application of written tests and personality assessments among children. As a further consequence of state-organised education, more interventionist social policy initiatives such as social work, health services and social care generally created a framework for psychological assessments of social functioning, in the home, the clinic as well as the school.

Thinking critically about research methods in developmental psychology

The study of development makes use of a range of methodologies. Within positivist research the main methods are cross-sectional designs, cross-cultural comparisons, longitudinal designs, observational studies and experiments. Each of these has its own rationale, advantages and disadvantages and we need to think differently about each one. Many of the principles relevant to assessing the advantages and disadvantages of research methods in general are applicable to developmental research methods, but there are additional considerations that have to be borne in mind. Additionally, many of these methods are used in psychology generally and their advantages and disadvantages are similar.

Cross-sectional designs

If, for example, we wanted to compare differences in moral reasoning between five- and eight-year-olds, we might use a cross-sectional design. This is where one group of subjects is compared with another group at the same point in time. In age-related comparisons, randomisation is impossible (we cannot 'allocate' our subjects to the five-year-old group or the eight-year-old group – their age is a subject characteristic which each child 'brings with them' and over which we have no control). This kind of study is relatively easy to do and provides basic information about developmental changes. If we found that the eight-year-olds displayed more advanced moral reasoning compared to the five-year-old group, then we could, in principle, conclude that understanding of morality increases with age. This conclusion could not be asserted as a strong *causal* statement of course, since there was no randomisation between groups.

Why does the lack of randomisation in cross-sectional designs prevent us from drawing causal inferences? The problem here is that the five-year-old group and the eight-year-old group might differ in many ways *other* than age alone. This means that any observed differences *could* be due to the age difference but it might be due to one of the other differences between the groups. Since we cannot rule it out deductively, it remains a logical possibility.

It is possible, however, to try to control the variables which are potentially affecting the two groups' moral judgements to allow more internally valid conclusions to be drawn. We could seek to use only five- and eight-year-old children from a particular family size, or social class or educational setting. An alternative approach to deal with this would be to try to match each of the children in one of the groups with children in the other group on family size, class and academic background. In this case, a repeated measures design (and associated statistical tests) would be appropriate since each child has its own 'control'. By using groups that are similar, we would be able to do a better job of comparing 'like with like'. In these circumstances, unless we have very good reasons to assume that the two groups *do* in fact differ in some significant way, it is reasonable to conclude that it is *likely* that understanding of morality increases with age.

Internal versus external validity in age comparisons

Although matching has the advantage of improving the internal validity of the study (because we are able to make stronger inferences about the variables of interest), it does weaken the external validity of the study (because our conclusions would only be applicable to the particular family size, social class or school used). It can be seen that the problem here is that by trying to keep the two groups as comparable as possible we are losing some of the diversity of the sample. Once again we see that attempts to improve the internal validity of a study compromise the external validity, and vice versa (see Chapter 3).

Of course we are never going to get two groups of children who are identical in every way apart from their chronological age so the matching will always be very imperfect. However, the *more* similar the two groups are the *more* internally valid the study and the *more* informative it will be. For example, Minter *et al.* (1998) wanted to test the hypothesis that visually impaired children's understanding of other people's minds was affected by their diminished visual experience. Minter *et al.* matched the 21 visually impaired children with 21 sighted children of the same chronological age and the same verbal intelligence. This meant that any differences between the two groups could not be attributed to differences in age or intelligence as these had been controlled. In the event it was found that the visually impaired children *did* score worse than the sighted children on the experimental tasks. Minter *et al.* were able to infer *deductively* that the differences were not attributable to age or intelligence differences. They were able to do this because they had ruled out the possibility of age or intelligence being a potential explanation of any differences between the groups by making those variables the same for both groups. Similarly, Wareing *et al.* (2000) were able to demonstrate that MDMA (ecstasy) users were less accurate information processors than non-users of the same age, health and educational attainment.

THINK IT THROUGH

Although Minter *et al.* controlled for age and intelligence, it is always possible that some *other* uncontrolled (that is, unmatched) variable is responsible for the observed differences. Can you think of any other variables on which the impaired and sighted children might have differed? Could the children have been matched on your variable(s)?

Does the Minter *et al.* result tell us *why* the visually impaired children have a less accurate idea of other people's minds? If so, how? If not, why not?

Cross-sectional designs which have large gaps between the ages of the groups being compared also run the risk of a particular kind of confounding known as *cohort effects*. That is to say, there may be special characteristics of almost all of one of the groups which is not a feature of most of the other group or groups with which it is being compared. An example of this is has been research on European adults who grew up during the Second World War. When comparing them with other adults, younger or older, whose childhood happened after or before the war, there is a danger that chronological age will be confounded with childhood experiences of trauma and dislocation.

'Broken down by age and sex'

Gender is another variable in developmental psychology that lends itself only to a cross-sectional design. We should avoid drawing strong causal inferences about the effect of gender on performance, as the empirical comparisons can only ever be cross-sectional. Again however, matching can serve to rule out alternative possible explanations for any differences between boys and girls that may be found. Particular thought must be given to studies which claim to show that girls achieve a specified level of functioning at an earlier age than boys, as this would involve at least two cross-sectional comparisons. Cross-sectional designs are essentially correlational, as many other variables are confounded with age. When statistics are broken down by age and sex, we need to think very critically indeed about any *causal* links that we are explicitly or implicitly being asked to believe.

Overall, cross-sectional designs have many well-known limitations caused by the confounding of age with other factors. They are informative, however, especially when possible confounding variables are identified and controlled for. Cross-sectional designs do not in themselves tell us very much about the *processes* of development. Even if we used six groups covering five, six, seven, eight, nine and 10-year-olds, we would still only be getting a series of snapshots of an ongoing process. However, when exploring an area of development that is relatively underresearched or when resources are limited, cross-sectional designs can be useful so long as they are interpreted properly.

Longitudinal studies

An alternative to comparing two or more age groups at one moment in time is to follow one group (that is, cohort) as they grow older. This allows better data to be collected on the process of development and not just its end product. A longitudinal study effectively enables each child to act as its own control, that is, the performance of a child at a given age can be compared with the performance of the same child at a later age. Such a study on moral reasoning was carried out by Colby *et al.* (1983), in which they interviewed the same group of people every two years between the ages of 10 and 36. Patterns of continuity within individuals can be observed in a way that is not possible in a cross-sectional study. Because the same group is observed across a number of years, there is no cohort problem (of differences between cohorts), since all the data comes from the *same* cohort. Hughes and Dunn (2000) for example, interviewed 40 hard-to-manage children at ages two, four and six, to assess the development of their moral awareness.

The disadvantages of the longitudinal method are also clear, however. To follow any sizeable group of subjects over many years requires substantial resources, commitment and organisation. There is also the difficulty of 'subject attrition', when participants drop out of the study after participating for some time, perhaps because of moving home or losing interest. The length of some studies is such that some subjects (and researchers) die during the period of data collection.

However, although longitudinal studies provide more interesting data than cross-sectional designs, they still do not allow us to draw *causal* conclusions. There is still no control over extraneous factors and many historical changes occur that are confounded with age. For example, the children in the Colby study were born just after the Second World War and grew up in the late 1940s and 50s, a time when there was generally a greater consensus about 'right' and 'wrong' than there is nowadays. Would children born in 1990 display the same patterns of conventional and postconventional reasoning as the Colby children? In other words, although the Colby study *is* informative, it still does not necessarily allow us to claim that as children develop between the ages of 10 and 14 in general they adopt a more conventional rule-based moral code. It might be the case that all we can claim is that between 1954 and 1958 children became more conventional in their reasoning. This is, however, an unlikely prospect overall. Typically, it is the integration from several different longitudinal studies covering the same age range, but, crucially, starting at different dates, that allows us to make stronger inferences about the impact of age on development. In this case, other, if more modest, longitudinal studies have confirmed Colby *et al.*'s interpretation of their results – that the development of moral reasoning is a function of age, not local historical factors.

Carrying out longitudinal research is not just operationally demanding, it is also conceptually complex to carry out properly. Several decisions have to be made at various key points and the choices made will affect the kinds of conclusion which can ultimately be drawn. For example, how frequently should the cohort be observed or measured, and at what age exactly? If the periods between observations are too long, it will be difficult to present a full picture of the processes of change. If the periods are too short, then many observations are likely to be redundant (especially if the developmental process being observed is a gradual one). Returning to interview or test children or adults too frequently will not only irritate them but lead to various forms of reactivity (that is, experimenter-induced effects – see Chapter 5), compromising the internal validity of the study.

Of course, we still do not know *which* aspect of age is important from these studies. If and when we conclude that age is an influential factor, it is still not clear from longitudinal studies whether maturational or social factors underlie that influence. In the case of moral reasoning, there is a strong case for social (nurture) factors (but there is nevertheless some possibility of an indirect role for biology).

Overall, longitudinal studies provide us with very useful data about developmental processes. Although extremely resource intensive, they can help us to assess the changes over time within individuals. When thinking about the results from a longitudinal study, we must always bear in mind the frequency of sampling, the impact of subject attrition and the historical factors affecting the experience of the cohorts involved. When several longitudinal studies carried out at different times come up with the same conclusion, then firmer conclusions can be drawn.

Cross-cultural research

Cross-cultural research is another form of cross-sectional design. Children's behaviour in two or more countries with differing histories and cultures is compared in order to assess the degree and type of variability across cultures. There can be no randomisation of exposure to different cultures but some attempt to control variables or match subjects is possible (although difficult). The basic rationale for cross-cultural studies is that, although societies around the globe might differ culturally, there are no significant biological differences. Thus if we observe substantial similarities in behaviour or thinking across cultures, that is on the face of it evidence for the role of biology rather than culture, for nature rather than nurture. If differences are found, this is taken to be evidence of the role of the social or physical environment in child development. For example, in relation to the study of moral reasoning, researchers have found that the first four stages of Kohlberg's scheme relating to fairness and duty do appear to be universal, whereas the fifth and six stages relating to recognition of the exceptions to moral rules are not found in all cultures. This has been taken to suggest that the first four stages, if not exactly biologically programmed into human beings, unfold in the same sequence at roughly the same ages, because they depend upon the emergence of particular cognitive abilities which are more directly influenced by the maturation of neurological structures and connections. By contrast, the fifth and sixth stages are taken to be dependent on local cultural factors.

We have to think very carefully about what we can and cannot infer from cross-cultural comparisons that demonstrate similarities before we can conclude that there is a specific *biological* foundation to the behaviour. We have to consider the deductive reasoning being used here. It might well be true that human groups throughout the world are similar genetically and biologically especially in relation to neurological maturation. However, it need not follow from this that *any* observed similarity in behaviour across cultures is attributable to this particular underlying similarity. The observed similarity might be caused by something *other than* the neurological similarity which all the observed groups share.

Affirming the antecedent

The logical reasoning error involved in concluding that cross-cultural similarity is indicative of biological similarity is an example of a deductive reasoning error known as **affirming the antecedent**. This is the error of concluding that because an effect has been observed a particular possible cause of that effect must have happened. In this case, although it is true that if biological factors determined development we would expect to find cross-cultural similarity, it does not follow that if we were to find cross-cultural similarity it is necessarily because of biological factors. An analogous reasoning error would be that although we know that if you poison someone they will die, it does not follow that if you find a dead body the poor wretch has been poisoned – there are various possible causes of death other than poison. Similarly, there are various possible causes of cross-cultural similarity other than biology such as kinship or survival needs. To develop your ideas here you might want to look again at the discussion of necessity and sufficiency in Chapter 3.

Experiments in developmental psychology

As we discussed in Chapter 4, an experiment involves the control of all potentially confounding variables in order that the effect of the manipulation of an independent variable X *and only variable X* on the dependent variable Y can be measured. As mentioned above, the main issue in developmental psychology is how individuals develop as they grow older, but age itself cannot be *manipulated* across subjects – we have to take age as we find it. However, researchers use experiments in child psychology to great effect to explore *why* children behave the way they do at certain ages and why different types of children (however defined) behave in different ways or are able to perform certain tasks. Experiments in developmental psychology are also useful in giving a better picture of exactly what it is that infants and children are doing when they perform some act or demonstrate some preference.

There are, however, some distinctive practical problems involved in the experimental study of children. When studying the perceptual and cognitive abilities of adults we can ask them simple questions such as 'What do you see', 'What do you think about that?' or give them simple instructions such as 'Press that button when you see a blue cross'. However, when working with young infants and pre-verbal children we cannot use language to convey such experimental instructions. Instead, researchers have to set up situations to capture the attention of the child which often incorporate an element of play. The child's response to different kinds of stimuli is then recorded objectively. It is necessary to make sure that the experiment is set up in such a way as to ensure that the responses can be interpreted unambiguously.

The habituation–novelty technique

One common experimental technique to test whether infants can tell the difference between two stimuli (let us call them stimulus X and stimulus Y) is to present stimulus X repeatedly until the infant shows signs of boredom. Stimulus Y is then substituted for stimulus X and a note is made as to whether the infant shows signs of renewed interest. If interest is shown, then the infant clearly is able to discriminate between the two stimuli. However, if the infant does *not* show renewed interest, this can only be taken as evidence that *either* the infant is not able to discriminate *or* is equally bored by the new stimulus – but we cannot say which.

Let us consider one of the classic studies by Baillargeon on infants' conception of the laws of physics and the properties of objects (for example Baillargeon, 1986). Baillargeon wanted to find out if infants younger than six months had some kind of knowledge of the fact that objects fall down when unsupported. She tested whether infants expressed surprise when shown physically impossible events such as a ball staying in mid-air when its support was removed. If children could be shown to express surprise at impossible events, they must have some model of *possible* events. If Baillargeon had simply shown children an impossible event and noted that even very young infants showed surprise, she could not have concluded that the children were surprised *because* the events were impossible. Such a deduction would not have been valid. Infants could have shown surprise because they were not expecting to see anything at all or were surprised to see objects moving. To rule out this possibility, Baillargeon showed children both impossible *and* possible events lasting the same number of seconds, using the same objects, the same distance away from the child. The two sets of events differed *only* in terms of one being possible and the other being impossible. Baillargeon was thus able to deductively rule out these other explanations – the infants were surprised not by the movement, not by the time elapsed and not by the distance from the screen but rather because the event depicted was perceived by the infants as impossible. This means that children must have some rudimentary expectations of the conditions under which things do and do not fall – or else they would not have found the gravity-defying ball surprising. Thus the function of the experiment here was to make sure that we could make inferences about underlying competence on the basis of performance, by demonstrating that the performance (surprise) happened under some conditions (impossible events) and not others (possible events). Only an experiment could have permitted this causal inference to have been drawn.

Another role of experiments in child psychology is to test whether children perform poorly or deficiently because they *lack* some particular skill or ability at a certain developmental stage. By training or providing this skill when it is spontaneously or naturally lacking and then checking to see whether the deficient performance improves, the cause and effect relationship between the deficit and the poor performance can be established. There is an example of this in several research studies carried out by Peter Bryant (1990), where he demonstrated that the reason children cannot perform some of the Piagetian conservation tasks is not because they lack the necessary cognitive schema (as Piaget argued) but because they *forget* information they are given initially about the task. By randomly allocating children to a 'reminder' condition or a 'no reminder condition', Bryant was able to test whether forgetting was a factor in the poor performance of preoperational children. In the event, Bryant found that reminding children did improve performance in some cases, suggesting that normal performance at the preoperational stage is often poor because of forgetting. Note that both Bryant and the Piagetians agreed that children at the age of about five would not understand that liquid in a tall thin glass was the same volume of liquid as in the short, wide glass. But the experimental structure allowed Bryant to show what it was that *caused* this misconception.

Dynamic assessment environments

Lev Vygotsky (1896–1934), a Russian psychologist, felt that traditional testing techniques were too limited to test children's real potential. He argued that psychologists should use 'dynamic assessment environments' where children's first answers to questions or first attempts at puzzles would not be the definitive record of their performance. He suggested that psychologists should probe further, especially after initial incorrect responses, in order to tease out the real underlying ability of children. This way, argued Vygotsky, fuller and more accurate measurement of children's underlying competence could be derived from the observed performance. Vygotsky's technique has still not been fully integrated into mainstream research despite a resurgence of interest in his work in the 1980s. The practical difficulty is that it can be difficult to assess how much 'help' a researcher is giving. There is also the problem of comparing children who demonstrate the same level of competence after different amounts of probing and prompting. Vygotsky claimed that the ability to use input from others to develop ability was central to cognitive development. Thus for him probing and prompting was not artificial but a typical and intrinsic part of the cognitive learning process.

What do you think are the implications of Vygotsky's methods in terms of *internal* validity on the one hand, and *external* validity on the other?

Thinking critically about theories in developmental psychology

General criteria

General criteria for assessing psychological theories are applicable to developmental psychology and should be applied as appropriate (Chapter 3).

1. Does the theory display *comprehensiveness?*
2. Does the theory display *parsimony?*
3. Does the theory display *clarity of constructs?*
4. Does the theory display *internal consistency?*
5. Does the theory display *testability?*
6. Does the theory have *empirical support?*
7. Does the theory have *heuristic value?*

In developmental psychology there is a wide range of different types of theory. Generally speaking, however, theories addressing the cognitive aspects of development tend to be as comprehensive, clear, consistent and testable as any in psychology. There is an established tradition of empiricism in developmental psychology and this is reflected in the relatively systematic theories that are produced. Traditional accounts of children's emotional development and personality such as those advanced by Freud fare less well on the clarity and testability dimensions. Recently, much of the research by Jean Piaget has been reassessed leading to the view that the theory is stronger on heuristic value than on empirical support.

Criteria specific to developmental psychology

In addition to assessing the usefulness of the theory in *general* terms, there are further considerations which are particularly relevant to *developmental* theories. Although different theories will emphasise different aspects to a greater or lesser extent, the issues in the box below need to be thought about when evaluating theories in the child psychology and lifespan area. Many of them focus on the extent to which the theory adequately deals with *change*.

Thinking critically about theories of psychological development

What is the theory claiming?

- How does the theory describe the process of change?
- What assumptions does the theory make about biology? About society?
- What differentiates the theory from other similar theories of developmental change?

What relevant evidence is available?

- What evidence is available which is consistent or inconsistent with the theory?
- What studies have been carried out which *might* have disconfirmed the theory, but did not?
- What methods were used to collect the relevant data and were the usual problems of developmental research addressed?
- If biological processes are emphasised, is there satisfactory cross-cultural *consistency* evidence available?
- If social/cultural processes are emphasised, is there satisfactory cross-cultural *diversity* evidence available?

How adequately is the process of change explained in the theory?

- To what extent does the theory account for *atypical* forms of change as well as typical forms?

Thinking critically about theories of psychological development (cont'd)

- How adequately does the theory *integrate* biological and environmental influences on development?

- How satisfactory is the theory in terms of modelling the relationship *between* biological and environmental factors?

- How satisfactorily does the theory account for periods of *stability* (within stages, if relevant)?

- How adequately does the theory describe the role of *triggers* or circumstances for change (to the next stage, if relevant)?

- Are triggers or circumstances adequately described in terms of being necessary and/or sufficient *conditions* for change?

- Does the theory relate change to chronological age or some other external milestone (for example starting school)?

It can be seen that developmental theories have the particular challenge of describing and explaining the process of *change* and the relationship between the biological existence of the child and the social world around it. We have addressed several of these issues in our review of developmental psychology but we should note that it is the link between theoretical models and actual studies that is the real test for the quality of a theory (as we shall see later in this chapter).

A further area where theories of development require carefully critical thinking is in relation to issues connected to the assessment of competence. In particular, many theories of child development claim that children do not develop certain competencies (such as fluent speech, basic numeracy or the capacity to make inner representations of objects) until a certain age or stage in development has been reached. The acid test of such theories is to investigate whether the competence can in fact be demonstrated at an age *earlier* than that specified. There are two issues related to this 'search for competence' research, however. The first is that if tests are too hard then children will not be able to show what competencies they do have and the erroneous inference will be drawn that they do not possess the competence. A second related issue is to do with theory. When explaining why a child does not have a certain competence, it is not always meaningful to say that they *lack* some specific foundation required for that tool. Defining a stage in terms of something being missing is conceptually problematic. It is rather like arguing that school pupils get a bus to school because they do not have cars or driving licences – it says nothing directly about how they *do actually* get from A to B. Similarly, describing five-year-olds in terms of their inability to conserve, while true, is also a definition in terms of *absence*. It says nothing about what they actually do when thinking. Both these complex but important issues are relevant to the study of Piaget and his theory of child development (see following box).

Thinking critically about children's competence – Piaget, toys, absence

Why Piaget's tasks were not appropriate: necessary and sufficient tests of competence

As with many of Piaget's experiments, his original task to test object permanence required the child to have additional skills to the one actually being assessed. Testing for the presence of object permanence by requiring an infant to find a hidden object is rather like testing for the presence of numeracy by requiring a person to complete a tax return. The successful completion of the task *would* indicate the presence of the competence, but unsuccessful completion would *not* indicate that the competence is lacking. Many numerate people fail to complete tax returns, and many infants with object permanence schemata cannot find hidden toys. In other words, object permanence is a *necessary but not sufficient* competence for the finding of hidden objects. Piaget mistakenly assumed that it was both necessary *and* sufficient.

And there it was – gone...

One interesting conceptual paradox associated with Piaget's theorising is the way he defined periods with reference to structures or processes that are *absent*. For example the preoperational child is largely defined in terms of what she cannot do (operational thought) rather than in terms of what she can do (for example make believe). Many psychologists have criticised this approach on epistemological grounds. It just does not seem right to define something in terms of what it does not have. However, a theory that states that a certain feature is missing in a process or structure meets Popper's criterion of falsifiability very easily (see Chapter 2). If a psychologist finds the supposedly missing feature where it should not be (in this case operational thought at the preoperational period), then the theory is clearly incorrect and can be rejected. Contrast this with the more common situation when a process or structure *is* posited to exist but is not found. What would Popper think of that? What would Kuhn? What would *you*?

From theory to experiment: thinking critically about research

In order to illustrate and extend some of the key ideas about critical thinking in developmental psychology which we have been discussing in this chapter, we will consider now a published research article on children's logical reasoning. The main theme of our analysis will be the way in which the need to translate abstract theoretical ideas into practical activities in the laboratory involves a range of compromises. Understanding the implications of these compromises will help us to think more critically about claims based on experimental research. This theme is particularly important in developmental studies, as reconstructing the informal world of the child in the structured experimental laboratory is not always straight-forward. However, the principles analysed here are general ones, important for all areas of experimental research in psychology and not just child development. Thus, although our example here is children's reasoning, the *general principles* of our analysis will illustrate ways of thinking critically about experiments in memory, vision or person perception as much as in child psychology.

The article we are going to look at is Roazzi, A and Bryant, P (1998) 'The effects of symmetrical and asymmetrical social interaction on children's logical inferences', *British Journal of Developmental Psychology*, **16**, 175–81.

In this article, Antonio Roazzi and Peter Bryant report the results of an experiment on the effect of social interaction on deductive reasoning ability in four-year-olds. In brief, Roazzi and Bryant tested the hypothesis that children's reasoning skills would improve if they interacted with other children of the same age who had better reasoning skills. This is a very interesting area because it involves testing the idea that social experience, and not just biological maturation, affects cognitive development. This article has been chosen because it is a well-thought out study which is clearly written. However, it is only by thinking critically about good research that psychological enquiry can develop. And that is exactly what we are going to try and do. Remember, we are just using Roazzi and Bryant (1998) as an example of how to think critically about psychological studies in general and not just child psychology (see following box). The questions that we will be asking are questions that can and should be asked of all psychological research.

Roazzi and Bryant (1998)

You will benefit most from the next section if you read the Roazzi and Bryant (1998) article first. Ideally, have it in front of you as you go through the rest of this chapter. The article reports a study where four- and five-year-old children who did poorly on an initial reasoning test were shown to improve after they were allowed to interact with other children who had done much better on the task. Interacting with children who had done just as badly or only slightly better did not have the same effect. The task used involved a set of scales and some sweets in boxes. In the study the test for each child was to work out how many sweets were inside a covered box, on the basis of weighing it up against other see-through boxes with sweets. The results clearly seem to indicate that children who had initially done poorly on the task did better in subsequent tests (both three days and three weeks later) when they interacted with peers who had done *well* on the initial test, compared to others who interacted with peers who like themselves had performed *poorly*. The background to the work relates to the claim that social experience affects the development of reasoning.

Now that we have read the article we can reread it critically. Let us consider this study in terms of the critical framework for reading empirical research reports we discussed in the Review section for Part I. We cannot consider all the questions but we will focus on the main ones that are relevant here.

First we must check that we have identified the *main claim* of the research. The simplest statement of the main claim is found in the abstract:

> We conclude that social interaction between less and more advanced children enhances the less advanced children's ability to make logical inferences. (p. 175)

Note that Roazzi and Bryant go on in the abstract to make an interesting *secondary claim* about why this enhancement takes place:

> ...we argue that this is probably due to the effects of discussion and of agreement rather than to social conflict, during the intervention period. (p. 175)

Consider the study in its own terms

This is an experimental study so we need to recognise that the philosophy of science being used is that of logical positivism with all that that entails. Since it is an experiment (rather than, say, an observational study), then the hypothetico-deductive logic of the experiment needs to be assessed, taking particular care to think critically about internal and external validity, sampling, operational definitions and ethics.

What is the hypothesis and how is it derived from previous research and theory?

The hypothesis in this study is not explicitly stated as such but can be identified without too much difficulty. In fact the hypothesis is presented as a 'research question', that is to say, the experiment is presented as a way of deciding which of two or more possible answers to a theoretical question is the more plausible. In the last paragraph of page 175 the authors state that 'One unsettled issue is whether social interactions between children at the same intellectual level... have a beneficial effect'. These 'symmetrical' interactions (that is, interactions between children at the same intellectual level) have previously been shown sometimes to be beneficial and sometimes not. The authors go on to suggest that if symmetrical interaction does have a positive effect then that would seem to suggest that social interaction of any kind helps cognitive performance. Note how the hypothesis/research question is derived from previous research – not in a strict inductive manner as the research methods textbooks say it should but in a more informal manner. This study, the authors are saying, will contribute to knowledge because it will hopefully answer once and for all whether symmetrical interaction really does aid cognitive reasoning in children.

Far from being tightly inductive, the introduction to the study proper has almost a narrative or story-like quality to it. The 'story' at the moment is incomplete but this article will help to fill in the gap. This is not a criticism of the paper but it does illustrate how the underlying logical structure of argument does not always appear explicitly in the written text. We should note that although the introduction is not explicitly structured as such, it is nevertheless heavily inductive in function. We should note too that it is a rather brief report of a fairly straightforward experiment (albeit one with important theoretical implications) and that in a longer, more detailed, research report the formal inductive structure would probably be more explicit.

Are the theoretical constructs adequately represented in the conceptual definitions?
In this study the *causal* theoretical construct is *social interaction* and the *effect* theoretical construct is *the ability to make logical inferences.* The relational proposition between these two constructs, as it nearly always is in an experimental study, is simply that of a causal relationship – social interaction *causes* changes in the ability to make logical inferences. The hypothesis/research question being derived from this theoretical claim is that manipulating the social interaction will affect the quality of reasoning observed. It is in this way that the study is attempting to help our theoretical understanding of the link between these constructs.

In Chapter 5 we noted the problems of operationalisation of theoretical constructs. In particular we have to check that the theoretical constructs are adequately captured by the variables used in the study.

Let us consider how we get from the theoretical to the practical in terms of the causal variable 'social interaction' (Table 9.1). We can see how the theoretical construct of 'social interaction' is turned into the much narrower conceptual definition of 'discussing a task with peers'. However, the conceptual definition of 'discussing a task with peers' has still got to be turned into a practical, feasible (not to mention ethically acceptable) activity which will be carried out in the actual experiment. By necessity, the conceptual definition is turned into the much narrower concrete operationalisation of 'receiving clues about the task from two other children while sitting at a small table with the experimenter'. The progressively more specific (and mundane) definition of 'social interaction' is repeated in relation to the effect construct 'ability to make logical inferences'.

Is there any 'operational slippage'?
If we look at the first sentence in the Discussion section of the article (p. 179), we can see that Roazzi and Bryant are quite clear about what they believe their study has demonstrated.

> The study showed that social interaction between less and more advanced children does improve performance of the less advanced ones on a simple logical task.

This is clearly a statement about *theoretical constructs* rather than *concrete operationalisations.* As we know from Chapter 3, such general conclusions are based on the assumption that the concrete operationalisations are fair expressions of the theoretical constructs. In a sense, all that we have actually observed is that 'receiving clues about the task from two other children while sitting at a small table with the experimenter' increases 'the number of correct guesses of the number of sweets in an opaque box based on information gained from weighing it against transparent boxes'. To assess the implications of this for the theory requires assessing how representative this is of the theoretical constructs.

Do the concrete operationalisations fall within the definition of the theoretical construct?
Although the authors do not provide a formal definition of what they mean by 'social interaction' or 'ability to make logical inferences' or what the other researchers they cite mean by these terms, I think we can safely say there is no problem here. Whatever else they might be, talking to two peers and working out

Table 9.1   Key features of the conceptual structure of psychology experiments

Key features of studies in general	As they appear in Roazzi and Bryant (1998)		Comment
Nomothetic structure	Cause	Effect	That cause and effect are being explored is implicit in the use of an experimental paradigm
Theoretical constructs	Social interaction	Ability to make logical inferences	These are derived from the main claim made by the authors in the abstract and introduction sections of the report.
Conceptual definitions	Discussing a task with peers	Performance on a deductive reasoning task	This is how the theoretical constructs are implemented in the design of the study. Usually these provide the bases for the experimental variables. In this paper we get this information from the introduction (p. 175, para 2)
Concrete operationalisations	Receiving clues about the task from two other children while sitting at a small table with the experimenter	Number of correct guesses of the number of sweets in an opaque box based on information gained from weighing it against transparent boxes	Concrete operationalisations are the ways in which the conceptual definitions are turned into practical activities or measurements in the experiment. We almost always get this information from the method section, particularly the procedure subsection

the number of unseen sweets from seen sweets are clearly examples of social interaction and logical inferencing, respectively.

Are the concrete operationalisations a fair example of the theoretical constructs?
As we have noted earlier, this is a key question in assessing the validity of an experiment or study. In this study we have to ask the question – is 'receiving clues

about the task from two other children while sitting at a small table with the experimenter' a 'fair' example of 'social interaction'. In other words, is it *representative* of the construct? We have already decided that it is *an* example of social interaction but the issue is what *kind* of example? In assessing this we need to consider both external and internal validity.

In relation to *external* validity, we should ask 'How representative is this concrete operationalisation of social interaction in the real world?' Is this the sort of thing which children do spontaneously in the real world? Probably not, although it is conceivable that some schools have small group work with just three children and an adult. This is where we need to draw upon our own real-world knowledge as well as our knowledge as psychologists. *To me* this example of social interaction seems to reflect rather formal and structured social interaction rather than the more informal and playful social interactions four- and five-year-olds normally engage in. It seems *to me* on thinking this through that the authors are slightly overstating their claim that these little three-way conversations are a fair reflection of 'social interaction' *in general*. Maybe a more appropriate claim would have been:

> The study showed that structured and directed interaction between less and more advanced children does improve performance of the less advanced children on a simple logical task.

In order to explore the original claim it seems to me that we would need to have a rather more *typical* example of four- and five-year-old social interaction or a *wider range* of examples. But what do you think?

In relation to *internal* validity, we can ask 'How representative are the concrete operationalisation and conceptual definition of the theoretical construct?' Since Roazzi and Bryant do not have any special technical meaning for 'social interaction', there is not a major issue here. However, in other studies, we do need to check that the theoretical construct being supposedly investigated by the researchers really is adequately captured by the conceptual definition, and, since all conceptual definitions are imperfect translations of the theoretical, we would need to check through what we have kept and lost with that definition. We might also note that, were this study to be cited by someone else as part of an inductive argument about the evidence for the claim that 'social interaction enhances logical reasoning', the original study was limited to a very specific situation, task and sample.

We might also note in passing that although the article talks about social interaction between children in the actual experiment, an adult male experimenter was present throughout. There is a lot more we could say about the effects of this, but we can see that the concrete operationalisation here seems to be adding an extra component to children's social interaction – an adult.

Of course Roazzi and Bryant are not claiming explicitly that social interaction of this kind does necessarily happen regularly in the real world, but rather that if it *were* to happen it would have the effects that we observe in this study. That is fine but if we read the first sentence of the Discussion section (p. 179):

> In conclusion, this is the first study to show that social interaction can improve children's ability to make simple logical inferences.

That word 'can' does seem to make this conclusion a rather weaker version of the claims made in the introduction. However, it is probably a more sensible claim, given that there are no strong arguments made in the paper regarding the representativeness of the task in relation to either the conceptual definition of social interaction or the nature of social interaction among children in the real world. In that context, this weaker conclusion of the study seems to be more appropriate, given the issues regarding internal and external validity. You might want to consider this more limited claim made at the end of the article in relation to our discussion of both 'indexicality' (Woolgar, Chapter 6) and qualifications to nomothetic laws (Billig, Chapter 7).

So far we have been considering the possibility of operational slippage in relation to the independent variable 'social interaction'. Now we need to consider whether there is any slippage in relation to the dependent variable, 'ability to make logical inferences'. The first issue to think about is 'To what extent is the conceptual definition a fair representation of the theoretical construct?' In this particular study that means considering the extent to which performance on a deductive reasoning task is a sensible example of 'ability to make logical inferences'. Again I do not think there is any problem here – deductive reasoning is certainly a form of logical inferencing. However, it is not just a matter of saying whether it is or is not *an* example, we have to consider what we are *keeping* and *losing* by deciding to use deductive reasoning as a conceptual definition of 'ability to make logical inferences'. By defining 'ability to make logical inferences' in terms of 'deductive reasoning', we *keep* the focus on all the cognitive activities implied by reasoning from knowledge of general principles to what must be true of specific cases (which is at the heart of deductive reasoning – see Chapter 4). However, we *lose* the focus on all the other types of logical inferencing such as inductive reasoning. Additionally, in this case the specific type of deductive reasoning was deductive reasoning about *number*. The children were asked to make inferences about the number of sweets in the opaque box given what they knew about the number of sweets in the other boxes. There are many deductive reasoning tasks that do not involve numbers. It is conceivable that a different kind of deductive task *not involving numbers* might have given different results to those actually found in the study. Of course it might have made no difference at all – we might have obtained exactly the same results. The fact of the matter is we do not know. Whether the use of something other than sweets and scales would have made a difference also remains an open question.

We should note that similar translation difficulties apply to the participants used in the study. The authors refer to 'children', and 'young children' when discussing their theoretical constructs. In the actual study only four- and five-year-olds were used. This age group is particularly interesting because they are in the preoperational stage in Piagetian terms and therefore their reasoning abilities are supposedly relatively underdeveloped. But we do need to think about the *representativeness* of this sample in relation to the more general claims made about the links between the theoretical constructs.

We are not criticising Roazzi and Bryant here, every study has to translate its abstract ideas into practical actions in the laboratory. But we need to think carefully about how each translation loses something of the original definition,

---

THINK IT THROUGH

Imagine you were designing a study *to follow on from and build on* the work of Roazzi and Bryant. What alternative conceptual definitions would you use in order to help fill in some of the gaps left by their conceptual definition of 'ability to make logical inferences'?

What kind of *other* possible conceptual definitions of 'ability to make logical inferences' could have been used in this study? In what ways would your alternatives have been (i) similar and (ii) different compared to that which Roazzi and Bryant used? Why do you think the researchers used the conceptual definition they did? What arguments would you put forward about the alternatives? You might want to consider using some of McGuire's heuristics for developing new theories and hypotheses discussed in Chapter 3 (see Table 3.3). What would you conclude overall if you found that social interaction affected the 'ability to make logical inferences' when the latter is defined in *your* way? On the other hand, if you *could not* replicate the Roazzi and Bryant result, what would you conclude then about the relationship between social interaction and the 'ability to make logical inferences'? You might want to look at the discussion of McGuire's heuristics (Chapter 3) and our discussion on Popper (Chapter 2) in this context.

---

but keeps other parts (and sometimes adds extra features). Let us continue with our critical thinking about the Roazzi and Bryant study.

What evaluation(s) of the claim is appropriate?

Generally the main claim of the paper is supported, but with the qualification that not all forms of social interaction or logical inferencing have been addressed. To that extent the claim is partially supported by the evidence presented. The implication, given the degree of support obtained, is that we can take seriously the idea that it is in principle *possible* for social interaction among peers to help logical reasoning involving numbers.

We will look briefly now at some aspects of synthetic (that is, creative) thinking about the research report.

How can this claim be applied?

The most obvious application here, in my opinion, would be to educational contexts, but you may be able to think of others. The results indicate that the difference between those who had social interaction with peers regarding the task was still apparent three weeks after the test, suggesting that the initially underachieving children had *internalised* some of the logical inferencing skills.

Does the claim cover all exemplars of the popular category?

The popular notion of 'social interaction' is probably connected to children's play – which is not what was at issue here. Similarly, working out the number of hidden sweets on a scale would not be considered 'logical' reasoning ability by most parents, but rather something to do with practical or possibly mathematical skills. This does not invalidate the experiment in any way whatsoever, but does alert us to how the study might feed into *policy* debates.

What are the implications for other claims?

There are no immediately obvious relevant other claims but we might want to note that generally the study suggests that cognitive abilities might be more fluid than we had thought. If logical reasoning skill can be shaped by social interaction, maybe other skills, such as reading and investigating, can be too.

What next steps does the study suggest, or lend itself to?

As we noted above, the precise way in which the study was operationalised, while valid, was not inevitable. There are other forms of social interactions and other forms of logical reasoning which could be explored.

Consider the study in other terms

Now we can stand back and consider the study in a wider context.

What is the historical context for the claim and the evidence?

As noted by the authors in the introductory section of the paper, the idea that the development of logical thinking is heavily influenced by social experiences has been around for some time. The idea that collaborative learning is effective and desirable is to some extent a legacy of 1960s' liberal educational theory which emphasised a shift away from hierarchical teacher–pupil relationships and towards lateral pupil–pupil relationships.

What is the cultural context for the claim and the evidence?

The study emphasises in principle the benefits of collaborative learning. Note that the model of social interaction for learning in the study does not involve a teacher – just other children. The history of education in most developed countries involves a movement away from an initial focus on curriculum/teacher-centred learning and towards child-centred learning, incorporating forms of discovery learning from the world around the child including other children.

THINK IT THROUGH

Ethics

Now that you have had a chance to think deeply about this interesting study, you are in a better position to consider the ethical aspects. What are your thoughts on the extent to which the main ethical issues in psychological research, such as doing no harm, informed consent, deception, freedom to withdraw, confidentiality and debriefing, were addressed (Chapter 5)? What aspects of ethics are reported clearly in this study? Which are less clearly reported? What would you want more information on if you wanted to carry out a full ethical evaluation on this study?

What is the argument not addressing? What is missing, ignored or excluded?
The argument presented in the paper is 'not' many things. The authors do not claim that children learn *exclusively* from social interaction with peers. Nor do they claim that children routinely teach each other about deduction. We have already noted that alternative forms of the concrete operationalisation to the ones used in the study might or might not have produced different results.

Overall, our analysis of this brief but important paper indicates that, even in the most carefully designed study, decisions have to be made about how to turn abstract theoretical constructs into real tasks and observations in specific experiments. These decisions have a bearing on the adequacy of the test of the theoretical constructs and the links between them. Making the operationalisations too narrow runs the risk of compromising the external validity of the experiment, while making them too broad runs the risk of compromising the internal validity.

SUMMARY

In this chapter we examined the main methods and topics of developmental psychology. We have particularly noted some of the enduring issues to which contemporary child psychology relates such as nature versus nurture. Our survey of the methods used by child psychologists indicates that great care is required to employ methods which are appropriate for children but which still enable useful inferences to be drawn. Theoretical models of cognitive development in psychology are generally robust and enable relatively direct tests to be made of their claims. We have also analysed a recent experimental research report in order to develop our thinking about the difficulties posed by translating theoretical constructs into concrete operationalisations. We found that considering the necessarily narrow conception used in the actual experiment helped us to think more clearly about the limitations of a study, both in terms of internal and external validity, but also in terms of what future research might be interesting.

KEY TERMS

Affirming the antecedent

FURTHER READING

Cowie, H, Smith, P K and Blade, H (1998) *Understanding Children's Development* (3rd edn) can be highly recommended for its comprehensive and critical coverage of biological, social and cognitive aspects of development including extremely thorough accounts of Piaget and Vygotsky.

The British Journal of Developmental Psychology from which the Roazzi and Bryant paper is taken publishes original articles on the 'development from infancy to old age, including: development during infancy, childhood and adolescence; abnormal development including the problems of handicaps, learning difficulties and childhood autism; educational implications of child development; parent–child interaction; social and moral development; and the effects of ageing.'

For a radical critical psychology perspective on development, try Burman, E (1994) *Deconstructing Developmental Psychology* (London: Routledge).

Coverage of recent thinking on Vygotsky and the kind of ideas he inspired can be found in the contributions to Faulkner, D, Littleton, K and Woodhead, M (eds) (1998) *Learning Relationships in the Classroom* (London: Routledge).

Bremner, G, Slater, A and Butterworth, G (eds) (1997) *Infant Development: Recent Advances* (Hove: Psychology Press) provides some much more recent ideas about how children's cognitive development can and should be modelled. A challenging but rewarding read.

USEFUL WEBSITES

Developmental Psychology links from Social Psychology Network
http://www.socialpsychology.org/develop.htm
Probably the best jumping off point for high quality links to developmental psychology on the web. Part of Scott Plous' Social Psychology Network project.

Child Psychology Page
http://www.york.ac.uk/inst/ctipsych/resources/dev.html
Computers in Teaching Initiative links to Child Psychology Sites.

Social Science Information Gateway (SSIG) to Child Psychology
http://sosig.ac.uk/roads/subject-listing/World-cat/abchild.html
One of many first-rate collections of web resources from SSIG.

European Society for Developmental Psychology (ESDP)
http://devpsy.lboro.ac.uk/eurodev/
The ESDP website with book reviews and further Internet links.

Lev Vygotsky Centennial Page
http://www.massey.ac.nz/~ALock/virtual/project2.htm.
Information and links based around the 100th anniversary of Vygotsky's birth in 1896.

Thinking about Cognitive Psychology

CHAPTER OVERVIEW

Previously we have considered how social psychology accounts for social behaviour and how developmental psychology accounts for individual growth. Both these areas have been influenced by the theories and concepts of cognitive psychology, to which we now turn. Cognitive psychology addresses the nature of human information processing as revealed in thinking, memory, reading, reasoning and perception, using laboratory experiments as its main methodology. However, computer simulations are also used to test potential models of information processing. In this chapter we will look at some of the key concepts and distinctions used in cognitive psychology and assess their importance for psychological theory. Both positive and critical accounts will be offered of how well the general criteria for good theories are met. We shall analyse some additional aspects of internal validity as it applies to cognitive psychology experiments and look at some of the problems of doing applied cognitive psychological research outside the laboratory. Finally, we will briefly review the links between cognitive psychology and other areas in psychology in order to provide a fuller picture of the central role of cognitive psychology in the discipline generally.

LEARNING OBJECTIVES

By the end of this chapter you should be able to:

- Indicate the main areas of cognitive psychological research and theorising
- Explain why the embodiment and content of thought are relatively secondary concerns to cognitive psychologists
- Think critically about the main features of experiments and computer simulations in cognitive psychology

LEARNING OBJECTIVES (cont'd)

- Compare and contrast the basic features of computational and connectionist metatheories in cognitive psychology
- Offer a balanced account of the strengths and limitations of theorising in cognitive psychology
- Give a brief account of the links between cognitive psychology and other areas of psychology, indicating examples of the application of ideas from cognitive psychology to other domains

What is cognitive psychology?

On 4 October 1992 a Boeing 747 took off from Amsterdam Schipol Airport with four crew members and a cargo. Within minutes it was discovered that both starboard engines had failed. The crew tried to return to the airport but lost control of the plane. The aircraft crashed into an 11-storey building and all four crew members and 39 people in the building were killed. The subsequent media coverage in the Netherlands was extensive, with all television companies and newspapers carrying news stories for several days and weeks after the event. However, there was no television footage of the actual crash *impact* itself, just the aftermath.

Less than a year later 107 out of 193 people questioned claimed, however, to have seen the actual moment of impact on television. How could so many people claim to have 'remembered' seeing footage that never existed? Cognitive psychology tries, among other things, to make sense of how human minds can make such errors of recall.

Cognitive psychology is the study of *human information processing* and as such investigates perception, attention, memory, thinking, reasoning and language. Some of the basic *issues* for cognitive psychology include:

- What is information and how do we organise it?
- Are humans rational thinkers?
- Are humans efficient thinkers?
- What kind of metaphors should we use to describe human information processing?

Some examples of *specific questions* which cognitive psychologists ask are:

- How do we recognise patterns?
- Why do optical illusions look the way they do and can they tell us about human visual information processing generally?
- How are we able to pick out and keep track of the sound of the human voice in the midst of a noisy environment?
- How do we retrieve previously learned information?

- Why and how do we forget things?
- What conditions are conducive to creative problem solving?
- How do we make decisions when faced with various alternatives, some risky, some safe?
- How do we produce and process writing and speech and make sense of it all?

THINK IT THROUGH

What themes do you see emerging from this list of questions? Do the questions seem focused on the content of thinking or the processes of thinking?

So much for the various questions, issues and topics of cognitive psychology. We need to consider now the underlying unity of cognitive psychology that brings all these areas together. By exploring a classical definition of cognitive psychology, we can think more critically about the area by providing a fundamental framework for all work that falls under this heading. Ulric Neisser (1967) offered a definition of cognitive psychology which is well worth repeating and exploring:

> Cognitive psychology refers to all processes by which the sensory input is transformed, reduced, elaborated, stored, recovered, and used.

The 'sensory input' referred to in Neisser's definition is any sensation in the visual or auditory channels such as a spoken word or a visual image (psychologists have only very rarely studied the processing of information in other modalities). We should note here the difference between sensation and perception and how Neisser clearly emphasises the latter. This definition also emphasises the dynamic manipulation of information in a cognitive system. This kind of definition shows how cognitive psychology rejects the behaviourist idea that humans respond instinctively, or through learned habits, to environmental stimuli. How this definition relates to issues which intrigue cognitive psychologists can be best illustrated by an example. Imagine you receive the following 'sensory input' in the form of an announcement at a lecture:

> The mock cognitive psychology exam scheduled for the 11th of December has been brought forward to the 4th of December.

You might write this information down on a piece of paper and then put it in your jacket pocket. You now have both a written record and a mental record of this information. The piece of paper lies in your pocket until discovered some weeks later (hopefully before the 4th of December). The piece of paper might become a bit crumpled, but it would still have the same information on it, no more, no less. If the same were true of your *mental* (that is, cognitive) record, life would be impossibly chaotic (but at least cognitive psychology books would be much thinner).

In fact the fate of the mental record is very different. You will have *transformed* the auditory sensory input (the lecturer's spoken words) into some kind of mental representation of this information. This representation might have linguistic or visual features. It might be represented as a record of fact (the exam is on the 4th) or as an action to perform (study for the 4th) or in various other ways. In both these representations the original input has been *reduced* (there is probably no explicit representation of the *original* date of the exam). Suppose further that the next day you overhear another student repeating a rumour that the exam has been brought forward because it is going to be a tough one. You might *elaborate* your representation now to 'the tough exam is on the 4th or 'study really hard for the 4th'. Of course you might also have elaborated on the strength of your inferences about previous exams you have experienced. You keep this representation in memory and when someone asks you the following week when the exam is you are able to say 'It's on the 4th of December'. You also remember to actually turn up on the 4th. It can be seen, therefore, that you have *stored*, *recovered* and *used* the representation just as anticipated in Neisser's definition. Usually the cognitive processes studied by psychologists occur over a much shorter time frame, sometimes only a few milliseconds. Additionally, cognitive psychologists have tended to look at each of the operations referred to in Neisser's definition (transformation, **storage**, recovery and so on) in *isolation* rather than as a coherent sequence. This is true of most of the topics studied in cognitive psychology, with perception, attention, memory, thinking and language studied as discrete rather than interconnected phenomena. Cognitive psychologists agree that this fragmentation is unfortunate but recently there have been signs that more integrative work is being carried out.

THINK IT THROUGH

Why do you think there has been such fragmentation of process and topic in cognitive psychology? What advantages and disadvantages does this bring?

Embodiment is irrelevant to cognitive psychologists

It is important to note that cognitive psychologists are not interested in which brain cells you used to store information, they are interested only in the abstract description of (i) the structure of the information stored and (ii) the processing that was carried out on that information. The physical embodiment of information processing is irrelevant to cognitive psychologists, in much the same way that aeronautical design is irrelevant to a travel agent, or textile production is to a supermodel. The emphasis is on the abstract properties of representations and their transformation rather than on the things which enable the representations to take place (that is, neurons), which is what makes it easy for cognitive psychologists to exchange ideas with computer programmers and those working in linguistics, mathematics and robotics. In all these disciplines it is the idea of symbols and their manipulation which matters rather than the fact that those symbols are mediated by nerve cells, floppy disks or larynxes.

Content is secondary

Cognitive psychologists are much more interested in how sensory inputs are represented rather than what they represent. This is why theories of episodic memory (that is, memory for sequences of events) look pretty much the same whether they are trying to account for how we remember a sequence of flashes of light, car journeys or vegetable purchases. Thus theories in cognitive psychology are generally context-independent. This makes cognitive theories, when true, very powerful, since in principle they have a very wide domain of application (see 'comprehensiveness' as a criterion for assessing theories in Chapter 3). This further enables the exchange of ideas between cognitive psychologists, computer scientists, engineers and so on, since the way symbols can be manipulated is independent of what they stand for. Most people know this is true from very basic algebra where if 2a = 4b, then a = 2b, whatever 'a' and 'b' stand for, but this arbitrariness of symbols is also true for many more complex symbolic manipulations such as recursion and iteration (see box below).

Recursion and iteration

Recursion is when a definition contains a version of itself, or when the instructions for carrying out a procedure include the instruction to carry out the procedure itself. A recursive definition is partially defined in terms of itself, specifically simpler versions of itself (Hofstadter, 1979: 127). For example, a definition of how to open a locked hotel room door might run as follows:

How to open a locked hotel door:

1. If you have the key, put it in lock and go in. END
2. If you do not have a key, then ask at reception for the key
3. If reception have the key, take it and go to 1 else END
4. If reception say the key is locked in the storeroom, then see instructions on how to open a locked hotel door else give up. END

Notice that step 4 instructs us to use the whole procedure.

In psychology an example of recursion might be the rule 'I like someone if they are nice or if I like someone they like'.

Iteration is when a process is applied to the result of its own operation. For example, when building a fence, a spirit level can be used to check that the top of the fence is even. Successive adjustments can be made until the fence is parallel with the horizon. The process of checking the level is applied to produce a slight adjustment

---

Recursion and iteration (cont'd)

of the fence. This resulting adjusted angle is the input into the next assessment of angle and so on. In symbolic processing, the result of the application of one mathematical procedure on a set of data becomes the input for the next cycle and so on.

In psychology, an example of iteration might be when a child repeatedly asks 'why?' in response to each successive parental explanation.

In computer and cognitive science, recursion and iteration are used all the time in much more mathematically complex forms than these trivial examples, but the basic principles are the same.

This emphasis on form over content is what cognitive scientists mean when they refer to the 'syntactic' aspect of cognition – the rules for the ordering of thought. One of the fundamental assumptions of cognitive psychology is that the mental level of information processing can be studied without reference to lower-level neural structures. Some theorists emphasise the separation of mind and body in strong terms:

> The amazing flexibility of our minds seems nearly irreconcilable with the notion that our brains must be made out of fixed-rule hardware, which cannot be reprogrammed. We cannot make our neurons fire faster or slower, we cannot rewire our brains, we cannot redesign the interior of a neuron, we cannot make any choices about the hardware – and yet, we can control how we think. (Hofstadter, 1979: 302)

However, 20 years after this passage was written, it turns out that hardware is not so inflexible as we thought, as we shall see in Chapter 11. We may not be able to control the hardware through thought, but the hardware is adaptive to learning.

The structure and processing of information

It would be a mistake to assume that our minds make sense of information by simply responding to the input as it comes in. It is clear that our minds approach processing tasks with all kinds of *expectations* about what kind of information is coming next and the best way to process it efficiently when it arrives. Take the processing of the verbal information in the announcement made by the lecturer about the date of the examination as an example. Your cognitive system will have used its knowledge of English grammar to anticipate that the last part of the utterance would be a date. A system which uses both the incoming information *and* its knowledge of what to expect is said to use both bottom-up and top-down processing respectively. It is very clear that the human perceptual system works in this way. Thinking *critically* about human perceptual processes often involves assessing whether any given theory has got the balance right in terms of the relative importance of, and interconnections between, these two aspects.

Cognitive psychologists emphasise the importance of accurately describing the structure of mental representations. One important form of representation is that of a schema. A schema is any cognitive representation which enables perceptions to be organised. For example, you might have a schema for television sets. The schema might specify among many other things that television sets must (i) have buttons at the front, (ii) have a screen, and (iii) have cables at the back. It might also contain information about the relationships between these features (for example that pressing a button makes a picture appear on the screen). This means that if you catch a *glimpse* of the front of a television set but do not see the cables at the back, you still 'know' that this object has cables at the back because your schema specifies that things such as televisions have things such as cables at the back. Similarly, if you saw a television which was otherwise perfect but had no buttons at the front, you would know it to be deficient. That we do have schemata and use them widely in both simple and complex processing tasks is very clear from research. Thus schemata allow us to categorise information, make relevant links and generate expectations about the world around us. Without schemata objects would need classifying from scratch each time. Note that a schema system is very much more powerful than just having some sort of list of all known features of the objects in the world. By clustering or chunking together the features relevant to a specific object, inferences relevant to that object can be made much more quickly, reliably and efficiently.

A further interesting and very common type of mental representation is that of a **prototype**. A prototype is any representation which is a *specific* case but which serves as a representation of a *general* class of objects. For example, you might have 'Mars' as a prototypical representation of the class 'planets', or Bruce Willis for the category 'Hollywood movie star', or 'wine' for the category 'alcohol', and so on. Note that prototypes are forms of schemata in that they encode information about the features that objects falling into that class will have. The fact that we have prototypes means that when we are asked about planets, movie stars and alcohol, we answer with reference to Mars, Bruce Willis and wine, without being particularly aware that we are doing so.

Thinking critically about methods in cognitive psychology

We turn now to consideration of the strengths and weaknesses of the various methods used in cognitive psychology. We shall consider experiments, verbal protocols and computer models.

Experiments

Cognitive psychologists use laboratory experiments a great deal. Since cognitive psychologists are typically interested in the ways in which individuals process information, most experiments involve groups of subjects responding to different versions of the same input. The independent variable in a perception experiment might be the length of the lines in an optical illusion. The independent variable in a memory experiment might be the instructions given to the subject to process the information in a particular way or the organisation of the to-be-remembered items.

In a reasoning experiment the independent variable might be the degree of 'realism' in the materials of the problem to be solved. For perceptual studies the dependent variable is often reaction time. This is simply the time lapse between the appearance of information (usually on a computer screen) and a button being pressed by the subject. In a memory experiment the dependent variable might be the number of words or items correctly recalled, while in a reasoning experiment the dependent variable would usually be the number of correct answers given. Often an experimenter will also use the number and type of *errors* made as a dependent variable, as this can reveal distinctive characteristics of the kinds of processing operation which have been carried out on the information presented to the subject.

Often the stimuli in cognitive psychology experiments are quite simple and require limited responses from subjects. For this reason, and because typically subjects are not able to work out precisely what the experiment is assessing, it is common for subjects in cognitive psychology experiments to be exposed to tests (or 'trials') from all the levels of the independent variable. Thus cognitive psychology makes use of within-subjects designs (see Table 5.1). This is an efficient method of data collection since more data can be collected, and because each subject acts as their own control it is easier to remove the random noise in the data.

In addition to these basic considerations, there are additional questions we need to consider when reading about and performing experimental cognitive research. Many of these considerations relate to the extent to which the independent variable really does amount to an operationalisation of the terms of the hypothesis as derived from the theory under consideration.

One of the first questions we can ask is 'Were the stimuli used representative?' It is crucial in any experiment that the stimuli presented to the subjects really are good exemplars of the category supposedly being investigated. For example, if we are interested in testing the hypothesis that recall for words decreases with the retention interval, then we need to use common words or else our findings will not have wide applicability. Test items that are too exotic or too familiar can lead to *artificially* slow or rapid processing which will lead to genuine effects not being picked up (see the discussion on concrete operationalisation in Chapter 9).

The setting up of cognitive experiments, especially perception experiments, can be a painstaking business. In addition to ensuring that stimuli are presented in the correct sequence, all other distracting stimuli need to be filtered out. The effect of the testing arrangements on subjects' motivation, concentration and attention needs to be carefully assessed in advance. Reading the procedure section of a research report you will see that researchers often report the size of the image, the visual angle, the distance the subject sat from the screen, the time in milliseconds the image was on the screen, where the subject was told to place his hands before pressing the button in response and so on. These details are given to help other researchers rerun the same study if they want to investigate the phenomenon further. However, in addition to checking that various potential confounding variables have been controlled for, we should consider what the experiment must have *felt like* from the subject's point of view. Most readers probably skip over the procedure sections of research reports too quickly but it is worth trying to imagine the experiment from the subject's perspective. Do the conditions seem cramped? Would this have been an interesting task? How long would each subject have been sitting doing the same task? Were the subjects paid? What was their motivation for taking part? Were the instructions to the subjects clear or were they overly complex? In other words, it is worth trying to put yourself in the shoes of the subject. If the task was boring or just too long, it might well be the case that a percentage of the data reflects bored subjects not paying attention.

Verbal protocol analysis

Verbal protocol analysis (VPA) involves the detailed analysis of the talk of subjects as they carry out complex tasks. This running commentary is tape-recorded and transcribed to enable reliable coding and cross-checking. Unlike the discourse analysis approach to the study of talk, VPA involves breaking the speech down into units (the segmentation phase) and then classifying each segment as an instance of a small number of predefined categories (the encoding phase). These coded segments can then by subjected to statistical analyses in the usual way. The strengths of VPA are that it can capture rich information about how different individuals tackle different kinds of task and the strategies used by the subjects can be made clear. The main difficulty of VPA (apart from its labour-intensive nature) is that there is always a concern that the spoken commentary is not always a direct, 'pure' printout of the internal cognitive processes of the subject. Thus there is a question mark over the validity of the technique. It is possible, for example, that subjects change their processing strategy because they are being monitored, an example of reactivity. The technique works best when the protocol is provided concurrently and the processes being examined are high level ones which lend themselves to verbalisation.

Computer models

With the rapid increase in the processing power of computers, psychologists and computer scientists have been able to implement their theories about human cognitive abilities as computer programs. The idea here is that since theoretical models about the kinds of processing carried out on internal representations are often very complex and can be highly mathematical, the only way to check that they are *possible* is to turn them into a program. If the program runs at all, that suggests that the theory or model is at least internally consistent – but it does not necessarily mean that the program describes how a *human* performs the task. In artificial intelligence (AI) programs, the aim is usually to do a cognitive task as efficiently as possible. For example, an AI program might be designed to recognise photographs of faces and classify them into categories such as male and female. Such a program would be deemed successful if it classified all the photographs correctly. Computer **simulations** in cognitive psychology, on the other hand, are generally designed to mimic human behaviour, warts and all. Thus a simulation program designed to recognise photographs of faces would be deemed successful if it classified correctly all the photographs which humans classified correctly but *misclassified* the same ones that humans misclassified.

Both AI and simulation programs do more, however, than force us to be explicit about our models. As we try to build ('write') a working system, we find that we have to specify procedures for subtasks that we did not think of explaining at the outset. For example, when we come to write the instructions for our face recognition program, we might realise only some way into the exercise that not all the features are always visible in photographs (for example ears hidden behind hair). We might have previously considered this a trivial technical distraction but it is precisely these 'distractions' which the human face recognition system deals with a hundred times a day. If we really think we have a full theory of face recognition, it should specify how occluded features are dealt with. While useful, being able to create computer models of thinking can lull us into thinking that we understand more about a process than we really do (Gregory, 1998).

Contemporary epistemologies in cognitive psychology

In cognitive psychology there are two major alternatives to mainstream experimental approaches – **computationalism** and **connectionism**. Both of these try to understand the mind by drawing upon computer models even to the point of building computer programs that mimic the way the mind works. However, computationalism emphasises the similarities between the mind and traditional computer architectures, while connectionism draws on more recent 'neural network' models of information processing. Experimental research emphasises the importance of cause and effect models, while computationalism and connectionism prefer models of systems of information processing. We shall see that both these alternative approaches have strengths and limitations.

Computationalism – the mind is like a computer

In order to make sense of the way the human mind manipulates knowledge structures, symbols and other representations, cognitive psychologists have employed a computational metaphor. That is to say, the question is asked 'How far can we get by assuming that humans process information in the same way as computers?' The answer is that we do get quite far but maybe not as far as we originally thought. One useful outcome from the attempt to consider human and computer processing side by side is that theories of human cognition have become much more precise. If we put forward a theory about how a human mind solves anagrams, we should be able to write a computer program which demonstrates that model working. Previously psychologists were often able to get away with papering over the cracks in their theories by the use of woolly language. We can test whether a theory is *internally consistent* by showing that it works on a computer. Of course showing that anagrams *can* be solved in a certain way is not the same as proving that humans *do* solve the problem in that way. Thus computational coherence is a necessary but not sufficient condition for a theory to be accepted as valid.

Maybe we need to think more critically about what we mean by 'thinking'. Since the early 1960s, the question has been most exhaustively examined in relation to whether or not computers can think. Some commentators have argued that computers cannot be said to be capable of thinking because they are incapable of the creative and unpredictable leaps of imagination characteristic of human thought. This is met by the objection that the failure to demonstrate imagination does not necessarily imply a lack of thought, it simply shows a lack of *human* thought. And it is not at all clear that computers are incapable, either in practice or theory, of being original and creative. Some chess computers, for example, are able to demonstrate moves which watching grandmasters would describe as innovative. A difficulty here, however, is that it is not always clear whether it is the computers or their programmers that are demonstrating the creativity.

As a way of dealing with the endless disputes about a definition of thinking against which a computer's performance could be compared, Alan Turing (1950) devised a simple test which sought to offer a practical solution to the issue of artificial intelligence (see box below).

The Turing test

Alan Turing was an Oxford mathematician and theorist of computers. He proposed a simple test to explore whether machines (that is, computers) really could be said to think (Turing, 1950). He suggested that a computer and a human being should be located in two separate rooms and away from a second human being acting as an investigator. The investigator would be allowed to send questions via a keyboard to the computer and human in the adjacent rooms – but without knowing which of the respondents is the computer and which is the human being. The investigator's task is to work out which is which simply on the basis of the typed replies coming to his monitor. The dialogue might go like this:

Investigator: Candidate 1, where is Paris?

Candidate 1: France.

Investigator: Do you like French food?

Candidate 1: No, it's too rich.

Investigator: Do you like French wine?

Candidate 1: No – I don't drink wine.

At the end of the questioning the investigator has to decide which of the two respondents is the computer. If the investigator gets it wrong, then says Turing, we might reasonably conclude that the computer can, for all practical purposes, be said to be able to think.

Nowadays many computers can pass the Turing test but there is dispute over its relevance. Some psychologists and philosophers argue that the test sets too high a threshold for thinking since, for example, a child could think but would not pass for an adult. Some argue that the test is too easy or at least misleading because the issue is not just about thinking but about *understanding*. In the example, even if candidate 1 is a computer that can pass for a human, the computer might have an internal encyclopaedia of information about food, wine and France – but it has never consumed these things or visited France. Its understanding is purely in terms of how terms such as 'food' are linked to terms such as 'rich' and 'French' – it is the *relationship* between predefined terms that it knows about, not the real-world *referents* of the terms themselves. That is, it only knows the rules about how features are related to *one another* rather than how they are related to the real world and an experience of it. In short, its understanding is purely *syntactical* rather than semantic.

What do we mean by 'understanding' something? We might say that we understand how to speak our own native tongue, we understand why it rains and why it gets dark in the evening. We might understand the rules of a game or perhaps how a particular piece of machinery works. Something in all of this relates to the connection between our thinking and our actions in the world. Computers that pass the Turing test do not necessarily need to 'understand' the answers they are giving to the questions they are being asked. For this reason, and in order to address other issues in discussions about what counts as thinking and whether computers can 'think' or not, John Searle, an American philosopher, proposed a 'mental game' called the Chinese room puzzle which would help to clarify some aspects of what we *mean* when we make the claim that a computer can understand something (see box below).

Searle's Chinese room puzzle

John Searle suggests that cognitive science does not help us explain human understanding in any meaningful way. Even though computers can receive inputs (for example from keyboards or sensors) and can process that information in such a way that it can produce outputs (for example via the monitor or through acting on some other computer) that seem to be similar to humans, Searle argues that such programs do not *understand* what they are processing in the way that humans understand what they are processing. Thus, says Searle, programs do *not* show us how understanding might be happening with human hardware (brains).

In order to present this point of view in concrete form, Searle asks us to imagine a situation in which you are locked inside a room, and you can only speak English and no other language. Inside the room there are two books each containing Chinese characters (which mean nothing to you), and a further book, in English, which tells you how to link the characters in the books to each other. It tells you which Chinese characters to write down and post *out* through the letterbox when any Chinese characters get posted *in*. And sure enough, Chinese characters come in through the letterbox, you look them up in the book, and it indicates to you which Chinese characters to post back out again. The people outside the room refer to the first book which contains examples of all the symbols that get posted through the door as 'questions' and to the book from which you are directed to pick the Chinese symbols to post through the door as 'answers'. *But you don't know this.* So, there you are happily receiving Chinese symbols, looking them up in the books, and following

---

Searle's Chinese room puzzle (cont'd)

the rules in English, working out which symbol from the other book should be posted out. And posting them out. The question which Searle asks us at the end of all this is simple: *does the person in the room understand Chinese?*

What is your answer to Searle's query? Why? Can Searle's question be answered by doing more experiments? Think carefully about your answers here.

According to Searle, the answer to the Chinese room puzzle has to be 'no'. Just being able to carry out operations on input and produce sensible even 'correct' output, does not necessarily amount to *understanding*. Of course Searle is not really interested in Chinese – he is interested in computers. He is saying that just because computer programs can deduce the correct output from inputs does not mean that they understand those inputs or what they are doing to them.

Searle's question cannot be answered by any kind of experiment because it is a query about definitions and the evidence we require to apply those definitions. This is a conceptual rather than empirical problem.

We need to think critically about cognitive science and the claims made on its behalf. If we come across a claim that a computer is able to be, say, creative, we need to ask whether what is meant is 'creative in the way that humans are creative' or creative in some other way. In either case we need to see clear statements of what the criteria for creative (or whatever) are taken to be. We need to look at these criteria and see whether they are *representative* of creativity (or whatever). Having identified these criteria and reassured ourselves about their generality, we need to assess whether the performance of the computer really does match those criteria. It can be seen then that operationalisation of theoretical constructs is as much a challenge for cognitive scientists as it is for experimentalists (see Chapter 9).

Connectionism – the mind is like a brain

A recent alternative to the computational approach is that of connectionism (also known as the parallel distributed processing or neural networks approach). Connectionism takes as its starting point the idea that the mind might process information *the same way the brain does*. This seems a strange kind of claim to make. How can the mind work in the same way as a brain? Is the mind not 'hosted' by the brain? And we thought cognitive psychologists were not interested in the specific brain cells that might be involved in any specific representation. All these concerns are understandable and it is worth thinking through what is going on here. Connectionists are suggesting that a useful way of thinking about how the mind works is to assume that its key components are organised and communicate with each other in broadly the same way that neurons in the brain are organised and communicate with each other. This is *not* at all the same thing as saying that we should try to work out *which* brain cells are

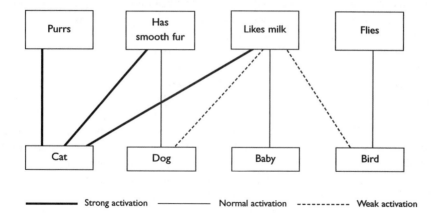

Figure 10.1   Simple connectionist model of activation patterns

actually involved in any given piece of information processing. Nor is it the same as saying that neurons and the units in the mind are part of one big system.

Unlike computational approaches which emphasise *serial* processing of information, connectionists emphasise *parallel* information processing. Similarly, unlike computational approaches which emphasise central control processes and knowledge being located in particular mental locations, connectionists emphasise that information about any one topic is spread ('distributed') across cognitive networks. Connectionists do not just present this idea as a general set of possibilities – they present many examples of how information can be processed extremely efficiently using neural networks.

Computational and connectionist accounts compared

The computational information processing approach as used in cognitive psychology has its origins in the developments of linguistics, engineering and computing of the 1960s. As such its models emphasise control of processing, knowledge structures and content-free processing (syntactical structures). By contrast, connectionism, with its foundations in studies of the processing architecture of the brain itself, emphasises how information and its processing occurs in several different parts of the system simultaneously. In the computational approach, the assumption is that all our knowledge about, say, cats is stored in a structured way in a specific place in the cognitive system, with all the information relevant to cats stored there or somewhere nearby. Thus our concept of 'cat' is that information at that location in our cognitive system. In the connectionist approach, our knowledge of cats is the *pattern of activation* of a particular neural network. The network is organised in such a way that the word 'cat' activates some parts of a network and not others. It is the set of links between units which contains the notion of 'cat', not any single specific unit. As such, our concept of 'cat' is distributed across the system and not located in any one place.

This distributed form of representation works because of the massive amount of activity going on simultaneously (that is, in parallel) across the whole system.

Although connectionism deals with the mind rather than the brain, some connectionists are tempted by the idea that the underlying principles for mental processing might be provided by neural structures. However, even staunch supporters of connectionism in psychology acknowledge that some of the main design features in connectionist models have no obvious counterpart in the brain. An example of this is the connectionist concept of 'back-propagation', which means that differences between predictions by the system and the feedback are fed back down the line. Thus while learning the concept 'cat', the system might initially treat any word beginning with 'ca' as 'cat'. As it experiences more input examples, it gradually refines excitatory/inhibitory links until it gets it right. (A much simplified analogy of back-propagation would be a shopkeeper receiving a box of goods from her assistant in the storeroom to give to a customer in the front of the shop. The customer rejects the box of goods because the box is too heavy to carry. The shopkeeper tells the assistant to pass out lighter boxes from now on.) Neurons cannot back-propagate the way the models do, however.

> For back-propagation to operate, neurons must compute exact differences in activation value between their current state and their desired state... store these differences and use them to compute differences in other units at earlier stages of processing. There is no evidence for transportation of exact activation values in the brain. (Ellis and Humphreys, 1999: 612)

Other differences between features of connectionist models and our current state of knowledge of neurological data are shown in Table 10.1.

Thinking about applications of cognitive psychology

The scope of applied cognitive psychology

Cognitive psychology has turned to real-world applications in a big way over the past 10 years. This research involves taking the theoretical models from laboratory studies and then applying these models to real-world problems. Cognitive researchers carrying out applied research also seek to learn from the environment in which they carry out their studies. Thus applied cognitive psychology involves both deduction (reasoning from established principles to specific cases) and induction (bringing together information from a range of cases). One of the useful functions of these studies is that by reworking abstract theoretical constructs in everyday terms, they enable us to think more practically about cognitive psychology generally.

The judicial system is a happy hunting ground for cognitive psychologists, as much of the civil and criminal legal system involves judgements, inferences, comparisons, reasoning and of course memory. We will look now at a particular area of applied cognitive psychology – eyewitness testimony (that is, memory for real-world events) – to help us to think about the strengths and weaknesses of taking cognitive psychology into the real world.

Table 10.1   Principles of connectionist models compared with neuropsychological data (based on Ellis and Humphreys, 1999: 612–13)

Connectionist models	Brains
Extensive back-propagation	No back-propagation
Processing units have both excitatory and inhibitory connections	Processing units have *either* excitatory or inhibitory connections but rarely both
Input from positive and negative units summed to determine output value	Inhibitory cells veto input of connecting cells
Units at each level densely interconnected	Units sparsely connected

Crombag *et al.* state (1996: 93)

> Reports by eyewitnesses are among the most important types of evidence in criminal as well as civil law cases. Many cases are decided exclusively on the basis of eyewitness testimony. It is therefore disturbing that such testimony is often inaccurate or even entirely wrong.

We shall see that while external validity is increased, allowing us to be reassured that cognitive phenomenon do exist in a non-laboratory setting, experimental control is limited, restricting our capacity to *explain* the data patterns we find. We will focus now in some detail on recent research by Crombag *et al.* (1996) into real-world eyewitness testimony to explore these points.

Until recently, events such as the 1992 Boeing Amsterdam Schipol Airport crash, mentioned at the beginning of the chapter, would have been examined by social psychologists in order to research the emotional effects of the crash on those who saw it. More recently, however, cognitive psychologists have started to look systematically at the *information processing* that operates in the aftermath of such high profile real-world disasters.

Ten months after the Schipol crash, Crombag and his colleagues asked 193 people the simple question 'Did you see the television film of the moment the plane hit the apartment building?' Respondents were restricted to answering 'yes' or 'no'. This was something of a trick question – there had been no television footage of the impact to see. The use of the word 'the' subtly encouraged the idea that there had been footage to see. Those subjects who said they had seen the impact on television were asked to complete a further question:

> After the plane hit the building, there was a fire. How long did it take for the fire to start?
>
> a. The fire broke out almost immediately
>
> b. It took a while, namely........ seconds/........ minutes
>
> c. I don't remember

Surprisingly, no fewer than 107 people (55 per cent) said they saw the video of the actual crash. The answers to the second question were also fascinating. Of the 107 people who claimed to have seen the footage, 63 (59 per cent) said the fire started immediately on impact, 24 (23 per cent) said it took a little while (between 2 and 30 seconds) and 20 said they could not remember. Overall, then, 87 people out of the total 193 claimed not only to have seen an event on television of which no footage existed, but went on to helpfully state how long it took the fire to start from the point of impact. This shows just how fragile episodic memory can be. It would seem here that subjects are drawing upon their general knowledge of plane crashes (that is, semantic memory) and applying it to their memory for observed events (that is, episodic memory).

In a follow-up study, Crombag *et al.* decided to see such how much bogus detail subjects could be subtly encouraged to 'remember'. This time they used law students as subjects, most of whom were under 25 years of age. This time they found that not only did even more people say they had seen the footage (66 per cent) but 41 per cent said they saw the plane catch fire on impact, hit the building

---

THINK IT THROUGH

Explaining sex differences in memory for non-events

Women appeared to be more likely than men to remember seeing television coverage that did not exist. Crombag et al. suggest five different hypotheses for this tendency of women to remember non-events:

1. Women may watch more television and therefore find it more difficult to remember what they have and have not seen.

2. Women may watch more television and know they watch a lot of television and are therefore more likely to guess that they probably did see it.

3. Women may be less cautious when they answer questionnaires.

4. Women may have a stronger wish to help the researcher.

5. Women may have a tendency to visualise dramatic events.

6. Women may be more susceptible to suggestion.

What assumptions do these possible hypotheses contain? How would we test these hypotheses? Are these hypotheses likely to be true of all women? Is just one of these hypotheses likely to be true? What do you think? Are there other possible explanations (you might want to consider using some of McGuire's heuristics for developing new theories and hypotheses outlined in Table 3.3)? The authors admit that their data do not help explain this pattern – clearly further research is needed. What kind of study would you carry out? Would it be important, for example, to use an incident which was of equal interest to men and women? How easy would it be to carry out a test of these hypotheses in the laboratory? In the field? Are there likely to be other studies that lead to hypotheses about why differences were observed?

horizontally (67 per cent) and that the body disintegrated (28 per cent) – all recollections of a piece of video that was never broadcast because it did not exist. Interestingly, females were found to be more likely to be affected by the leading question than males. In discussing the results of the study overall, Crombag *et al.* (1996) suggest that people cognitively confuse post-event hearsay with first-hand knowledge in such a way that the processes of constructing memory representations are not stored with the final representation itself. People do not keep a 'mental record' of how they came to know something.

We can see from this unexpected sex difference finding both the attractions and limitations of real-world research. On the one hand interesting and unexpected results turn up which cannot be said to be caused by the artificiality of the laboratory. On the other hand, because we lack the *control* of the cognitive laboratory we are often unable to replicate or manipulate the effects that we do find.

Cognitive psychology then is turning much more to cognition in the real world of courtrooms, memory for news and line-ups of suspects. However, while the content and context of the cognition is different, the underlying models of thinking remain the same. Generally, cognitive psychology, even in the real world, focuses on the *individual's* recall of collective events (rather than collaborative recall) and the recall of information for unambiguous events (rather than, say, recall for messy processes of social interaction). Nevertheless, there are exceptions to this rule, with some psychologists looking at collaborative recall in applied settings (for example Anderson and Ronneberg, 1996).

Thinking critically about theories in cognitive psychology

General criteria

Theories in cognitive psychology should be assessed in terms of the criteria identified in Chapter 3 as relevant to all psychological explanation.

1. Does the theory display *comprehensiveness?*
2. Does the theory display *parsimony?*
3. Does the theory display *clarity of constructs?*
4. Does the theory display *internal consistency?*
5. Does the theory display *testability?*
6. Does the theory have *empirical support?*
7. Does the theory have *heuristic value?*

Every theory in cognitive psychology must be assessed on a case-by-case basis. There are good and bad theories in cognitive psychology just as there are elsewhere. It is possible to consider theorising in this area in general terms so long as we note that all generalisations miss the details of specific examples. There are two kinds of perspective of the quality and function of theories in cognitive psychology. One is the positive assessment based on the tight definitions and testability of cognitive theories. The other perspective emphasises the artificiality and measurement obsession of laboratory-based cognitive psychology.

A positive view of the quality and functions of theories in cognitive psychology

In terms of comprehensiveness, theories in cognitive psychology perform quite well. Theoretical constructs such as schemata and prototypes do appear to cover many areas of knowledge representation (rather than just one or two aspects). In terms of parsimony, cognitive theories do well, since theories are explicitly content free, meaning that, for example, a successful theory of memory will be applicable irrespective of the content of what is being remembered (rather than a different theory of recall for every type of content). In terms of clarity of constructs, cognitive psychology has developed significantly with the advent of computer simulations and computer models. Where theoretical constructs are specified in an explanation, there is often pressure to specify the internal structure and relationships with other processes in sufficient clarity to enable a program to be written or a mathematical equation to be drawn up.

The influence of computer science on cognitive psychology is also evident in relation to the internal consistency of a theory. If a program is internally inconsistent, it will 'crash'. In terms of testability and empirical support, theories in cognitive psychology lend themselves to direct testing in controlled laboratory settings. Thus they are generally testable and good theories will get the empirical support they deserve. In experimental cognitive psychology theories can and will be tested and will stand or fall by their results. Cognitive theories are relatively highly formalised and use technical definitions rather than metaphorical flourishes and as a consequence tend to have less heuristic value than theories in other areas of psychology. However, the metaphor of the computer and the use of mathematical models, such as catastrophe and chaos theory, and the free interplay of ideas between linguists, neuroscientists and psychologists means that there are plenty of imaginative, bold ideas in circulation to stimulate intellectual creativity.

A critical view of the quality and functions of theories in cognitive psychology

It is possible to take a more pessimistic or critical view of theories in cognitive psychology. Theories in cognitive psychology, it might be argued, are 'comprehensive' only because cognitive psychologists define phenomena in narrow terms. For example, theories of problem solving tend only to use problem types with well-defined starting circumstances and clear-cut solutions. Theories of problem solving are comprehensive so long as we do not try to apply them to ill-defined, everyday, messy problems with unclear criteria for success. In terms of 'parsimony', computer programs may look parsimonious on the surface, but if we look at the detailed programming instructions there are often a whole set of 'fixes' and 'patches' which tie up the loose ends where the theory is underspecified.

In terms of internal consistency, cognitive psychological theories are more consistent than most but this claim may be overstated. In terms of testability and empirical support, the problem is that cognitive psychologists produce theories only about things that are easily measurable rather than develop general theories which present new measurement challenges. For example, there are theories about button-pressing reaction times, word-list recall and attention to taped voices, but less on the more messy 'making up your mind on difficult life-decisions' time, or 'remembering to keep verbal promises' recall or 'getting bored during conversations'. As for heuristic value being low, it should be remembered that cognitive psychology, despite its claims to formal mathematical methods and computational models, in fact uses woolly, metaphorical terms more than is acknowledged. For example, attention and concentration are characterised in terms of cognitive 'effort' but there is little analysis of what this effortfulness might mean. Is it exhausting? Does it involve the use of energy? Similarly, problems arose with the notion of 'depth' of processing (Craik and Lockhart, 1972). Of course it is only a metaphor but what kind of extra information does the notion of 'depth' provide for a theory?

Similarly, ideas such as 'capacity' of short-term memory (of plus or minus seven items) may have stimulated plenty of research but it also reinforced an unnecessary notion of static storage of 'items' rather than dynamic and flexible information management as would seem to be the way memory works. Thus, despite cognitive psychology's claims to be formal (and therefore immune from the fuzzy aspects of theory building), it does in fact use metaphors and terms with particular connotations quite regularly.

Links with other areas

Cognitive psychology enjoys strong links with other areas of psychology, consideration of which helps us think through the ways in which ideas circulate within the discipline.

Links with social psychology

Cognitive psychology has strong links with social psychology. We saw in Chapter 7 that Petty and Cacioppo's elaboration likelihood model of attitude change was strongly influenced by information processing models. In particular, they suggested that the more we think about an attitudinal statement the more we will elaborate on that statement and generate further information and arguments consistent with it, giving the original input more persuasive power. Indeed, cognitive social psychology is now a recognised subarea of social psychology. Nisbett and Ross (1980) described many ways in which cognitive biases underlie much of our processing of information about the social world. For example, we have a tendency to be strongly influenced by the first impressions we form of other people largely because these first few pieces of information serve to trigger schema about the target individual into which later pieces of information are made to fit. Generally, the application of cognitive psychology in social psychology has emphasised the errors to which our cognitive systems are prone when processing information in complex multifaceted social environments, suggesting possibly that we have evolved to deal with more basic tasks (see Chapter 11).

Similarly, much research activity in developmental psychology is informed by the assumptions, theories, methods and findings of cognitive psychology. Piaget's ideas on internal representation predated the explosion of interest in cognition in the 1960s. Recently, however, developmental psychologists interested in children's thinking have tried to offer information processing models of cognitive development to replace Piaget's classical approach, which was heavily influenced by ideas from biology and emphasised structure. For example, it is generally believed that, while children's cognitive capacity (that is, the maximum number of chunks that can be handled simultaneously in working memory) does not increase significantly with age, the efficiency of processing does.

Cognitive models have also become very closely incorporated into biopsychological research. For example, clinical work in cognitive neuropsychology, with patients suffering from brain injury caused either by trauma or lesions (such as accident damage) or through disease (such as viral infections), has yielded fascinating insights into how different cognitive functions appear to be located in different parts of the brain. Second, advances in brain mapping and scanning equipment and their wider use in medical contexts have allowed psychologists, neuroscientists and clinicians to 'photograph' the living brain as it processes information. The functional neuroimaging studies provide detailed information of brain activity as it occurs, without the need for surgery. Subjects can be asked to perform various cognitively demanding tasks and readings can be taken of parallel neural activity.

How should we think critically about the link between cognitive psychology and other parts of psychology? First and foremost we need to consider whether or not the very best ideas are being transported from cognitive psychology to the other area. If we are trying to answer the question 'Are infants affected by the Müller-Lyer illusion in the same way that adults are?', we need to make sure that our theoretical understanding of the Müller-Lyer illusion is the best one available. We also need to be aware of the subtle factors which affect the perception of this illusion (see for example, Predebon, 1998). We should also be aware of the difference between looking at cognitive processing as a lower-level explanation for social phenomena (as in Nisbett and Ross's work) and looking at cognition itself as the thing to be explained by reference to even lower-level systems (as in neuropsychology). In the former, cognitive systems are seen as the underlying regularity offered to explain diverse patterns of social behaviour, while in the latter underlying neural structures are offered as the underlying regularity to explaining diverse patterns of cognitive activity (see levels of explanation in Table 3.1).

SUMMARY

Cognitive psychology involves the study of transformation, reduction, elaboration, storage, recovery and use of information. As such it involves the analysis of perception, reasoning, memory and language usually through experiment but also occasionally through computer simulation. Cognitive psychology is much less interested in the format or content of storage and processing of information, a fact which enables collaboration about symbol and information systems with theorists working in other domains. Models of the mind as a computer have been extremely influential in cognitive psychology, although newer models are emerging which suggest that the mind, somewhat paradoxically, can be thought of as operating much as the brain itself does. Theories in cognitive psychology are widely regarded as meeting the main criteria for useful theories but this might be at the expense of exploring cognitive activity in relatively artificial environments. More recently, however, applied cognitive psychology has developed with a focus on cognition in the real world. Cognitive psychology continues to be an influential force in psychology as illustrated by the range of links it has to other areas of the discipline.

KEY TERMS

Computationalism ■ Connectionism ■ Iteration
Prototype ■ Recursion ■ Simulations ■ Storage

FURTHER READING

There are many excellent books on theorising in thinking, judgement and reasoning but among my favourites is Garnham, A and Oakhill, J (1994) *Thinking and Reasoning* (Oxford: Blackwell) which is as clear and authoritative as they come. For a stimulating introduction to cognitive science, Hofstadter, D R (1979) *Godel, Escher, Bach: An Eternal Golden Braid* (London: Penguin) is a classic account of thinking conveyed through the works of three geniuses from mathematics, art and music. Hofstadter demonstrates the power, paradoxes and universality of symbol systems emphasising how the same basic patterns emerge in all areas of everyday life. Not especially technical but some chapters ask more of the reader than others.

Recent critiques of the cognitive science enterprise can be found in Paul Thagard's (1996) *Mind: An Introduction to Cognitive Science* (Cambridge, MA: MIT Press), which argues, among other things, that cognitive science needs to evolve to take into account the criticisms made of its early development.

USEFUL WEBSITES

Cognitive and Psychological Sciences on the Internet
http://www-psych.stanford.edu/cogsci/
A joint UK–US venture to bring together Internet resources on cognitive psychology. Links are also provided to electronic discussion groups.

'CogPrints'
http://cogprints.soton.ac.uk/
An electronic archive of articles in psychology, cognitive science, neuroscience and linguistics.

Cognitive Science Dictionary
http://web.psych.ualberta.ca/~mike/Pearl_Street/Dictionary/dictionary.html
A useful resource for keeping track of terminology in cognitive science.

Thinking about
Biopsychology

11

CHAPTER OVERVIEW

Our bodies, including our brains, are machines and like most machines we do not really take much notice of them until they break down or do not work in the way we expect them to. We know that our brains underlie everything we do and we know that if an individual suffers brain damage they will, in many cases, not be able to function in the same way they did previously. Nevertheless, we normally tend to treat the relationship between our brain and our sense of self as unproblematic. Most of us also lack any intuitive sense of how the brain works, since so much of it is on a microscopic scale and is tucked away inside the skull. In this chapter we will be exploring ways of thinking about the biological side of psychology, with special reference to the relationship between mind and body. We will consider how to think critically about evolutionary analyses of human behaviour and individual differences. We will also consider the difficulties of mapping the output from highly sophisticated systems for measuring the brain onto the less precise theoretical constructs of mind and behaviour.

LEARNING OBJECTIVES

By the end of this chapter you should be able to:

- Describe the scope of biopsychology and its relation to other areas of the discipline
- Outline the mind–body problem and indicate its relevance to psychology
- Think critically about the contribution of cognitive science to the understanding of the mind–body problem
- Identify the assumptions of biopsychology and how they are revealed in the methods employed

Brains, bodies and biopsychology

We think of ourselves variously as perhaps a father or a mother, son or daughter; as someone with beliefs about politics, religion or art. We may be talented musicians, we may prefer strawberry ice cream to vanilla, and we may amuse small children at parties with deftly executed card tricks. But whatever identity or sense of being we have about ourselves, each of us has a body. A body that can get cut, get tired and have sex. As we grow older, our body will become a progressively less efficient system and one day we will die. It is important that we do not forget this because the questions that we have as psychologists, be they about memory, social interaction, language, vision or thinking, are questions which arise about *embodied* persons and answers to those questions must therefore be meaningful within that context. Whatever else has shaped our experience of the world, we cannot escape the fact that we are the products of millions of years of evolution. We are (at least in part) the way we are because our genes are the way *they* are. And yet we cannot simply say that we are *only* our genes, or that all of our behaviour can be explained entirely in terms of our genes. The real issue is: *In what ways is our biology relevant to our understanding of ourselves as persons?* As psychologists we want to discover whether we can better understand, say, memory by understanding the way the brain works as an organ when we are carrying out the activity of 'remembering'. Although as of 26 June 2000 we know through the Human Genome Project 97% of the human genetic blueprint, we still lack a clear understanding of the link between genes and behaviour.

The investigation of the ways in which our brain and its associated systems underlie psychological processes is known as biopsychology (or biological psychology). Under this general heading, we sometimes also come across *physiological psychology*, the study of the physiological processes such as endocrines which underlie behaviour, *neuropsychology*, the study of brain function often in the context of damaged brains, and *comparative psychology*, the study of the behaviour of non-human animals. The main focus of all of this research is the nervous system – the networks of billions of interconnected nerve cells which communicate and store information.

Across all these approaches is an emphasis on the *adaptive* nature of the human nervous system in relation to psychological functioning. That is, the nervous system has evolved over millions of years in such a way as to maximise our chances of survival and reproduction. Consequently, the human nervous system is the way it is now because it has helped the survival of thousands of preceding generations. Thus our hearing is sensitive to a particular range of pitch and volume and our eyes are sensitive to particular wavelengths in the electro-magnetic spectrum because precisely those ranges contain the information (about predators and prey) which help us to survive. Of course this process does not happen by *intentional* design. Rather it is the nature of the survival of the fittest that any organism which has sensory systems tuned to the wrong wavelengths is more likely to die before having offspring to carry their characteristics forward than an organism which is tuned to the right wavelengths.

What kind of relationship should psychology have to biology?

Is knowledge of biology a necessary foundation for the study of psychology in the same way that, say, physics is a necessary foundation for the study of aviation engineering? Or is the relationship more analogous to that between printing and literature? There would be no novels without papermills but our understanding of narrative form, character development, irony and bathos is in no way dependent on our knowledge of pulping and inking. Literary criticism as a form of knowledge is entirely independent of the physical medium of the texts it analyses. But can psychology stand in that same kind of relationship to biology as literary criticism stands to printing?

Some psychologists argue that it can. In particular, social psychologists argue that the social level of analysis of psychological phenomena is entirely indepen-dent of the biological level of analysis and thus they reject the reductionism implicit in biopsychology. The arguments that are used by anti-reductionist psychologists to resist the dissolution of psychology into biology often involve pointing out that the questions we ask of behaviour are only meaningful at the social level of analysis. For example, if we ask 'What is the main cause of jealousy?', a social psychologist, especially one of a social constructionist bent, would point out that such question can actually only be *meaningful* if it refers to a form of social interaction, a way of speaking, a form of social organisation and a set of rules within which 'jealousy' is a meaningful category. One could not even *in principle* point to a part of the brain and say 'there, it's that bit there, look, see it twitch, he is being jealous, *right now*'. No one would seriously suggest looking for the biological component of being 'cool'. Being 'cool' is a social category which only makes sense in a particular culture at a particular time. On the other hand, it *does* seem to make sense to look for the biological dimension to hearing. 'Hearing' (unlike 'cool') is not socially or historically contingent (or at least not in the same way). The problems arise of course for less clear-cut forms of behaviour and experience such as 'love', 'anger' or 'fear'. Which of these are socially constructed? Which are biological universals?

The orientation of biopsychology

Let us think now about the assumptions of biopsychology, that is to say, what it takes for granted about human behaviour and what we can know about it. In other words, we shall look at its angle on ontology (the nature of the world) and on epistemology (what we can know about that world).

Biopsychology is almost by definition reductionist. That is to say, biopsychology typically involves the assumption that behaviour needs to be explained in relation to more underlying 'basic' aspects of the system. Thus memory, for example, according to biopsychologists can and should be explained by reference to the operations of parts of the brain (such as the hippocampus) and depression can and should be explained by the operation of neurotransmitters (such as dopamine). Some psychologists would argue that an exclusively biological, reductionist account of human behaviour is possible and desirable, while others would argue that while a biological account is a necessary part of a full account it can only ever be a part of a full account. According to biopsychologists then, the best form of knowledge about behaviour is knowledge about the *lower-level* structures and processes that underlie behaviour. According to biopsychologists, this emphasis on microstructures and microprocesses has yielded fascinating and complex insights into behaviour which no other approach could have provided.

THINK IT THROUGH

When coming across the reductionism of biopsychology for the first time, there is a temptation to reject it simply because it does not sound very uplifting. Are our memories of our first childhood sweethearts really reducible to a few neurons firing, a bundle of connections in the hippocampus? Is our despair after our first romantic heartbreak really just no more than the squirting of dopamine across a couple of million synapses?

We have to make sure our emotions do not cloud our thinking here. The *personal meaning* of those experiences is not to be found at the neurological level but that is not an argument against reductionism per se. We cannot reject reductionism just because we do not *like* it. We can avoid getting ourselves into this mess if we think carefully about the language we use to specify the thing that needs explaining. If we label our first love affair as 'a tender, foolish, exhilarating life-affirming experience', then we are *never* going to receive a sensible answer from a biopsychologist along the lines of 'neurons and synapses'. This is not simply because of the relationship between the experience of love and the biology of the brain but because of the relationship between *words* such as 'tender' and words such as 'synapses'. Thinking about biopsychology requires us to think very carefully about the *language* we use to describe our behaviour and experience. If we want a reductionist account, then the behaviour to be explained needs to be defined objectively and in terms which do not depend upon personal, cultural and historical linguistic labels. Whether behaviour can be defined in such terms is another matter, of course.

Recently biopsychology has developed models that also incorporate holist assumptions into its thinking. That is to say, explanations are sought by looking at the broader, more 'macro' systems in which individuals are located. In evolutionary psychology, individual behaviour is explained in terms of the dynamics of the gene pool for that individual's species. Such accounts are interesting because they are reductionist in the sense that they consider the individual as made up of the underlying genetic material, but holist because the focus is on how the gene pool *overall* reproduces itself. Similarly, Wahlsten (1999) argues that extreme reductionism, which involves trying to explain behaviour in relation to single genes, is now giving way to analyses of how *sets* of genes interact with each other in systems.

Another important aspect of biopsychology is its assumption about the nature of the world it investigates. Biopsychologists operate on the assumption that they are developing theories and models about real objects. For biopsychologists, 'neuron' is not just a 'useful construct' – it is a real entity. In this sense biopsychology is realist in orientation. Similarly, biopsychology operates on the assumption that brains, neurons and neurotransmitters are defined by specific properties which are essential and intrinsic to those things (and not just projected on to them by scientists). As such biopsychology is strongly essentialist in nature.

Biopsychology is concerned with how overt behaviour is produced by underlying biological mechanisms, structures and processes. Thus there is no scope in biopsychology for free will. The underlying systems and *nothing else* are seen to cause the behaviour we observe. Thus biopsychology is strongly deterministic in its orientation. That is to say, biopsychology operates on the assumption that *in principle* if we had all the information about the state of a human brain and all incoming stimuli at any given point we would not need to know anything else in order to predict what it would do next. Recently, however, there has been a concession that even if biopsychologists knew everything about the prior state of, say, a nervous system (and that is a big 'if'), the next state of the system could only be predicted probabilistically, that is, what it is likely to do next rather than what it is certain to do next. This general modification of the traditional deterministic position is characteristic of theorists working in engineering, mathematics, computing, geology and other sciences which prefer to think in terms of inherently non-determined but still predictable stochastic (that is, probable) systems.

Evolution, instincts and learning

Making sense of biological psychology depends upon understanding the phenomenon of **evolution**. Evolution is the process whereby species develop over many generations by virtue of the process of **natural selection**. Natural selection, in turn, is the process whereby from among the diversity of members of a given species there are those which are highly suited to the immediate environment and will therefore evade being eaten by predators, will catch more prey and, crucially, will have more offspring with similar genetic material to themselves. By contrast, other members will be less well equipped to survive in their environment and will have fewer offspring (if any). Over many generations the genes of the fitter organisms spread through the species. Generally the process of evolution is gradual. Each mutation (that is, spontaneous alteration of genetic material in an offspring), if it is to improve reproductive fitness, has to confer an advantage to the organism in such a way that existing features are not rendered useless. There are two camps in biology regarding whether evolution has to be gradual or dramatic. Some psychologists such as Steven Pinker (1994) argue that evolution is essentially gradual, while some biologists such as Stephen Jay Gould (2000) suggest that evolution is better thought of in terms of *punctuated equilibrium*, with periods of stability punctuated by periods of dramatic development.

Mutations

When coming across concepts in evolution for the first time, the idea that *mutations* could be the foundation for evolutionary development seems bizarre. But we must set aside the science-fiction model of radioactive mutants wandering around with grotesque deformities. A mutation is *any* kind of specific structural change in genetic material. These can occur due to radioactivity, but occur more frequently on a spontaneous basis. Most mutations may be trivial and have no direct or indirect reproductive consequences at all. Many are *regressive* in that they reduce rather than improve reproductive fitness. The small number of *adaptive* mutations take many generations to spread through a species but in evolutionary terms the process is irresistible.

There is no doubting that evolution happens and that its main mechanism is natural selection. The question for psychologists is – How *important* is it in explaining human behaviour? And, more challengingly – In what *way* is it important for explaining human behaviour?

We need to begin by recognising that most of our brains are devoted to learning, not to innate instincts. We may have evolved a healthy fear of darkness but most of us now turn the lights out before going to sleep. In simplified terms, we are able to do this because our cerebral cortex (which deals with planning and judgement) overrules our limbic system (which deals with emotion). It has long been known that one way or another learning leads to changes in neural connections and that such changes are the basis of memory (Rosenzweig *et al.* 1972). More recently, with sophisticated contemporary methods there is now some very specific evidence about the precise way in which experience alters neural connections. Kolb and Whishaw (1998) have identified several important aspects of brain **plasticity**, that is, the capacity of the brain to rewire itself. The brain even in adulthood is not a static entity, it responds to the environment and to input generally by reorganising aspects of its own functioning. Plasticity can be shown in relation to the chemical changes in the brain, with new experiences leading to greater or lesser amounts of neurotransmitters being produced.

More striking, however, is evidence suggesting that the very *structure* of neurons is itself open to change as a function of learning. Kolb and Whishaw point out that in enriched environments, training in specific new skills and general recovery from brain injury leads to fundamental, structural neural changes such as an increase in the length of dendrites and the number of new synaptic spines formed. Interestingly, various supporting cells such as blood vessels and glial cells also increase in number when dendritic structures develop. This suggests that changes in response to environmental change are systematic rather than haphazard. We *have* evolved but we have not evolved into slaves of instincts, we have evolved into learning machines that can process information flexibly and, within limits, even restructure themselves when necessary.

Evolutionary psychology

Evolutionary psychology claims that the structure and functioning of the contemporary human mind reflects the fact that it evolved through natural selection to solve adaptive problems faced by our hunter-gatherer ancestors. Evolutionary psychology claims that aspects of social behaviour and forms of human social organisation, as they are today, can be explained in terms of the 'adapted mind'.

Cosmides and Tooby (1997) have suggested five principles of evolutionary psychology:

1. The brain is a physical system. It functions as a computer. Its circuits are designed to generate behaviour that is appropriate to our environmental circumstances.

2. Our neural circuits were designed by natural selection to solve problems that our ancestors faced during our species' evolutionary history.

3. Consciousness is just the tip of the iceberg; most of what goes on in our mind is hidden from us.

4. Different neural circuits are specialised for solving different adaptive problems.

5. Our modern skulls house a stone age mind.

Adapted from: Cosmides and Tooby (1997)

Evolutionary psychologists argue that the mind as it is today is first and foremost an adapted mind, adapted to meeting the basic demands of reproduction, warmth, acquiring food and generally staying alive in an untamed, unpredictable and dangerous environment.

Some evolutionary psychologists go on to claim that, since males and females have different challenges in relation to these basic demands (most obviously in terms of reproduction), their *minds* are different. For example, it is claimed that modern male sexual behaviour (supposedly more promiscuous, more often attracted by physical features, more easily aroused) can be explained by reference to the fact that the only constraint on male reproduction is the brief delay before the next erection. By contrast, sociobiology claims that females' more cautious sexual behaviour (supposedly less promiscuous, attracted by enduring qualities, less easily aroused) reflects the fact that reproduction requires a nine-month investment during pregnancy. Generally then, evolutionary psychologists in general and sociobiologists in particular argue that our genes drive our behaviour. We might think that we love that person, the argument goes, but in fact it is just our desire for reproduction dressed up in local culture and conventions.

How should we think about such claims? What evidence is relevant?

Critics of evolutionary biology argue that contemporary patterns of behaviour are *not* due simply to the influence of our genetic inheritance but are due at least in part to social institutions and culture values.

Arguments in favour of sociobiology are essentially confirmatory – and arguably therefore weak. For example, Buss *et al.* (1992) predicted that, since men are motivated to have several partners (in order to spread their genes widely), they would feel more jealousy by the idea of their partner having sex with another man than the idea of her developing a deep emotional attachment to another man. By contrast it was predicted that women (biologically more motivated to secure ongoing support for childbearing and child rearing) would be more jealous by the idea of their partner developing a deep emotional attachment to another woman than by the idea of him having sex with another woman. The results supported this prediction, with 60 per cent of men indicating more jealousy for sexual infidelity, while 85 per cent of women reported more jealousy for emotional infidelity.

However, we should recall here Popper's concern that gathering evidence which is consistent with a theory is not really enough in itself (see Chapter 2). There might well be another theory which also explains this pattern of data. For example, women might be *socialised* to value emotions more than men. And women might be *socialised* not to express their sexual desires (and disappointments) as openly as men.

One claim of evolutionary psychologists is that men have better spatial abilities than women because being hunters men had to develop a better sense of distance, perspective and orientation. Clearly hunting does involve specific spatial abilities (Calvin, 1993) and the paleontological evidence suggests that males rather than females did most of the hunting, so this claim seems superficially at least to be plausible. But we need to think critically about all claims. While there has been much debate on this theory, we will focus here on the simple matter of evidence for the original assumption. Do men really have better spatial abilities than women?

In fact it is clear that men are not better than women at *all* spatial tasks and for some spatial tasks women are actually better. Silverman and Eals (1992) found that women were better than men in a test involving recognising when objects had changed places. Postma *et al.* (1998) found no sex differences when subjects had to replace 10 objects in 10 original marked locations or when a single object had to be replaced in one of 10 marked locations. However, they did find males performed better when no marked locations were presented and subjects had to remember precisely where the object had originally been located.

Results like these make us ask the question of evolutionary psychologists – Why do men perform better on some spatial tasks, women perform better on others but there are no differences on yet other tasks? And how can this *specific pattern* of different spatial abilities between males and females be explained by reference to evolution? What specific reproductive advantage is there for men (but not for women) to be able to remember the precise location of objects? What specific reproductive advantage is there for women (but not for men) to be recognise when two objects have exchanged locations? Thus although there are complex conceptual issues in relation to making strong inductive inferences about biological foundations of cognition on the basis of sex difference, in this case we need to make sure that the *premises* are true first (see Chapter 4).

Of course, complex patterns of difference pose a challenge for all theories and not just evolutionary psychology. For example, if, as some feminist psychologists propose, women perform poorly on spatial tasks because they have been *socialised* to believe that they are weak on spatial tasks, then it still has to be explained why women are worse on some spatial tasks, but *as good* as men on some others and *better* than men on others still.

We need to consider whether the evidence provided shows that the behaviour is caused by evolutionary processes or is it only showing that in principle the behaviour *could* be caused by evolutionary processes? In other words, does the evidence support evolutionary theory and *only* evolutionary theory or is it merely *consistent* with it without ruling out other theories?

In Chapter 3 we identified ways of thinking about theories which try to explain a behavioural phenomenon in general with 'eight questions about the heterogeneity of behaviour for general theories'. Evolutionary psychology certainly seeks to explain behaviour in general so the questions are relevant here. Using the eight questions as a template, we can replace 'behaviour X' with 'spatial ability' and 'the theory' with 'sociobiology'.

1. Is the diversity of forms of spatial ability addressed by sociobiology?
2. Is the prevalence of spatial ability addressed by sociobiology?
3. Are the differences and similarities between males and females, young and old and across species in terms of spatial ability addressed by sociobiology?
4. Are the cross-cultural differences in spatial ability addressed by sociobiology?
5. Are the historical differences in spatial ability addressed by sociobiology?
6. Are the differences in the criteria for identifying examples of spatial ability addressed by sociobiology?
7. Is spatial ability a composite behaviour which requires its components to be explained first?
8. Is spatial ability an individual behaviour, dyadic behaviour, a group behaviour or societal 'behaviour'? Are all these levels addressed by sociobiology?

THINK IT THROUGH

Using the information provided in this chapter and your psychology textbook *start* to answer the eight questions above. Aim to go through the questions on the list and *identify what evidence you would have to collect or read about* in order to answer the questions. The books at the end of this chapter will also help you find the relevant evidence but this is primarily an exercise in identifying what kind of evidence is important in assessing the limits of theories that try to explain everything.

Overall then we need to be clear about the evidence base for evolutionary claims, the extent to which evolutionary claims rule out other possible explanations, the patterns of evidence overall and the language we use to describe the behaviour we seek to explain.

The mind–body problem in psychology

One of the fundamental issues in biopsychology, and for that matter psychology in general, is what is known as the **mind–body problem**. Specifically this issue relates to attempts to reconcile the fact that we all have subjective mental experiences (happiness, imagination, self-awareness and so on) but that we also have brains (with neurons, blood cells, neurotransmitters and so on).

Most people do not see why there might even *be* a problem here. We do have a brain and we do have thoughts – the former produces the latter. This position is sometimes referred to as **naïve dualism**. Much of this is reflected in everyday language about the mind and the brain. The problem for philosophers and latterly psychologists is the issue of *how* could our subjective experience or consciousness of self and the world arise from that biological machine, that mass of blood and cells we call a brain? Or, as the philosopher Colin McGinn puts it, 'How can technicolor phenomenology arise from soggy grey matter?' (1991: 1). How could something mental arise from something physical? And in that context, what indeed do we mean by 'mental'? That is to say, what precisely is this thing that we do not consider to be part of our physical brain? Or are 'mind' and 'consciousness' just illusions?

The two main positions on this issue are **dualism** (that is, the belief that there is a physical dimension and a separate non-physical dimension) and **monism** (that is, the stance that there is only one dimension). While monism in principle could be the view that the single dimension is abstract/ideal/spiritual/subjective, in practice, at least in psychology, monists assume that the one dimension is a physical one and that there is no other dimension. The challenge for dualism is explaining how the physical and the non-physical might *interact*. Thus the question for dualists in psychology is 'How does the brain interact with the mind?' The challenge for monism, which denies anything beyond the physical, is to explain apparently non-physical experiences such as subjectivity, consciousness and personal identity.

A particular monistic view of the mind–body problem is **mind–brain identity theory** which argues that for every mental property there is a corresponding physical (that is, neurophysiological) property. Thus hearing a middle C is just neural activity in the inferior colliculi, a feeling of anger just excitation in the amygdala, and a sense of bliss might just be an overactive hypothalamus. The problem with this point of view is that it is never the *same* set of neurons which are seen to be active every time we hear a sound, feel angry or feel elated. This is a complex area, but once the one-to-one correspondence between specific mental experiences and specific physical events is dissolved, identity theorists have to weaken their position in some way. A further view is to see consciousness as an **emergent property** of a physical *system*, not a separate or parallel feature, or as a feature which can be mapped onto specific physical events, but as something which grows out of, yet remains fundamentally rooted in, the physical dimension; much as music emerges from a CD player – the music is not in the CD, the laser, the speakers or the power source and it does not exist alongside it, it emerges *from* this system.

Many debates around this issue have been and still are further confused by thinking of the mental as something to do with a human *soul*. Many philosophers before the 19th century dealt with the mind–body problem as a puzzle about human spirituality and the idea that something of humans lived on after bodily death. What was this 'something' that lived on? Where did it live during the body's lifetime? How did the soul interact with the body and brain? These questions, whatever their religious significance, muddied the waters for many years for psychologists and most philosophers, who realised that even if we dispense with the idea of the 'soul' we are still left with the spectacular phenomenon of subjective *consciousness* that demands explanation – a phenomenon which is no less spectacular simply because it stops when we die.

The modern form of the mind–brain problem can be usefully summarised in terms of the following two very different questions:

1. What is the relationship between the cognitive, mentalistic capacities of our mind and our brain?
2. What is the relationship between our subjective experience of consciousness and our brain?

The first question relates to the link between our capacity to reason, draw inferences, read and speak, and our brains. That is to say, how are we to explain our symbolic processing capabilities given that they occur within a physical brain? The second relates to the fact that we do not just reason, infer, read and speak but that we are *aware* that we do these things, that we have a distinctive and seemingly personal subjective experience which occurs alongside that symbolic (cognitive) processing. We are not aware of the vast majority of our cognitive processing and such cognitive processing as we are aware of is not the only feature of our consciousness. What is this consciousness thing? Even if we accept that consciousness does not *cause* the processing that we do and is just a side effect, it is still *one hell of a side effect*. Cupboards do not have it, trees do not have it, and although some other animals seem to have it, they do not seem to have it at anything like the same level we do.

The fact that our minds seem to provide a representation of things such as the world, the past and our plans in such a way as to allow us to reason, act and communicate is sometimes referred to as 'A-consciousness', meaning 'access consciousness' (Block, 1995). This kind of consciousness is the inner representation of our relationship with the world. By contrast, 'P-consciousness' ('phenomenal consciousness') is the term used to describe the distinctive, *subjective* awareness which seems to be a characteristic *of* those inner representations but which is not reducible to them. P-consciousness is *what it is like* to have the experience of any state.

The A-consciousness/P-consciousness distinction helps us to recognise that, while many systems, including computers, are capable of inner representations which underlie intentional action (that is, A-consciousness), it seems more difficult to argue that they have, or ever could have, the subjective awareness that they *have* these representations (that is, P-consciousness). In terms of the view that consciousness is an emergent property of some physical systems, we need to ask whether the consciousness that is allegedly emerging is A-consciousness or P-consciousness. While it is possible to see how A-consciousness might emerge from physical systems, it is much less clear how P-consciousness might do so.

Discussions about the first form of the mind–brain problem have been dominated since the 1950s with debates and issues arising from the assumptions and demonstrations of cognitive science with a particular role for computers. The mind–brain problem becomes at this point very clearly a discussion about the relationship between information processing and biological structures. Cognitive psychologists and those mathematicians, philosophers and linguists working alongside them in cognitive science have argued that computers can offer useful metaphors for the brain. For example, the relationship between software (the programmed instructions about operations) and hardware (the chips and processors by which those instructions are performed) is often offered as a useful metaphor for the relationship between thinking and the brain. This metaphor, although flawed, does provide a novel way of thinking about the connections between judgement and neurochemistry.

Computers are able to process large amounts of information very easily. The two main features of computers in this sense are their capacity to store large amounts of data and to perform complex operations on that data. These storage and computational features respectively can be exploited through carefully written programs that specify instructions for the computer to carry out. As discussed in Chapter 10, computers can be programmed very easily to answer simple questions in natural language, recognise complex shapes, perform actions when given human spoken commands and recognise letters and words and much, much more. In short these computer programs are simulations of human thinking and other higher-level information processing tasks. *Thus a fundamental contribution of computers to psychology is to show that we do not need to invoke any special rules of nature to explain how complex symbolic representations and associated mental activity can arise from physical machines.*

Cognitive scientists argue that the achievements of computers show that what we would intuitively describe as 'mental activity' can in principle arise very easily from physical entities. There is no need to agonise over formulating special types of reality for thoughts; they are just types of computations. Although there remain many queries about how uncritically we should accept the computer metaphor of the mind (see Chapter 10), cognitive science does demystify the discussion about minds and brains. In particular, the debate is now cut off from speculation about souls and cosmic idealism.

THINK IT THROUGH

Colin McGinn (1991) offers a very interesting, if somewhat pessimistic, angle on the mind–body problem. He argues that humans, because of our evolution, simply lack the cognitive structures required to understand the way consciousness emerges from the brain. McGinn believes that consciousness is ultimately a physical phenomenon such as gravity, light or energy, but that our brains are wired in such a way that we are 'cognitively closed' to that phenomenon. So, if your tutor complains that you have not grasped the basics of the mind–body problem, you can always reply that McGinn says that our brains are not wired to do so. (No doubt undergraduates around the world wait with baited breath for future books from Professor McGinn in the same vein including *Why our brains can't understand statistics* and *Evolution and the limits to our comprehension of modern French philosophy*.)

Do you agree with McGinn? What would it take to prove McGinn wrong?

Thinking critically about methods in biopsychology

Biopsychologists, and those working in closely related fields such as neuroscience, use a wide range of neuroimaging (brain recording) techniques and neurobiological research methods to explore the structure and functions of the brain. Among the most important of these are electroencephalography (EEG), magnetic resonance imaging (MRI) and positron emission tomography (PET). They each yield different kinds of information about the brain but each has distinctive advantages and limitations which we shall discuss later. We shall begin though with consideration of experimental research in biopsychology, with particular reference to animal studies and then the use of studies of human twins. When reading about the use of these different techniques and methods, you should apply your knowledge of such advantages and limitations when you critically assess any claims being made about the biological dimension of behaviour.

Experiments

The experiments carried out by biopsychologists are characterised by the usual design considerations of randomisation, counterbalancing, control group, double-blind testing and so on. However, these experiments often involve complicated technical procedures which need careful preparation, checking and execution. For example, Rosenzweig *et al.* (1972) in a classic study tested the hypothesis that animals raised in a rich sensory environment would display more brain growth than animals raised in a poor sensory environment. Rats were randomly allocated to either (i) a large *stimulating* cage of six rats (full of play objects which were changed once a day), (ii) a smaller *dull* cage on their own with basic food and water or (iii) a standard *control* cage with two or three rats of a normal size and adequate food and water. Results indicated that on average the cerebral cortex of rats in the enriched environment had become thicker and heavier than that of the rats in the smaller dull cage.

However, and most importantly from our point of view, Rosenzweig *et al.* were criticised on the grounds both of internal and external validity. Interestingly, the way in which subsequent studies by Rosenzweig *et al.* addressed some of these problems is instructive and demonstrates how criticism can improve the quality of research.

In terms of internal validity, it was claimed that Rosenzweig *et al.* could not infer that the environments had caused the changes to the brain because there were other differences in the experience of the rats that had not been controlled for. Specifically, it was argued that when the toys were changed each day the rats from the stimulating environment were handled – once to take them out for the toys to go in and then again when the toys were replaced. It might have been the *handling* which had stimulated the cortical changes, not the cage.

Rosenzweig *et al.* dealt with this criticism in two ways. First, in a subsequent study they made sure that *all* rats, and not just the ones having toys replaced, were handled equally often. The results were the same as before. Second, in order to determine whether handling was having any effect at all, they ran a separate experiment where all rats lived in the same standard cages but one group was handled more often than others. In this study, no differences were found between the two groups. Thus concerns about internal validity were addressed through better controlled experiments.

Rosenzweig *et al.* were themselves concerned that their studies lacked external validity. The rats they used in their study, like most research rats, had been specially bred in captivity for many generations. Further, the range of stimulation provided by different types of laboratory cage is not necessarily similar to the range of environments an animal might experience in the wild. To test this idea, Rosenzweig *et al.* captured a set of deer mice from the wild. These were randomly allocated to the stimulating cage or placed in outdoor conditions. It was found that even after only four weeks the brains of mice allowed to run about outdoors were even bigger than the mice placed in the stimulating cage.

This attempt to assess the external validity of a study of laboratory animals is the exception rather than the rule. Rosenzweig *et al.*'s results provide further evidence that brains are not just produced by genes, but by experience as well.

Case studies of brain damaged individuals

Cognitive neuropsychology involves the analysis of the performance of individuals who have suffered brain trauma (that is, damage) in order to better understand the nature of cognitive processes generally. The idea here is not simply to work out which part of the brain is responsible for which cognitive processes (although that is important and interesting), but also to work out the relationships between different parts of the *mind* on the basis of the different types of deficit that go together. Central to reasoning about what deficits tell us about the structure of the mind is the idea of *dissociations* and *associations*. If a patient can do task A (for example recognising rhymes) but not task B (for example recognising synonyms), this would be a dissociation between rhymes and synonyms. It is tempting to infer in such circumstances that the cognitive processes underlying task A are separate from those underlying task B. But that could be an error. Maybe the patient is just not able to perform the slightly harder task of recognising synonyms. In other words, the evidence from such *single* dissociations does not rule out the possibility that the two tasks reflect different *levels* of processing demands, rather than different *types* of processing. To deal with this, cognitive neuropsychologists sometimes seek out a patient who has a deficit pattern *which is the other way round* to a patient which they have already tested (for example a patient who could recognise synonyms but not rhymes). These 'double dissociations' provide much stronger evidence in favour of the two processes being separate.

When patients display two or more deficits, we have a slightly different reasoning problem to deal with. If a patient could not recognise complex patterns and could also not recognise symmetrical patterns, it might be tempting to infer from this *association* that the two processes are related in some way in cognitive terms. But that inference would be dubious because the two processes might simply be *located in the same part of the brain*, anatomically related but not cognitively related. For that reason conclusions based on dissociations are stronger than conclusions based on associations (Ellis and Young, 1988).

Twin studies

Studies of identical twins (also referred to as 'monozygotic', meaning 'from the one egg') are typically motivated by the nature–nurture question. If identical twins develop in a similar way, then this is normally interpreted as evidence in favour of the nature side of the argument, while if differences are found this is normally taken as evidence for the nurture side. However, since monozygotic twins share not only identical genetic material but also typically almost identical social environments (for example same family, school and being dressed similarly), inferences from such studies are problematic. Studies of identical twins separated and brought up in *different* social environments (for example after adoption) in principle offer more reliable inferences but these are extremely rare and fraught with practical problems. There has been a recent resurgence of interest in the study of twins and heredity generally in developmental psychology, due to greater documentation and access to twins for psychologists, the recognition of the severe limitations of early twin studies and the developing ideas around evolutionary theory and psychology.

Studies of identical twins separated at birth *in principle* provide a chance to compare the relative roles of genetics and the environment. It is found that the IQ of such twins remains very highly correlated (although not as high as identical twins raised together). Similarly, identical twins share effectively 100 per cent of their genetic material, whereas non-identical twins (so-called dizygotic or fraternal twins) only have approximately 50 per cent of their genetic inheritance in common. We find that the IQs of identical twins are much more similar than the IQs of non-identical twins. Finally, IQs of adopted children are found to be much more similar to the IQs of their biological parents than to those of their adoptive parents. On the face of it, a clear pattern emerges here: the closer the genetic link the closer the IQ scores. This would suggest that there is a clear genetic factor in IQ.

The problems with such studies, however, are well documented. First, in cases of separated identical twins it often transpires that the twins were not really 'separated' at all – merely living with relatives in the same neighbourhood. Additionally, it is often the case that the twins are not separated at birth but some time later – often several years later – meaning that they will have shared a similar environment as well as the same genes at an early and critical phase of their development. When thinking about studies comparing identical and fraternal twins reared together, we need to consider the ways in which the parents of identical twins treat them very similarly, whereas parents of fraternal twins do so less excessively. Thus the greater similarity between identical twins may be due to the more similar environment they are exposed to and not simply the common genetic make-up. When considering adoption studies, we need to bear in mind that adoption agencies tend to place children with families similar to those the children came from originally. Taken all in all there would seem to be some evidence that intelligence (or at least IQ) has an inherited component – but the methodological issues remain significant.

We turn now to specialist techniques used in biopsychology. We need to consider some of the technical detail in order to make sure that we are in a position to reason clearly about what these procedures do and do not tell us about cognition and behaviour.

Electroencephalography

Electroencephalogram recordings are based on the output of several electrodes placed in (or in the case of humans, *on*) the head. The readings give a general picture of electrical activity in the brain, usually in response to specific stimuli presented to the subject. The outputs of EEG are often difficult to interpret, however, as there is no way of telling precisely which *part* of the brain is responding. Reading EEG printouts is often compared unfavourably to standing outside a pop concert and trying to tell who is sneezing inside. What EEG records *are* useful for is providing information about the *speed* of response by the nervous system. The analyses of responses can be made clearer with the use of computers to average readings across several presentations of the same stimulus (called average evoked potentials).

Magnetic resonance imaging

MRI provides detailed information on the *structure* of the brain. The subject is exposed to a very strong magnetic field, which affects the molecules in different parts of the brain influencing their energy states. These energy changes are recorded by computer and turned into high-resolution images with artificial colouring digitally added to improve clarity and informativeness of the three-dimensional image generated. The MRI systems produce extremely detailed images differentiating structures less than 5 mm apart in some cases.

MRI involves monitoring the pattern of radio waves as they are passed through a brain which is already in a magnetic field. These radio signals allow a map of the brain structures to be generated. Although it sounds rather daunting for the subject, the technique is safe, with none of the problems of CAT scan X-rays. Most textbooks point out that the technique requires no special preparation by which they mean nothing has to be done in advance to the brain to make it show up on the image. However, many subjects undergoing a MRI scan can be very anxious about the procedure which typically involves sliding into a huge steel magnetic cylinder while lying flat on their back. Thus participants need reassurance and support before the scan. The disadvantage of MRI, apart from the cost, is that participants need to lie very still or the image will be 'blurred' and unusable.

More recently, *functional* magnetic resonance imagining (fMRI) systems have been developed which are sensitive to the *activity* of the brain and not just its structure. The system exploits the fact that brain activity leads to increases in blood flow in excess of what is actually required by tissues. This has a number of consequences including a reduction in deoxyhaemoglobin which crucially has certain magnetic properties. The fMRI computer systems are calibrated so that *lower* magnetic readings are recorded as a stronger signal indicating *higher* neural activity in that area. Most modern systems involve collecting one full brain image 5 mm across every 200 milliseconds. The scan produces data points known as voxels with each voxel indicating the degree of neural activity through colour coding. For example, Hernandez *et al.* (2000) used fMRI in a study of Spanish–English bilinguals and demonstrated that different language skills were represented in the same brain area.

Positron emission tomography

PET scans involve displaying the location of radioactive substances injected into the brain. The limitations of this approach include the fact that rapid activity in the brain cannot be tracked and the images are not of the same high resolution as MRI output. Nevertheless, the degree of specificity provided by PET scans can be good enough to test hypotheses about which part of the brain in general terms is responsible for the processing of different kinds of information. For example, Grady *et al.* (1995) found less neural activity than normal in the hippocampus (and only the hippocampus) of elderly subjects when processing faces they had never seen before. Using the PET method, Schacter *et al.* (1998) compared the brain activity in subjects who had to say whether or not they recognised a piece of information with a control group which simply looked at a cross. While carrying out this memory task, the experimental group showed more activity in several specific brain areas compared to the control group. Indeed, there was some evidence in those trials that the brain activity was different when the subject was *correct* compared to when the subject was wrong. Schacter *et al.* argue that this difference arises because the brain carries out post-retrieval monitoring.

Increasingly the data from different techniques are being combined to produce even more revealing images of brain activity. MRI scans can be combined with either PET or fMRI scans in order to integrate the structural detail provided by the former with the functional details offered by the latter.

Technical and conceptual issues in interpreting neuroimaging

There are both technical and conceptual aspects to be considered in evaluating neuroimaging studies. These are closely related to each other in several ways.

For PET scans, which depend upon tracing the location of radioactive material, we need to be sure that sufficient radioactive material was injected in the first place for it to appear during a scan. This is especially important if we are looking at small areas of the brain or at low activity processes. If we predict activity in brain area X, but not brain area Y, we need to be sure that if we do see this pattern on the PET scan it is because of different neural activity levels and not because there was insufficient radioactive material injected to show up at brain area Y.

One of the main issues for fMRI is ensuring that the presentation of a stimulus is matched to the recording of the response. Since the stimulus may be presented for no more than 250 milliseconds (or less), it is crucial that the record of activity correctly records when the stimulus was presented. Thus *synchronising* the electronic record of the presentation of stimuli with the computed brain images of the response is essential as very small errors can lead to misleading results. One of the main technical problems of fMRI scans is subject head movement. It is no good having £3,000,000 worth of equipment sampling a whole brain at four times a second if the subject keeps fidgeting. Subjects are normally restrained in order to make sure that the final images are stable and useable. The general technical issue for PET, MRI and fMRI scans is the sheer computational load involved. High-powered computers are required to collect, store and present the data gathered from successive scans. Special software is available to ensure that successive images are matched together correctly to produce accurate displays over time without compromising the structural detail. Nevertheless, the faster that images are captured the greater the amount of noise which threatens to overwhelm the signal (Menon and Kim, 1999).

Gabrielli (1998) points out the need for caution when interpreting results from PET and fMRI methods. First of all we have to remember that the images generated by PET scans or fMRI are not images of neural activity per se, but of nearby (local) blood flow or metabolic changes which are *indicative* of neural activity. With fMRI techniques, some aspects of the response to the magnetic field depend upon the blood-oxygen levels. According to Gabrielli, it is often not clear precisely *what* the activity around nerve cells is actually indicative of. Neuroimaging studies of scans from subjects' brains often compare the activity levels in response to two or more tasks. Some tasks are not only different in kind but also different in difficulty or duration. Thus the observed differences in scan *might* be due to the different processing being carried out, but it might be due to different levels of *effort* required or slightly longer *processing* times.

We can see here that Gabrielli is questioning the internal validity of some neuroimaging studies. A further difficulty is that both fMRI and PET techniques need to allow the activation levels to 'clear' before the next trial can be presented. This can lead to complications as subjects anticipate future trials or keep on thinking about previous trials. Gabrielli also points out that residual activity can be found in parts of the brain that are severely damaged. These traces may be of processes not directly involved in those being studied but merely correlated with it. It might be the case that in undamaged brains much of the activity we observe has nothing to do with the critical processes that *produce* the behaviour the subject is engaging in. Thus neuroimaging data from PET and fMRI scans might be likened to someone observing cars and noting that the little light on the front to the left is what *makes* cars turn left – rather than merely being correlated with the manoeuvre. The main notion we can take from all of this is that fMRI and other scans can only describe brain activity, not brain function. To describe brain function requires further interpretation of the stimuli presented to the subject and of the patterns of responses to those stimuli over several trials. A further problem with functional neuroimaging studies is that different studies identify different 'hotspots' or maxima of neural activity for the same task. Farah and Aguirre (1999) found that 17 studies reviewed indicated no fewer than 84 different candidates for the precise part of the brain involved in recognising objects.

It is worth remembering the advice of Gabrielli next time you look at those impressive colour plates in your psychology textbook. Nevertheless, overall there is no denying the advances that have been made possible using neuroimaging techniques (see Posner and Raichle, 1995, and Menon and Kim, 1999 for reviews).

Thinking critically about theories in biopsychology

Theories in biopsychology are generally more consistent with traditional models of theory building and experimental testing in the traditional positivist model than most other areas of psychology. We should be able to make judgements about theories in biopsychology without too much trouble, but we shall see. Remember we need to apply to biopsychology the key criteria for theories which we discussed in Chapter 3.

1. Does the theory display *comprehensiveness?*
2. Does the theory display *parsimony?*
3. Does the theory display *clarity of constructs?*
4. Does the theory display *internal consistency?*
5. Does the theory display *testability?*
6. Does the theory have *empirical support?*
7. Does the theory have *heuristic value?*

As always, although it is difficult to generalise, we shall consider the extent to which theorising in this area broadly meets the criteria implied by these questions.

In terms of comprehensiveness, biopsychology theories tend to do well. The models put forward do tend to cover all the evidence associated with the phenomenon in question. In areas such as the biopsychology of sleep and dreams, the evidence seems so diverse that theories struggle to deal with all of it. In other areas, such as the mechanisms of colour vision, the evidence is much more coherent and theories can and do cover it all. In relation to parsimony, the conciseness of biopsychological theories is also generally good but the complexity of the subject matter and the use of extensive technical terms make theories look overelaborate. Biopsychological theoretical constructs vary greatly in terms of clarity partly because many different levels of explanation are involved. The construct of 'punctuated equilibrium', for example, refers to the process of stop-start evolution covering millions of organisms over millions of years, while 'neuron' refers to a specific physical structure in the nervous system sometimes as small as a thousandth of a millimetre in size.

Often in biopsychology constructs are broken down into subdivisions and sub-subdivisions and so on, as in the case of the nervous system, which is broken down into the central nervous system (brain and brain stem) and the peripheral nervous system (sympathetic and parasympathetic systems). Sometimes the subdivisions are overelaborate for the questions we are trying to address. Biopsychological theories tend to be internally consistent, since there is limited speculation beyond the evidence to hand. Testability and empirical support tend to be good but the difficulty is that the volume of research is high and theoretical models find it hard to keep up with empirical findings. We often need to ask whether or not a theory has evolved to keep up with new discoveries. The heuristic value of biopsychological theories varies from theory to theory. Some evolutionary theories are presented in striking and accessible formats which trigger controversy and debate, while theories of neurological functions tend to be very technically precise and dependent on specific forms of instrumentation (for example fMRI) with little scope for application outside a rather circumscribed domain.

SUMMARY

In this chapter we have considered the ways in which biological psychologists think about the mind and behaviour, and reflected on how we can think critically about the epistemology and methodology of biopsychology. The fact that we have brains which have evolved and adapted over millions of years provides a context for our analyses of many areas of psychology. The deterministic, realist and essentialist assumptions of biopsychology align it with the natural sciences more closely than any other area of psychology. Biopsychologists, cognitive psychologists and philosophers have argued over the most meaningful ways to conceive of the relationship between mind and brain for many years. However, the approach of cognitive science offers us a workable model of the mind that will help us to make sense of biopsychological investigations of the brain. At the heart of our analyses of biopsychology is the issue of reductionism, the assumption that higher-level processes of behaviour and ability can be explained by reference to lower, more fundamental processes and structures. In biopsychology, reductionism is most dramatically illustrated by fMRI scans which offer the promise of allowing us to map cognitive and behavioural processes to activity in specific areas of the brain. And yet such reductionism limits our understanding of how thoughts and activities link into wider systems of functioning and interaction.

> ## KEY TERMS
>
> Dualism ■ Emergent property ■ Evolution
> Mind–body problem ■ Mind–brain identity theory
> Monism ■ Naïve dualism ■ Natural selection ■ Plasticity

FURTHER READING

An accessible account of language in general and of Pinker's theory in particular that language is essentially a type of instinct which has evolved like any other is Pinker, S (1994) *The Language Instinct: The New Science of Language and the Mind* (London: Penguin). Pinker reviews research on animals taught to sign, the evolution of language and the relationship between language and the mind.

Barkow, J H, Cosmides, L and Tooby, J (eds) (1992) *The Adapted Mind: Evolutionary Psychology and the Generation of Culture* (Oxford: Oxford University Press) is a useful collection of key articles on the role of evolutionary constructs in the explanation of human behaviour.

A good example of the heuristic value of evolutionary theory is Buss, D M (1994) *The Evolution of Desire: Strategies of Human Mating* (New York: Basic Books). Buss applies evolutionary psychology principles to the areas of interpersonal attraction and sexual behaviour, incorporating empirical studies of contemporary attitudes and preferences.

USEFUL WEBSITES

Origin of the Species
http://infidels.org/library/historical/charles_darwin/origin_of_species/
The full text of Darwin's classic *On The Origin of the Species* including a glossary 'which has been given because several readers have complained to me that some of the terms used were unintelligible to them'. Bless him.

Psyche
http://psyche.cs.monash.edu.au/
The pages of the excellent Monash University journal *Psyche*, which publishes articles on issues regarding consciousness and its analysis. The articles are peer reviewed and authoritative. A wide range of topics is covered from animal consciousness to vision and consciousness.

Consciousness Studies Web Page
http://www.consciousness.arizona.edu/
The University of Arizona pages on consciousness studies encourage the promotion of 'open, scientifically rigorous and sustained discussions of all phenomena related to

the mind'. The pages cover conferences, publications, lists of relevant web pages and online courses on contemporary consciousness studies. While the primary focus is on neuroscientific approaches, a balance is sought between the 'hard' approaches of artificial intelligence and the 'soft' approach of humanism and philosophy (their terms, not mine).

The Wellcome Department of Cognitive Neurology

http://www.fil.ion.ucl.ac.uk/

Images, interactive experiments and detailed study notes on brain structure and function with particular reference to neuroimaging techniques, from University College, London. Try the 'neuroscience resources' link for the most comprehensive cognitive neurology list on the web.

Brain and Behavioral Sciences

http://www.cogsci.soton.ac.uk/bbs-bin/bbskeywords

Searchable database of articles from the leading international journal of neuroscience and related fields.

The Sanger Centre

http://www.sanger.ac.uk

Comprehensive website giving full coverage of the Human Genome Project. Not only can you check to see the running total of documented DNA sequences, you can download and search through them.

Thinking about Personality and Individual Differences

12

CHAPTER OVERVIEW

In the study of personality and individual differences the emphasis is on diversity and distinctiveness, and how different people respond in different ways to the same situation. When studying personality we need to be clear about what we mean by 'unique' and 'different'. We also need to be careful about how we measure personality. How, for example, do we make sure that our measurements are consistent and meaningful? At the extreme end of the personality scale are those suffering from mental illness. What should we be thinking about when considering definitions of mental illness and research reports for new treatments? We need to think carefully about what we take for granted in our thinking about personality and individual differences. Do we have the right model of the 'individual' or 'self'? In this chapter we will be reviewing both traditional and contemporary theories of personality and intelligence and considering how best to think about the claims they make. We shall consider in particular detail the use of the main criteria for assessing theories, as the issues that arise in the study of personality are typical of most areas of psychology. We will conclude with a brief review of some recent ideas from radical constructionist psychologists which question whether the assumptions we make in everyday life and in psychological theorising about personality and individual differences are necessary ones.

LEARNING OBJECTIVES

By the end of this chapter you should be able to:

- Think critically about everyday ideas regarding 'uniqueness', 'personality' and 'individual differences'

- Define and illustrate the features of idiographic, hermeneutic and psychometric approaches to personality and individual differences, and how they all differ from nomothetic psychology

> **LEARNING OBJECTIVES (cont'd)**
>
> ■ Assess both classical and modern models of personality in relation to the main criteria for assessing psychological theories
> ■ Think critically about attempts to define 'mental illness'
> ■ Critically assess the implications of research reports on new therapeutic interventions
> ■ Specify and contrast the assumptions of mainstream psychology and constructionism regarding the nature of 'self'

Thinking critically about some basics of personality and individual differences

Why are some people outgoing and confident while others are withdrawn and shy? Why is it that some people can suffer a seemingly never-ending stream of misfortune yet carry on regardless, while others crack at the first sign of pressure or hardship? Why is there such an apparent range of performance on intelligence tests and other supposed indicators of intellectual functioning? What makes one person become schizophrenic but not another? Why do some war veterans suffer post-traumatic stress disorder but not others? Are we each unique in our view of the world and our responses to it?

These questions and many more of a similar nature are what interest psychologists who work in the broad area of what we will refer to as personality and individual differences (PID). In popular media discussions and in literature there is and always has been a fascination about what makes one person different from another. Subjectively, too, we often feel as though we are in some important if inexpressible way different from everyone else. Indeed much of modern life is organised around assumptions that people are different from one another in terms of motivation, attitude, ability and emotional response. 'Individuality' is one of the great taken-for-granted assumptions of the 20th century. It is embodied in education systems that exploit such assumptions through differentiation of provision and reward. It is embodied in liberal philosophies of freedom and choice. The fashion and lifestyle industries promote particular varieties of individualism as a commodity. We are all given individual names, National Insurance numbers and email addresses. We do not like to be seen to be conforming (and yet we know we do). Our individuality is sometimes part of our sense of *separateness* from other people. We are not other people and they are not us. We are inside our head, and they are somewhere 'out there'. We are individuals and not part of some wider undifferentiated sea of humanity and being. *Intuitively* we feel that there is something irreducible about our individuality, that it cannot be explained away by reference to some other more basic level of analysis. Of course these intuitions might be completely wrong, but we do have them.

Most people, who do not know and do not care about what psychologists do, often assume that the *only* things psychologists do is look at the distinctive, unique aspects of each individual – the *specific* ways *this* individual came to be the way they are, the *particular* motivations and preoccupations which explain why this individual does what they do and so on. This image is perhaps attributable to the high profile of psychoanalysis in Western culture which seeks to dig deep into the hidden past of an individual. In fact, of course, nothing could be further from the truth. Psychologists, whether they are developmental, social, cognitive or biological, typically begin with the assumption that everyone is *similar* and that individual variation is an anomaly. To some extent this is part of the positivist legacy. Physicists do not waste their time trying to explain why *this* brick falls in the distinctive way that it does, but rather they concern themselves with the general properties of gravity. Biologists are not particularly interested in why or how *this* plant turns sunlight into nutrients, but rather in the general process of photosynthesis. Similarly, psychologists typically are less concerned about how Mr Smith hears his car radio in noisy traffic and are more concerned about the process of selective attention in general. You will remember from Chapter 3 that psychology, especially social and cognitive psychology, is characterised by a search for general, that is nomothetic, laws of behaviour. Nomothetic psychologists are much more interested in the ways in which situations affect behaviour rather than in the ways in which individuals affect situations or how characteristics of individuals affect behaviour. Nevertheless, many people reading about traditional experimental psychology remain unconvinced by this **situationism**, declaring simply 'but everyone's different, aren't they?' Some even go as far as to present these differences as evidence of the impossibility of psychology. In other words, claiming that the uniqueness of each individual simply precludes any attempt at systematic analysis of the kind that emphasises situations as causes.

Some psychologists from the nomothetic approach argue that although there are differences between individuals they are small differences, and that the similarities between people are much more interesting and revealing. It is also argued that those differences are typically not theoretically or conceptually significant. The analogy of the motor car might be useful here. We might acknowledge, due not only to the original design, materials and construction but also wear and tear, driving styles, irregularity of maintenance and weather conditions, that every car engine is different from every other car engine. And yet the kinds of variation which these factors create in an engine are largely irrelevant to understanding how engines work and what their *function* is. Whether these variations were present from the start (such as design and construction) or come about later (such as 'wear and tear'), what the engines have in common (internal combustion) seems to be more meaningful than what they do not have in common (for example materials, scratches, size). According to nomothetic psychologists, we need to know the general 'core' principles of the dynamics of human motivation, attitudes and thinking rather than how these principles manifest themselves in different ways in different individuals. Nomothetic psychologists further argue that to some extent the significance of individualised differences depends on psychologists' level of understanding of a phenomenon at the outset. If we do *not* know the principles of the internal combustion engine and its relationship to traction, it is pointless in a very fundamental way to keep banging on about scratches on the pistons. At the moment psychology is still looking at the basics of the human 'engine'.

THINK IT THROUGH

We have mentioned before in this book how analogies can be helpful but also misleading. The engine analogy conveys the point about similarities reasonably well I think, but analogies are *not evidence*, they are *ways of thinking which may or may not be useful*. You might want to assess this analogy in relation to the questions identified in Chapter 2. We can certainly think here of a **counter-analogy**, that is, an analogy that illustrates the opposite of what the first analogy demonstrates. Can you think of a counter-analogy here? That is to say, an analogy of a system, object, procedure or whatever where the shared features are *less* significant than the differences? Think about this before reading on.

One possible counter-analogy would be books. What books have in common — paper, covers, illustrations, indexes, chapter headings and so on — is surely less significant than what each book is *about*, or the *story* it tells. In this case the differences between the items are the more interesting. Of course it depends on our point of view. To a mechanic whose job it is to fix engines it is no good just knowing about engines in general, she needs to look at why *this* engine has gone wrong. If you are a publisher of trash romantic fiction, the general presentation and adherence to genre conventions is more important for achieving higher sales than the specifics of this story of boy meets girl.

We are already familiar with the idea of nomothetic approaches to psychology which emphasise the similarities between individuals and which attempt via experiments to establish general laws about behaviour (see Chapter 7). By contrast, **idiographic** approaches to psychology try to understand single individuals in depth, focusing on what is distinctive, even unique, about them. This does not mean that attempts at predicting behaviour or establishing regularities in behaviour are abandoned but rather that such predictions and regularities will be derived from and applied to that specific individual. The idiographic approach was originally associated with Gordon Allport (1961) who coined the term as part of his humanistic trait theory of personality. The idiographic approach to personality is associated with qualitative methods of assessment such as interviews, analysis of personal documents, projective tests and Q-sorts. In principle quantitative idiographic analyses are possible but in practice most are qualitative. This is largely because many classical theories of personality are derived from their close links to clinical practice.

In light of the above, we need to address some basic general points in order to keep our thinking clear when we come to look at specific theories and studies. There are four basic principles, in my view, which are worth bearing in mind when thinking about the area of PID in general.

1. *Individual differences do not necessarily imply uniqueness.* To argue, as personality psychologists do, that we need to study individual differences does not amount to a claim that each individual is *unique*. There might be wide

variability between individuals but we might be similar to many others of the same kind rather than unique, more like raindrops than snowflakes.

2. *Even if each individual is unique, it does not preclude interpretability.* Sometimes the idea of human uniqueness is taken as an insurmountable barrier to comprehensibility. This is an unnecessary inference. Even if each individual has a unique configuration of characteristics, the nature of those characteristics and the types of possible configuration are in principle something which psychologists could investigate and say meaningful things about. A good example of this would be Kelly's personal construct theory or some versions of humanistic personality theory. In both cases the possibility of uniqueness is taken seriously – but that uniqueness is not seen as being uninterpretable. To some extent the idea that uniqueness rules out interpretability is based on the notion that the only kind of understanding possible in psychology is a scientific understanding and that the only kind of interpretability is in terms of pigeon-holing and *simplifying* individuals. This is unfortunate since, as we shall see, many different forms of understanding are advanced in the study of personality in addition to a strictly scientific one, including many theories which do not seek to simplify at all. However, it has to be said that some quantitative personality psychologists argue that their techniques can deal with the idea of uniqueness just as well. The precise idea here is that an individual could have a unique combination of 'strengths' or 'levels' of factors giving a unique profile – even if all individuals can be interpreted in relation to the same predefined set of factors. An analogy here might be the uniqueness of an individual's National Insurance number which can still be understood in terms of the structure (or grammar) of national insurance numbers (in the UK, two letters followed by three pairs of digits and ending with a letter).

3. *Uniqueness is ultimately indeterminable.* How can we ever *know* that someone is 'unique' in the literal sense? We would have to know the personality of every individual in the world (and possibly every individual ever born) to say in a strict sense that such-and-such a person is 'unique'. Those who would argue in favour of entertaining some notion of uniqueness would not want to go quite this far, however. The claim being made is that each individual is qualitatively different from every other individual to such an extent and in such a way that there is no information about *other* people which we could *meaningfully* bring to bear on our understanding of that individual before actually finding out about that individual directly. The fact that people might be different to each other does not rule out the possibility that they can be studied *systematically*.

4. *Personality and experimental psychology are not mutually exclusive.* Although most introductory textbooks present the study of personality and the study of (nomothetic) experimental psychology as separate enterprises, the truth is that increasingly the two areas are coming together in interesting ways. There has always been fierce debate between those who emphasise the role of situations in producing behaviour and those who emphasise personality. Many

psychologists emphasise an *interactionist* position such that both are seen to be relevant to predicting and understanding behaviour. And of course our personality influences which situations we expose ourselves to.

This chapter reviews the ideas and methods of the study of individual differences in behaviour, thinking and emotions. This area incorporates the study of personality, psychopathology (mental illness) and intelligence. We will consider the kinds of claims that are made by theorists in this area as they relate to the issues of understanding individuality, but also in terms of how they relate to the possibility of integration with nomothetic, situationist psychology.

The scope of PID in psychology

The study of personality and individual differences in psychology covers a wide range of aspects of behaviour and experience. In a sense PID can cover any area of psychology, since we could in principle consider any behaviour, experience or competence in terms of 'How do people *differ* in terms of this phenomenon?' or in terms of theory 'To what extent does this theory apply to different people in different ways?' Traditionally, however, the area of PID can be broken down into classical personality theories, modern personality theories and intelligence and ability.

Classical personality theory includes psychodynamic, humanist and behaviourist accounts of personality. These theories tend to be global theories that seek to account for all aspects of an individual's personality. Psychodynamic and humanist theories are generally best regarded as attempts to interpret the nature of human personality in a qualitative fashion and as such are often therefore considered to be hermeneutic in nature. This indicates that they are attempting to capture the *meaningfulness* of human personality rather than measure and make predictions about it. Hermeneutic analyses try to interpret behaviour by reference to the context in which it occurs and the structure that it displays. By contrast, behaviourists attempt to apply the approach of logical positivism to the study of human personality in order to establish a scientific model based on learning theory principles of conditioning and reinforcement. Behaviourist analyses are thus interested in cause and effect and objective measurements of behaviour rather than what that behaviour means.

Modern personality theories tend to address much narrower aspects of personality using sophisticated quantitative psychometric methods. Topics covered in these theories include individual variations in self-esteem, sense of control over the world, optimism and self-consciousness. Some modern theories do, however, seek to be global theories. For example, Eysenck's personality theory argues that extraversion–introversion, neuroticism–stability and psychoticism–normality are the three fundamental axes of personality and all other personality constructs (and measures) can be subsumed under this model. One personality theory, which has emerged in the last 15 years, is what is modestly known as the Big Five personality theory of Costa and McCrae (1988). Their model brings together many findings that indicate that five (and only five) dimensions can account for almost all differences in adult personality. The five dimensions in the Big Five are neuroticism, extraversion, openness, agreeableness and conscientiousness. 'Neuroticism' here involves anxiety and impulsiveness while 'openness' refers to the tendency to be open to new ideas and values and to unexpected ways of looking at things. 'Agreeableness' refers to being trusting, helpful and compliant. It can be seen that there is significant overlap between the Big Five and the Eysenck model in terms of the first three main factors. Eysenck's constructs are measured using the Eysenck Personality Questionnaire while the Big Five is measured using the NEO-FFI ('NEO' from the first three factors, 'FFI' from 'Five Factor Inventory').

Subscales are dimensions along which people vary

When coming across the idea of factors and the names of subscales for the first time, it is easy to forget that these are *dimensions*. That is, when Costa and McCrae say that neuroticism, extraversion, openness, agreeableness and conscientiousness are important factors in personality, they do *not* mean that people in general are neurotic, extravert, open, agreeable and conscientious. What they mean is that these are the key dimensions along which people *vary*. That is to say, some people will score highly on the scale, others will be much lower and yet others will score somewhere in-between, indicating a broad spectrum of *degrees* of 'openness' in the population. It is this variation which psychometricians are interested in.

The study of individual differences in mental abilities has focused largely on variation in intelligence. Despite continuing disputes about the definition of intelligence, how it should be measured and, for that matter, whether it really exists or not, much research has sought to describe the structure of intelligence and to assess individual and group performance on tests which purport to measure those structures. A central idea here is that of a normal curve indicating the normal distribution of 'intelligence' in the normal population. The mean is artificially defined as 100 and other scores above and below this point are calculated on the basis of that reference point.

There has always been argument about the precise definition of intelligence and how it should be measured. Much of the discussion has centred on how many basic dimensions are involved. Some theorists such Spearman in the 1920s argued that there was just one important underlying general dimension to intelligence. Other theorists have argued for two, seven or even 120 'basic' factors. Such discussions are caught up in the different methods used to measure intelligence and different ideas about what a basic factor is. The question 'How many basic intelligence factors are there?' is a bit like asking 'How many basic places are there in the United Kingdom?' We might say four if we mean Scotland, England, Northern Ireland and Wales, or we might say '20' if we mean major cities, or we might say 12 if we mean major counties and so on. The original question is just too ill-formed to permit a sensible answer but it *looks like* a sensible question because it has the same overall grammatical structure of sensible questions (such as 'How many buttons are on this table?' or 'How many corners has a square?').

Theory in PID

The nature of theory in PID is different depending on which of the three areas we are considering. In the classical personality models, theories are often closely and explicitly allied to clinical practices and value-based assumptions about human nature. For that reason, psychodynamic, humanist and behaviourist accounts draw upon very different world views and, crucially, very different ideas about what psychology is and should be to those of modern theorists. In that context it should come as no surprise that each theory has different ideas about *how* personality should be studied, that is, they disagree about *methodology*. The reason why they have different views of methodology is because they have different views about the nature of knowledge that is possible or desirable in psychology, that is to say, they disagree about *epistemology*. Indeed since they disagree also in terms of what is true in the world, they disagree on *ontology*. It follows from this that it is difficult to compare classical theories except at the most abstract level, noting for example that psychoanalysis emphasises determinism while humanistic theory emphasises free will. Nevertheless, it is important to analyse the structure, function and adequacy of theorising in classical personality models, as they remain, in broad terms, influential across the discipline.

Modern personality theories tend to be more similar in terms of ontology, epistemology and methodology. They all broadly accept the assumptions of positivism and take for granted the 'technology' of paper-and-pencil questionnaires. In some respects personality questionnaires are a paradigm within psychology (see discussion of Kuhn in Chapter 2). Disputes within contemporary psychometrics tend to be limited to the appropriateness of particular forms of factor analysis. The idea of the legitimacy of quantification or correlation is not itself seriously questioned. Thus in that context it is possible to make more specific comparisons of theory.

Mischel and Shoda (1998) have argued that there are essentially two different types of theory in contemporary personality research. On the one hand is the traditional dispositional model which emphasises that theories of personality should aim to describe the content and structure of stable underlying traits. These stable traits in turn explain the stability of behaviour across different situations. On the other hand there is the more contemporary processing dynamics view which argues that personality is made up of various cognitive and emotional systems which process information in consistent ways and produce stability in behaviour. Examples of this processing would include encoding biases, expectancy biases, affective tendencies, distinctive values and personal competencies and plans. Thus the dispositional model argues that observed behavioural consistency is essentially a *reproduction* of the underlying personality structure, while the processing dynamics view argues that observed behavioural consistency is essentially a *consequence* of regularity in the way individuals deal with information and challenges in different social situations. Mischel and Shoda further argue that these two approaches are not in fact necessarily contradictory and can be reconciled. In particular, they argue that rather than focusing exclusively on traits, personality theorists should try to explain patterns of 'if... then...' conditionals. For example, where the traditional dispositional account would say 'Tom is shy', processing models would say 'If Tom is with strangers, Tom is shy'. Since the dispositional model draws largely on psychometrics and the processing model draws largely on experimental social psychology, this reconciliation opens up a range of interesting reformulations of existing personality theories and integration of research methods.

This shift away from structural accounts and towards process accounts of individual differences is to be found in the study of intelligence also. Most contemporary theorising of intelligence and intellectual aptitude generally has emphasised differences in computational capacities or strategies between individuals. Individuals who score highly on traditional IQ tests appear to perform simple processing tasks such as recognising numbers and letters quicker than those who score lower. However, there is some evidence that more intelligent individuals *spend longer* on encoding information in preparation for future processing (Sternberg, 1981; Sternberg and Kaufman, 1998).

If we are looking for ways of keeping our thinking fresh in the area of intelligence, we could do worse than consider the ideas of Howard Gardner. Gardner (1983) has suggested that too much of our thinking about intelligence is based on a very narrow range of assumptions about what 'intelligence' is, often reflecting traditional educational values which may or may not be relevant to all people and all cultures in the same way. Gardner argues that there are seven distinct forms of intelligence and that theorists need to acknowledge these alternative forms in their models. Gardner's seven forms are linguistic (for example verbal ability), logical-mathematical (for example solving mathematics problems), spatial (for example thinking about size, volume and space), musical (for example musical composition), bodily-kinaesthetic (for example in dance or sport), interpersonal (that is, understanding others) and intrapersonal (that is, understanding oneself).

It is well worth thinking carefully, and critically, about Gardner's ideas. Clearly, his definition of intelligence is very wide and challenges our understanding of exactly what we mean by 'intelligence'. For example, some people might argue that while we can respect the artistry, style and skill of a dance, it is nonetheless not 'intelligence' (but we should ask ourselves 'What is the foundation of a definition of intelligence that rules dance out?'). It is also not clear if each of these different kinds are wholly independent of each other. Possibly bodily-kinaesthetic is a special form of spatial intelligence? Or vice versa? And is 'intrapersonal intelligence' a wholly separate form of intelligence or just the application of the other six forms to the self? In particular there is a long tradition in social and developmental psychology which argues that understanding the self is essentially the skills for understanding others applied reflexively. More radically, it is possible to argue that linguistic intelligence underlies all forms of intelligence, since all the 'objects' relevant to the other forms of intelligence are constructed and experienced only through language (see Chapter 8). Nevertheless, not only does Gardener offer us a broader notion of intelligence, he suggests novel methods for identifying and assessing it. For example, he suggests that evidence from studies from brain-damaged patients might provide evidence for the independence of a particular form of intelligence inasmuch as it could be found that, say, musical intelligence might be severely damaged while some other type of intelligence, say intrapersonal, might be intact (see dissociation in Chapter 11). This test could be argued to be too conservative, however. That is to say, if we did *not* find such *modularity* of function among the intelligences, it does not necessarily follow that they are not independent. The neurological structure or substructure could conceivably support more than one intelligence. A key issue here is that the *observed* deficit would need to correspond fairly closely to the *theoretical construct* of 'musical intelligence' or whatever before we could take this kind of neurological evidence as being strongly in favour of the theory. It is all too easy to propose that two functions are separate and then find a function missing that is only vaguely similar to what was previously theorised, and then declare that *that* was what we meant all along.

An intelligence too far?

Recently Gardner (1998) has gone one step further in terms of broadening the scope of multiple intelligences. He has suggested that theorising about intelligence should also address the hitherto neglected area of 'naturalist intelligence'. Broadly, this intelligence relates to the ability to recognise, encode, retrieve and manipulate information about patterns in nature. Botanists, farmers, ornithologists and biologists might possess this intelligence more than most but there are no studies yet examining naturalist intelligence. Finally, for those who feel that there are never enough intelligences, Gardner has proposed (more tentatively) the idea of 'spiritual intelligence' (involving an awareness and ability to reason about 'cosmic' issues) and 'existential intelligence' (involving an ability to comprehend, imagine and reason about ultimate issues of life, death, being and nothingness). With Gardner's proliferating intelligences, we come a long way from 'What is the next number in the sequence 2, 4, 6...?' For some theorists 'spiritual' and 'existential' intelligence will no doubt be 'an intelligence too far'.

Gardner's work illustrates an issue we have come across several times already (for example Chapters 10 and 11). Whenever we read about a new theory, a new computer simulation, a new brain location or gene for behaviour or ability X, we need to look very, very carefully indeed at what definition of X is actually being used by the researchers. Is it the same definition as used in everyday language? Is it the same definition used previously by researchers in that area? Is it a narrow or broad definition of X? Even if we do not agree with all of Gardner's new intelligences, the emphasis on diversity in his work makes clear that when we read of anyone claiming triumphantly that they have discovered the gene for 'intelligence', we should recognise that there is still an awful lot of thinking to do.

Sternberg has offered a more broadly based idea for rethinking intelligence. He suggests that we need a notion of *successful* intelligence that involves adapting, shaping and selecting environments which match the intelligences the individual has. Sternberg's model strongly emphasises the idea that abilities per se are not what predict achievement but the way in which an individual *applies* those abilities in specific situations, having reflected upon what abilities they do and do not possess:

Successful intelligence involves an individual's discerning his or her pattern of strengths and weaknesses, and then figuring out ways to capitalize upon the strengths and weaknesses and at the same time to compensate for or correct the weaknesses. People attain success, in part, in idiosyncratic ways that involve their finding how best to exploit their own patterns of strengths and weaknesses. Sternberg and Kaufman (1998: 494)

Which just about brings us back full circle to uniqueness and individuality.

Thinking critically about theories of personality

Theories in personality come in many shapes and sizes and include both hermeneutic and nomothetic approaches. This diversity of approaches in PID makes it a particularly useful area to think a little more deeply about how to apply the criteria identified in Chapter 3 for assessing theories in psychology generally.

Comprehensiveness

Classical personality theories such as those of Freud, Skinner, Rogers or Kelly appear to have very broad application and therefore score highly on comprehensiveness. We have to remember, however, that these traditional personality theories set themselves the ambitious project of accounting for *all* aspects of adult psychological functioning. To be satisfactory on this criterion, a theory must cover all the aspects of the phenomenon it set out to explain and do so in a fairly thorough manner. Classical personality theories typically have very broad ideas about adult personality and what its functioning involves. However, the actual theories themselves do not always cover in detail the very general definitions of personality that are initially offered. For example, it could be argued that psychoanalysis purports to be a theory about adult personality generally but tends to offer explanations only for dysfunctional (that is, abnormal and debilitating) behaviour. Similarly, it could be argued that Kelly's personal construct theory sets out to deal with our general understandings of the world but only explains how we categorise our relationships. These are indeed matters for debate. It is not a straightforward matter to assess whether a theory really does cover all the things it says should be covered. Those who support a theory will argue that the theory does offer an account of all the significant aspects of a phenomenon, while the detractors will point out that some significant aspects are ignored.

A general issue here is the extent to which *the theories redefine what is to be explained*. In the area of personality, as with many areas of psychology, there is sometimes no consensus about what precisely the phenomenon to be explained is. And since the topic under analysis here is the entire adult personality system, there seems little prospect of a consensus emerging any time soon. What tends to happen is that each theorist offers their *own* definition of personality. Some theories such as Kelly's seem to be unable to meet their own definitions of what needs to be explained by a good theory of personality. Other theories, most notably Skinnerian behaviourism, seem more than able to account for the phenomenon of personality – so long as we are prepared to accept the narrow definition that patterns of learned habits and learned habits alone constitute 'personality'. Thus the issue of whether or not a personality theory is comprehensive depends upon what kind of definition of 'personality' the theorist offers at the outset. The more narrow the definition of personality, the more likely the theory is to be 'comprehensive', whereas the more inclusive and broad the definition, the more the theory is likely to fail to account for all the phenomena implied by that definition. Thus comprehensiveness is very much in the eye of the beholder. To the theorist who has offered a narrow definition, the theory is very comprehensive, to everyone else who has a wider definition, the theory is not comprehensive at all. For example, humanistic psychologists are often criticised for dealing only with the personalities of those who face no oppression, poverty or prejudice, preferring to concentrate on 'existential boredom'. Humanists say their analyses apply to everyone while their critics say they apply only to the affluent middle classes with comfortable lives.

In considering contemporary personality theories, the issues are similar but present themselves to us slightly differently. The Big Five theory, for example, is comprehensive in that it seeks to cover all aspects of the healthy and dysfunctional personality. Its claim to be comprehensive, however, depends upon an inductive argument, specifically, one that says 'All the personality traits we have looked at fit onto one of the five dimensions. We have not found any that do not'. Inductive arguments can never be decisive, they can only be suggestive. The cogency of this argument depends on how vigorously we feel researchers have looked to find significant personality characteristics that do not fit into the model.

Parsimony

The principle of parsimony states that *everything else being equal* the simpler theory is to be preferred. In this way unnecessary theoretical constructs and relational propositions are removed or at least kept to a minimum. This is a fine principle that will keep us on the right track whether we are constructing or dismantling theories. However, the area of personality research shows us that everything else is very rarely equal. We do not have in the red corner Freud's psychoanalysis and in the blue corner a version of psychoanalysis that is the same in every respect *except for the fact that it is based on fewer constructs and propositions*. Oh no. In the blue corner we have the very simple but also *completely-different-in-almost-every-conceivable-respect* behaviourism. The classical theories of personality differ from each other in so many fundamentally different ways that relative parsimony is rarely an issue. Even when the psychoanalytic theorists coming after Freud tried to develop the theory, the changes made were substantive and not to do with the presentational economy. Of course there is no evidence that Freud would have preferred a simpler version of his own theory. He clearly considered the details and variations to be significant and not just indulgent overelaboration. Whether it is possible to simplify psychoanalysis without finishing up with some kind of psychoanalysis-lite is a matter for debate.

Contemporary personality theories score highly on parsimony. The Big Five in particular seeks to reduce all significant variation in personality traits to just five dimensions. The claim is that behaviour, as far as it can be predicted from personality at all, can be predicted on the basis of the five NEO dimensions and no more. We *could* add on extra dimensions but, the argument goes, the increase in predictive power would be so small that it is not worth bothering about. Thus we see that parsimony and comprehensiveness are often in conflict – the more aspects of a phenomenon we try to explain the more theoretical constructs we require and the less parsimonious our theory becomes. There are no hard and fast rules about when we should favour parsimony over comprehensiveness and we have to ask as Costa and McCrae asked themselves when constructing the Big Five, 'Does the increase in comprehensiveness justify the loss of parsimony?' If the extra constructs provide improved understanding of the general *features* of the phenomenon, and not just the explanation of one or two additional *cases,* the answer would be in the affirmative. To add an extra factor to the Big Five would give the theory 20 per cent more theoretical constructs but would almost certainly not lead to explaining personality 20 per cent better.

Clarity of constructs

Most classical personality theories score badly on clarity. There is a whole range of constructs in psychoanalytic and humanistic personality theory which are difficult to define except in relation to other, often equally fuzzy, concepts from the theory itself. For example, Freud's concept of a 'defence mechanism' can only be defined in relation to *his* concepts of the 'ego' and the 'id', which in turn can only be defined in relation to *his* concept of the 'unconscious' and so on. These concepts can be illustrated by anecdote or case history but cannot easily be defined in ways which lend themselves to formal and objective testing. A further problem here is that Freud and other psychoanalysts claim that only trained psychoanalysts can detect the presence or absence in patients of psychological phenomena such as defensiveness. This makes the constructs completely inaccessible to outsiders, effectively insulating psychoanalysis from serious scrutiny. Constructs in other areas such as Kelly's personal construct theory and behaviourist accounts of personality arguably have an apparent clarity, precision and formality to them which can turn out on closer inspection to be rather superficial. When assessing the clarity of constructs of classical personality theory, we need to recognise that many of the constructs were not set up to be clear in the particular sense of positivistic theories of science. The clarity sought by humanists in particular is a purely communicative therapeutic form of clarity, designed to aid insight by clients and their humanistic therapists. Nevertheless, if we are to assess them as psychological theories and not just therapeutic devices, we need to judge the clarity of these constructs in terms of whether they are sufficiently clear to enable new (and potentially disconfirming) evidence to be collected about them.

Psychometric approaches to personality are generally much clearer about constructs. The main constructs are the dimensions of personality which emerge from the inductive process of factor analysis, involving large volumes of data collected through personality questionnaires. The constructs that are identified in this way are labelled retrospectively, once it is clear that they reliably emerge under different testing conditions with a wide range of samples. The dimensions which constitute the Big Five, (neuroticism, extraversion, openness, agreeableness and conscientiousness) are labels for the patterns of association which have emerged from a series of studies. While the patterns of correlations between test items and the dimensions that emerge from these (the factors) are usually clear, what is not so clear is whether the labels *given* to these dimensions are appropriate. We could in principle argue that the label applied to one of the dimensions is not the best label and that there is a better label to be used (for example we might argue that 'extraversion' should be relabelled 'confident'). Alternatively we might argue that one-word labels do not do justice to the complexity and nuances of the traits which appear to go together under that heading. For example, 'openness' is meant to be a superordinate term for, among other things, 'original', 'creative', 'independent' and 'daring'. Now, 'openness' captures something of the underlying disposition that might be being revealed by these terms but it does not, for me, capture some of the other qualities that seem to be implied. For example, there seems to be an element of 'risk' here and something to do with *actively* seeking and engaging opportunity rather than simply being 'open' to it. Of course simply labelling this dimension 'boldness' would lose some of the connotations of 'openness'. Perhaps this labelling of dimensions that emerges from factors *always* leads to a degree of misdescription. Possibly the only way to be clear about what we mean by 'openness' would be to *list* the traits it is trying to label. The labelling or naming of any set of items makes their existence as a set clearer, but masks their distinctive features and nuances. Often labelling factors with just one word gives a spurious sense of purity about the construct and the accuracy with which it is measured.

We can see then that classical personality theory demonstrates the difficulties of being clear about constructs that have been derived *deductively*, while psychometric personality theories demonstrate the difficulties of being clear about constructs that have been derived *inductively*. Deductive constructs need to be clear in order that they can be tested, while inductive constructs need to be clear in order that they are informative about the data from which they have been derived (see Chapter 4).

Internal consistency

A theory which is internally contradictory makes no sense, or at least makes no sense as a theory designed to inform understanding about a phenomenon and direct relevant research into it. Freudian psychoanalysis is particularly problematic in this respect since, among other things, it argues that underlying motivations can manifest themselves in many different partial and contradictory ways in the adult personality. Similarly, every conscious act can have several underlying motivations. Thus any attempt to measure these underlying motivations or the links between them that relies upon explicit behaviours is clearly doomed from the outset, as there is no one-to-one mapping between measurable behaviour and underlying psychological processes. Psychoanalysis comes across as contradictory in this sense because it argues, for example, that affection for another person could be, variously, a sign of underlying desire, a sign of underlying hate, or a sign of underlying something else entirely. No matter what results are found from any attempt to test a proposition from psychoanalytic theory, the theory can be defended by saying that the opposite of what was predicted is *also* consistent with psychoanalytic theory. No finding is inconsistent with psychoanalytic theory and for that reason can never be disproved. As we saw in Chapter 2, the philosopher of science Karl Popper used psychoanalysis as an example of how *not* to construct theories for precisely this reason.

A further problem with psychoanalysis is that Freud developed his theory over the course of his lifetime, shifting the emphasis dramatically on some of his major concepts. His early work focused on repression and trauma, while later work dealt with the stages of psychosexual development. His later work is more pessimistic than his early work and focused on relationships between individuals. Supporters of psychoanalysis criticise those who attack Freud by claiming that this develop-ment of his ideas is not given adequate recognition. The detractors counter by pointing out that the changes in his thinking are not always explicitly documented so it is difficult to keep track of different meanings of the same term. Although he changed his views on some topics, he usually does not explicitly state 'I used to believe X and now I believe Y'. The changes are subtler than that. The loose and open format of his writings (and of other psychoanalysts since) in the form of case histories and broad analyses makes it difficult trace the changes in the overall theory.

Testability

Given the lack of clarity in theoretical constructs and relational propositions of much psychoanalytic and humanistic personality theory, it should come as no surprise that many of the theories resist testing in any normal sense of the term. We have already noted the problems with constructing tests of principles here, which will yield results which cannot be 'reinterpreted' by the theory's supporters to show that the theory is in fact consistent with the findings. There have been some attempts to construct experiments which might test some principles of psychoanalysis in the laboratory and through questionnaires. It is fair to say, however, that those who carried out the tests never believed for one moment that a negative (that is, disconfirming) result would have made one psychoanalyst change their mind about anything, but the studies are valiant attempts at exploiting the heuristic value of psychoanalysis (see below). There have, for example, been studies designed to test whether anxiety leads to forgetting as described by the Freudian notion of traumatic repression (where information associated with some frightening event is buried in the unconscious and cannot be retrieved). These studies report contradictory findings, with some indicating that where subjects are made fearful (say with the possibility of receiving an electric shock), sometimes they do and sometimes they do not forget the words they were trying to memorise at the point they were made fearful. Of course the laboratory cannot reproduce the extreme levels of trauma to which Freud was referring. No electric shock in a laboratory can come close to simulating the horror of sexual abuse Freud stated his patients had gone through.

Humanistic personality theory suffers similar problems. Attempts have been made to measure some of the key humanistic constructs such as Maslow's notion of self-actualisation through questionnaires such as the Personal Orientation Inventory (for example Shostrom, 1964). These attempts to create psychometric instruments on the basis of hermeneutic theories are generally inadequate as:

- they do not capture the richness and subtlety of the original construct
- they are designed partly for use in clinical contexts rather than for theory-testing research
- they do not capture the *function* of the construct in the original theory.

It should be remembered that psychoanalytic and humanistic constructs were never designed to be turned into questionnaires, so the fact that the questionnaires, which have been compiled to measure these constructs, are unsuccessful should not come as a surprise. Generally speaking, the empirical versions of these constructs are bland and circumscribed compared to the passages of purple prose that inspired them.

What inferences can we draw from this? What conclusions can we come to from the fact that hermeneutic personality theories generally fare poorly on the testability criterion? We should remember that the testability criterion is part of the ideology of the logical positivism, even if textbooks and commentators often present it as a universal criterion independent of any particular epistemological position. By 'testability' we mean a very narrow way of matching particular kinds of description of the world (that is, cause and effects laws) on the one hand with specific ways of getting information about the world (that is, experiments) on the other. For some theories, 'testability' in the logical positivist sense is not a meaningful criterion.

Psychoanalytic or humanist theorists who adopt a hermeneutic approach are generally unconcerned by their theory's inability to be tested in the laboratory, because to them the ontology and epistemology of positivism is irrelevant. However, the problem with this anti-positivistic position is that the 'testability is irrelevant' claim can be used as a fig leaf to cover up all sorts of really, really bad and indulgent speculation on human personality masquerading as psychoanalytic, phenomenological or humanistic insight. Many hermeneutic personality theorists advance clinical practice as a more useful test of theories but resist rigorous experimental tests of such practice, arguing that the subtle processes and outcomes of, say, psychoanalysis or humanistic psychotherapy just do not lend themselves to quantification. In fact, however, there are plenty of studies that have translated the nuances of clinical practice into well-defined and measurable constructs in such a way as to test a range of hypotheses about the relative effectiveness of different schools of personality theory. Generally speaking, the one enduring finding of such research is that the theoretical orientation of the therapist (humanistic, existential, Rogerian and so on) is one of the least influential variables affecting client well being and outcome.

Assessing the testability of contemporary theories of personality is on the face of it much more straightforward. Indeed, trait theories of personality are constructed with the express purpose of being tested empirically. However, the problem with theories such as the Big Five is that they are in a sense *only* a set of statements that can be tested empirically. The statements do not in themselves derive from some prior and separate theoretical model. The constructs have been arrived at inductively. Eysenck's personality theory is a combination of inductive and deductive methods, inasmuch as he not only gathered data supporting his three main dimensions of personality, but also formulated a theoretical model to explain these factors which draws upon biological psychology and learning principles. The criticism which can be made about contemporary psychometric approaches to personality in relation to testability is the same criticism that can be made about positivistic research generally in relation to testability (see Danziger, 1985). The structure of the theories has come to mimic the structure of the instrumentation and format of the statistical techniques employed. That we have theories of personality which are phrased in terms of a small number of independent dimensions is largely to do with the fact that the statistical analysis of questionnaires by factor analysis yields, well, a small number of independent dimensions. It is important that theorists have a good understanding of instrumentation but there is more to theory construction than describing what the world looks like through instrumentation. By analogy, it would be a very sorry kind of astronomy indeed that only made claims about the shapes of light that come out of telescopes.

Empirical support

There have been studies that attempt to provide empirical support for some of the claims of psychoanalysis and humanism. While the constructs of psychoanalysis are largely unique to psychoanalysis itself, much of humanist psychology resonates with aspects of social and developmental psychology and indeed with everyday talk about personality and self.

However, researchers tend to find it easier to study those constructs which, while part of the humanistic model, are not the distinctive elements of the theory. So, for example, there are many empirical studies of 'self', 'motivation' and 'esteem' which could be said to show that these elements are significant in understanding human personality. But accepting that these constructs are important does not necessarily lead us specifically to a humanistic theory – there are many other theories that use these constructs. The difficulty is that those constructs which are most *distinctive* about humanistic psychology such as 'self-actualisation', 'genuineness', 'unconditional positive regard', 'conditions of worth' and so on are almost impossible to test directly through scientific methods. Further difficulties arise when constructs such as 'empathy' are studied through mainstream empirical methods using simple operational definitions of constructs which originally meant something very specific and complex within humanistic psychology. More generally, we need to be aware of studies which, while presented as providing support for the theory, could never have done anything else.

It is important, therefore, that when thinking critically about studies that seem to provide some empirical support for hermeneutic theories we ask ourselves the following questions:

1. Is the theoretical construct or relational proposition supported distinctive to the theory under scrutiny or is it common to several theories?

2. Is the definition of the theoretical construct in the study the same as in the theory? If not, which aspects have been set aside in order to make the construct testable?

3. Was there any possible outcome from the study which could *not* have been accommodated by the theory? Or could any result be construed as supporting the theory? In other words, was there ever any possibility of *disconfirmation* of the theoretical constructs or the relations between them?

Heuristic value

The heuristic value of a theory relates to its capacity to capture the imagination of researchers and provide stimulating ideas about what kind of research might be interesting to do. Hermeneutic personality theories are crammed full of stimulating ideas and new ways of looking at the world – but few of them have any clear-cut empirical consequences. Sometimes theories in PID work at a deeper level helping to establish a climate where a particular *kind* of idea becomes more acceptable rather than any particular version of that idea. While Kelly's personal construct theory has always been noted as distinctive and novel, the ideas contained within it have never been directly picked up by mainstream psychology. This was in part due to the historical context of Kelly's work. Published in the 1950s when behaviourism was still the dominant mode of theorising and clinical practice, and before the advent of the cognitive revolution, Kelly's cognitive model of personality had little impact. However, the *general* idea embodied in Kelly's work, that relationship problems could be reworked as *cognitive* problems, probably made it easier for researchers to propose experimentally based cognitive theories of disorders. Similarly, Altemeyer (1998) has argued that while early theorising about the authoritarian personality emphasised psychoanalytic explanations, more recent research emphasises a social learning theory interpretation. It can be seen in this case that the early psychoanalytic account motivated researchers to look more closely at the phenomena of submission and dominance, even though they did not accept the psychoanalytic theory originally advanced as an explanation.

Novelty

When considering the heuristic value of personality theories we need to consider whether what is being claimed is actually new. It is often said of Freudian psychoanalysis that 'what is true is not new and what is new is not true', and it is worth asking whether this applies to any theory we come across. In some senses, nothing is completely 'new'. Humanistic personality theory draws on many aspects of psychoanalysis, which in turn drew on the philosophical writings of Nietzsche, Schopenhauer and others. Behaviourism drew on the associationist tradition in the philosophies of Hume and Mill. In psychometric research, the 'new' contribution is partly the rationalisation of several different strands of interpretation into one overall framework, as is the case with the establishment of the Big Five theory. A danger with any new element of a theory is that it addresses the flaws of previous theories without incorporating their advantages. In such cases there is proliferation of different kinds of theory and no accumulation or progression of theoretical understanding. Theories need to be better than all the theories that have gone before and not just the most recent one.

Counter-intuitiveness

To what extent do the classical theories of personality offer anything that is counter-intuitive? You will remember that counter-intuitiveness is an important aspect of the heuristic value of theories, because not only does it stimulate us to carry out research but it makes us think more carefully about what it is we are trying to explain. We need to bear in mind also that it is not just our everyday intuitions that are at stake here but our intuitions *as psychologists.* Our lay intuitions are based on our personal experiences of living in the world. Our 'intuitions' as psychologists are based on our reading of previous studies, and perhaps our work in the laboratory or field setting.

Freudian psychoanalysis is counter-intuitive in both ways. It suggests, among other things, that children have a form of sexual desire, that aggressive behaviour may be motivated by love (and loving behaviour motivated by hate), that adults' emotions are caused by childhood conflicts, that most of our actions are caused by motivations we know nothing about and, not to put too fine a point on it, we are *all* in fact psychologically disturbed. There are basically two instinctive responses to counter-intuitive theories, both of which can be clearly seen in responses to psychoanalysis. Either take the theory on board and rethink everything that has gone before (because the theory reveals a deeper form of understanding than we have hitherto enjoyed) or dismiss the whole thing as gibberish (because the theory is just plain wrong and our intuitions are right). Of course the most sensible course of action is to test the theory to see whether its counter-intuitive observations are valid (whatever our criteria for establishing *that* might be). With psychoanalysis this sensible option is not available because psychoanalysis does not lend itself to that kind of formal objective assessment. Humanistic personality theory is much less counter-intuitive, seeking as it does to begin from our sense of being a human. A counter-intuitive humanistic psychology is almost a contradiction in terms. Humanistic personality theory tries to make our perceptions of the here and now of our subjective reality meaningful, *confirming* our sense of free will and personal development. In that sense, humanistic psychology is seeking to articulate a clearer version of intuitions we *already* have but at a higher level of understanding and could almost be said to be 'para-intuitive' (on the same level as our intuitions) rather than counter-intuitive.

Overall, then, we can see that assessing theories in PID (or anywhere else in psychology for that matter) depends upon a broad consideration of several very different types of criteria. It is unlikely that any one theory will do well on all of these, so we need to weigh up the overall strengths and weaknesses of each. Having looked at theories of personality in general, we turn now to consideration of how we should think critically about the study of mental disorder.

Mental disorders

The experience of mental disorder is one of the most personally challenging episodes anyone could endure. Correspondingly, interpreting mental disorder in a coherent and useful manner is one of the most professionally challenging problems for any psychologist. Almost every school of psychology has attempted to offer its own accounts of depression, anxiety, personality disorders, psychoses, drug dependency and neuroticism. The study of mental disorder is often linked to the study of personality for many reasons, including the fact that psychoanalysis began with consideration of how to explain the disturbed individual. It might be argued that locating discussion of mental disorders in the context of personality gives undue emphasis to the idea that a psychological disorder is definitive and decisive in terms of characterising someone's personality now and forever. Some radical psychologists argue that there is a need to get away from the assumption that anyone who has ever suffered a psychological disorder can only ever be thought of as 'psychologically disordered', when in fact they might have completely 'recovered' and their previous mental history is of no relevance to a comprehensive understanding of their current psychological status. In any event, the issue of mental disorders is clearly an issue normally considered within psychology to be relevant to the study of individual differences and we shall discuss questions relevant to critical analyses of psychological accounts of it in that light.

THINK IT THROUGH

Nomenclature

Abnormal psychology? Mental illness? Mental health? Mental disorders? Atypical psychology? Psychopathology? What do we call this area of the study of depression, anxiety, psychoses and so on (even assuming we accept *those* diagnostic labels as meaningful)? In the US, 'abnormal psychology' remains popular at least within psychology, while the terms 'mental health' and 'mental illness' are often more common in social policy and sociology texts. 'Atypical psychology' is a recent and largely European term that has yet to attain widespread currency. 'Mental disorders' is found in textbooks in both Europe and the US. 'Psychopathology' is a term most common in research periodicals particularly those with a biological emphasis. Each of these terms carries with it connotations derived partly from the perceived meanings of the words themselves and partly from the groups who use the terms. The labelling of this area of psychology is a minor but significant skirmish in the larger battle over the definition of 'normality' and 'madness' in society. What term do you feel is most appropriate?

Thinking about definitions and diagnoses of mental disorder

Most textbooks on psychological disorders begin with a review of the difficulties in defining the concept – and then spend the next 300 pages or so operating on the assumption that the definition presents no serious difficulties. Many attempts to capture the distinctive features of psychological dysfunction emphasise the deviant, unhappy and dysfunctional characteristics of the mentally disordered. The culture-driven stereotype of a mentally ill individual is probably of a rather dishevelled, wide-eyed, unshaven itinerant who is vaguely menacing but largely incoherent. Surprisingly, many textbooks draw upon this kind of stereotype and talk about the difficulty of distinguishing the mentally ill from the merely eccentric.

But what kind of mentally ill person are we likely to confuse with someone who is *eccentric*? Clearly not the depressed middle-aged woman who fears the imminent loss of her husband, or the man who suffers excessive anxiety and inhibition in social situations due to feelings of inadequacy. One of the difficulties that pervades definitions of mental disorder is that the discussions about mental disorders in general tend to focus on *absences*, while actual diagnostic categories for specific disorders usually focus on the presence of symptoms. For example, general discussions of people who are mentally ill focus on the fact that they do *not* follow the behavioural and attitudinal norms of society (that is, they are deviant) and do *not* function effectively (that is, they are dysfunctional), in the sense that they cannot hold down a job or a relationship. Most specific diagnostic criteria are much more focused on things that are present and identifiable such as hearing voices, anxiety, anger displays, drug consumption and so on (although there are also some diagnostic absences such as social withdrawal, weight loss and so on). What can we deduce from the fact that individual disorders can be differentiated from *each other* in terms of what sufferers display, while the 'mentally ill' are typically discriminated from the 'mentally well' in terms of what the mentally ill *lack*? One thing we probably can infer is that, according to psychologists, the mentally ill do not seem to have anything in common *with one another*, apart from the fact that they are different from some notional standard of normal functioning. If this is the case, then we should treat very sceptically any *general* claims about the 'mentally ill'.

In terms of thinking clearly about different types of psychological disorder, there are some basic issues that should always be examined:

■ To what extent is there *cultural and historical variation* in the prevalence of this disorder? Cultural variation can occur within a country or across countries. Historical variation needs to be assessed carefully as the criteria for different disorders change over time. The more variability observed the more likely the disorder has a social origin. On a national scale, variation in social class is also significant.

■ To what extent are there *sex differences* in the prevalence of the disorder? This does not in itself necessarily tell us anything about potential origins but helps us to focus on the distribution of the disorder in society.

■ What is the real prevalence in *children*? Some disorders, such as schizophrenia, almost never appear in children below the age of 14, whereas other disorders, such as depression, have only recently been acknowledged as occurring in preadolescence. We cannot assume that because children do display symptoms of a disorder, that disorder is entirely or even largely caused by biological factors. Children's psychological disorders can be as much a reaction to experience as it can be for adults. However, it can be difficult getting valid and reliable data from children and studies often run the risk of underestimating prevalence.

- To what extent is the disorder *responsive* to different kinds of treatment? Disorders which respond exclusively to drug treatments probably have a largely biological foundation, whereas disorders which respond to more behavioural or cognitive interventions are more likely to be social or interpersonal in origin.

Thinking about causes and treatments of mental disorder

There is a huge literature on the causes and treatments of mental disorders. Currently the majority of studies relate to clinical trials of drugs. Drug trials involve a lot of careful preparation and administration but are usually very well funded. Also common are organised experiments on psychotherapeutic methods such as cognitive-behavioural therapy. The following issues need to be thought about carefully if a thorough evaluation of any research report or claim about treatment is to be possible. (Note that almost all the questions are applicable both to drug trials and tests of psychotherapeutic interventions.)

- Have there been any clinical trials of the treatment?
- Were all potentially confounding factors controlled for?
- Were double-blind procedures used where relevant?
- Were there enough participants/clients to make the results reliable?
- Was the independent variable assessed at the appropriate levels (for example dosage levels for drugs and number of therapy sessions for psychotherapy)?
- Was the treatment administered *consistently* (for example the same batch of drugs and similar training for therapists)?
- How strong was the size of the effect obtained?
- What were the outcome measures (that is, dependent variables)?
- Are the outcomes measures assessed in relation just to symptomatology, or also to general psychological functioning and general social functioning?
- How valid and reliable are the outcome measures?
- Were the correct statistical procedures carried out (especially where multi-centre or other complex design issues are involved)?
- Were the correct ethical procedures adhered to (for example informed consent, freedom to withdraw, confidentiality and debriefing)?
- Was the assessment of the outcome measures carried out by a specialist, the patient or the patient's carer or family? What was the rationale for the selection of measures?
- Are the results from the outcome measures convergent? Or is the treatment working on some aspects of the disorder better than others?

■ When were the outcome assessments carried out? Is there evidence of both short- and longer-term alleviation of the disorder?

■ What are the side effects of the treatment? Are they manageable by the patient?

■ To what extent is the treatment being presented as a stand-alone treatment or as a complement to some existing treatment?

■ Is the treatment likely to be practical in the life circumstances of the patient, given the patient's lifestyle, age, gender, ethnic group and financial circumstances?

■ Is the overall treatment likely to be part of a better overall package than that which it replaces?

■ How was the research financed and what was the relationship between the sponsoring body, the researchers and the researchers' host institution(s)?

■ Are there published studies of the same or similar treatments which found no effect or weak effects?

■ Are there studies of the same or similar treatments which found no effect or weak effect which have *not* been published?

Overall, then, when thinking about claims regarding mental disorder we need to think about the assumptions being made about definitions, diagnoses, prevalence and clinical support for any treatments being proposed.

Radical alternatives

The study of personality and individual differences has recently faced new challenges from radical theorists who question some of the fundamental assumptions of the area. Mainstream psychology takes as its point of departure the idea of the *individual* person: a separate and autonomous entity, not just in a physical sense, but in a very fundamental social sense. The individual is seen as a self-contained, emotionally distinctive and internally coherent individual who is generally consciously aware of the world and of taking decisions to act within it. The model of the individual used by psychology is in most ways the model of the individual used by all of us in everyday life. In short, it is a common-sense view of the individual which seems to be the only model of the individual which our culture permits (part of a 'psy-complex', see Chapter 8). The issue this chapter has been addressing is 'What is the nature of differences between individuals?' but recently some psychologists have taken a lead from anthropologists and sociologists and asked the question 'What do we mean by "individual"?'

> The Western conception of the person as a bounded, unique, more or less integrated motivational and cognitive universe, a dynamic centre of awareness, emotion, judgement, and action organised into a distinctive whole and set constrastively both against other such wholes and against a social and natural background is, however incorrigible it may seem to us, a rather peculiar idea within the context of the world's cultures. (Geertz, 1979: 229, quoted in Nightingale and Neilands, 1997)

Gergen (1997b) has traced the ways in which scholarly ideas about person-hood have drawn on popular cultural conceptions of individuality throughout history. Nineteenth-century Romanticism built on medieval ideas of 'deep interiors' of the mind. The model of the person then was that of a hidden but powerful force which found expression in inspiration, devotion, grief or commitment. According to Gergen, Freud's idea of psychoanalytic theory needed this backdrop or else the concepts would have failed to connect with the culture as a whole. In the 20th century, argues Gergen, Romanticism gave way to Modernism and with it new assumptions about the person have emerged. Gone are the dark and mysterious forces of psychoanalysis, to be replaced by the observable aspects of behaviour examined by the harsh light of reason. In that context, the emphasis in both popular and scientific psychology is on the mechanical processes of learning and information processing. Of course scientific psychology has to go beyond the popular psychology but it does so, argues Gergen, by merely giving a more elaborate account of the implications of popular models rather than by replacing them. These conceptions of what it is to be an individual inform scholarly analyses, which in turn define an agenda for the methodologies and instruments that are relevant to the conception of person being examined. These instruments yield results that can only be interpreted in relation to those conceptions and so the process becomes self-fulfilling.

At the core of much research and theorising in personality and individual differences is a particular conception of the self. Reviewing this use of 'self' as a construct in cognitive, psychoanalytic, social and humanistic theorising, Wetherell and Maybin (1996) argue that they all essentially share (to greater or lesser degrees) an idea of the self that is separate, self-contained, independent, consistent, unitary and private. This model of the self is thus largely *asocial* and underpins much of the individualism of experimental research.

Rejecting all these formulations and arguing for a social constructionist approach to the study of the self, Wetherell and Maybin contend that the self is *emergent* (that is, not reducible to a lower biological or cognitive level), *contextual* (constructed in and for different situations and circumstances), *discursive* (constructed in language), *multiple* (has variable rather than unitary manifestations), *relational* (constructed with others) and *distributed* (participating in many roles, relationships and representations simultaneously). In short, Wetherell and Maybin are offering a *postmodern* account of personality that takes us away from the modernist view of coherent, rational, self-contained individuals.

The shift away from a self-contained, fixed self to a more fluid, socially constructed self poses profound challenges to the traditional agenda of personality research. It makes it difficult, for example, to give answers to questions such as 'What are the main underlying stable differences among individual personalities?', since the categories of 'underlying', 'stable' 'individual', and 'personality' are simply meaningless once the modernist, rationalist assumptions which gave them meaning are dissolved. For constructionist psychologists, the question 'What are the main underlying stable differences among individual personalities?' does not actually raise *empirical* issues at all. That is to say, neither the question nor any of its possible answers will be better understood simply by collecting more data. Rather, the question demands a conceptual response, which recognises the cultural, historical and linguistic contexts in which it is meaningful to even pose such a question.

Some social constructionists, especially those such as the critical psychologists influenced by Michel Foucault, consider the very sense of individuality to be an illusion created by language and perpetuated by a society which has a vested interest in encouraging individuals to take responsibility for themselves. The term commonly used to denote this sense of individuality is subjectivity (see Chapter 8). The impact of such radical accounts of personality and its epistemological foundations on traditional psychometrics has been limited. However, there is some evidence that ideas about the self as *contextual* are beginning to slowly become accepted in information processing models of personality of the kind described by Mischel. Nevertheless, it will be some time (if ever) before ideas of an emergent, discursive and distributed self are taken at face value in mainstream psychology, largely because there are no clear experimental tests of those claims.

SUMMARY

The study of personality and individual differences in psychology has involved a wide range of methods and theories, ranging from questionnaire and clinical interviews, the hermeneutic theories of Freud to the factor analytic models of Costa and McCrae. Models of personality vary considerably in terms of the extent to which they meet the standard criteria for assessing the quality of a theory. Among the more common and significant problems is the difficulty of testing claims from theories in such a way that the claims can be clearly disconfirmed. However, some theories, such as psychoanalysis and humanistic personality theory, claim that such criteria are irrelevant to their aims. In terms of methods it is essential that instruments used to measure theoretical constructs display satisfactory reliability and validity. The analyses of theoretical definitions and research reports of psychological disorders considered as a form of individual difference raise questions of what is 'normal' and require us to assess treatment outcomes in broad terms. Recently radical alternatives to traditional models of what psychologists mean by 'individual' have been proposed but have had limited impact on mainstream research and theorising.

KEY TERMS

Counter-analogy ■ Idiographic ■ Situationism

FURTHER READING

Yalom, I D (1980) *Existential Psychotherapy* (New York: Basic Books) is an accessible introduction to humanist thought and therapy.

The journal *Personality and Individual Differences* publishes articles on Eysenckian personality theory, the Big Five, IQ testing and psychometric issues generally.

Articles by Cernovsky, ('IQ testing'), Sloan ('Personality') and Hare-Mustin and Maraceck ('Clinical psychology') in Fox, D and Prilleltensky, I (eds) (1997) *Critical Psychology: An Introduction* (London: Sage) offer various critiques of mainstream PID research and theorising following a radical social constructionist line.

USEFUL WEBSITES

The Personality Project
http://pmc.psych.nwu.edu/personality
An outstanding collection of authoritative resources for all aspects of the study of personality, including tips for students, links to research laboratories and definitions of key concepts.

Personality – An Electronic Textbook
http://www.ship.edu/~cgboeree/perscontents.html
A handy guide to all the main personality theories.

Great Ideas in Personality
http://galton.psych.nwu.edu/GreatIdeas.html
Less comprehensive than the Personality Project, but it still provides good coverage of the main aspects of personality.

Sigmund Freud and the Freud Archives
http://plaza.interport.net/nypsan/freudarc.html
This contains links to full texts of some key early works by Freud.

Sigmund Freud Museum, Vienna
http://freud.t0.or.at/freud/index-e.htm
An interesting site which contains, among other things, 'amateur movies showing Freud with his family and friends between 1930 and 1939 in Vienna, Paris and London'.

Freud Museum, London
http://www.freud.org.uk/
Take a virtual tour of Freud's main home in London.

Mental Health Directory
http://mentalhelp.net/
This site effectively combines information on academic, clinical and support group work.

Review of Part II

In Part II we have applied the ideas reviewed and developed in Part I to six key areas of psychology. We have in particular considered how concepts related to induction, deduction, ethics, the philosophy of science and experimental design can be applied to theoretical models and empirical research.

It is important to note of course that many of the ideas we discussed in different chapters in relation to specific topics have application beyond those areas. For example, our discussion of ethics in Chapter 7 (experimental social psychology) is relevant to consideration of ethics in developmental, cognitive and personality research also. Similarly, our discussion of the challenges of the diversity of aggressive behaviour for evolutionary psychology in Chapter 11 provides a framework for thinking about, say, the challenges to developmental psychology of the diversity of children's play behaviour. You should actively think for yourself about the application of ideas from each chapter to other areas of psychology. We can review now some of the main ideas we have identified in our journey through psychology.

In Chapter 7 we considered the way in which scientific (that is, logical positivist) ideas have been used in social psychology and identified the main assumptions underlying the theories and experiments of that approach. We considered in particular the assumptions of reductionism, determinism and individualism evident in experimental social psychology. We saw how difficult it is to resolve ethical issues that depend upon some sort of trade-off between costs and benefits, when society involves many different interests and values. All of this we discussed in relation to social psychology, but it should make us think about the limits of the scientific method in developmental and applied cognitive psychology too. In Chapter 8 we considered an alternative model of social psychology, social constructionism, which argues that social life is played out across public conversations rather than in the private mind. The radical agendas of discursive and critical psychology make us think again about the relationship between psychology and society.

So, how should we *think* about social psychology? First of all we need to recognise the tension in social psychology between, on the one hand, the desire to see just how far an experimental model will take us and, on the other, the idea that social structures and language do not lend themselves easily to experimental methods. Second, we need to recognise the difference between thinking about a study in its own terms and when we need to stand back and think about it in a more detached manner. For example, we might assess the internal validity of an experiment on attitude change, but then we might also assess the way reductionism in attitude research generally reflects wider social assumptions about the responsibility of individuals in a democratic society to 'know their own minds'. In relation to social constructionism in Chapter 8, it is similarly important to think critically about the quality of research both in its own terms and more broadly. Simply because qualitative approaches reject the traditional criteria of scientific standards does not mean they should be allowed to get away with any old pseudo-journalistic rubbish masquerading as research. It is all too easy for those jaded by questionnaires, visual illusions and the like to find in constructionist research a breath of fresh air so invigorating that they leave their critical faculties behind.

In Chapter 9 we considered particular ways of thinking about what developmental psychology research methods do and do not allow us to infer about causality. However, we also paid close attention to how we should think about the relationship between theory and experiment, using a recent study as an example. We already knew from Chapters 2 and 3 that hypotheses need to be derived from theories in such a way that they can be disconfirmed (as Popper says). However, in this chapter we saw how the practical business of turning a general theoretical construct into a specific operational definition means that something of the original formulation can be lost. We noted that this 'operational narrowing', as we called it, is potentially a characteristic of *all* experimental work and not just developmental research.

In Chapter 10 we looked at how we might analyse theory and research in cognitive psychology, noting the impact that computers have had, not just in terms of providing more complex ways to present stimuli and analyse results, but as an analogy for the human mind itself. We saw how cognitive psychologists are less interested in the content or embodiment of cognition, and more in the structure of information and how it is processed. Thinking critically about theories in cognitive psychology involves considering whether the theory has (among other things) got the balance right between bottom-up and top-down processing, and between processing and storage. These issues are further complicated by the emergence of connectionist accounts which turn our ideas of 'processing' and 'storage' (especially storage) on their heads. We also found that, although cognitive psychology is looking more carefully at real-world cognition, in the field it often lacks the control necessary to decide between competing causal hypotheses.

In Chapter 11 we looked at the kind of issues we need to think about if we are to make sense of biopsychology. We considered the relationship between mind and body and the implications of different ways of thinking about that relationship. We saw how the deterministic, realist and essentialist assumptions of biopsychology raise complex issues when we try to explain complex higher-level personal and social behaviour in its terms. Of particular interest was our analysis of how we should think about claims that contemporary human behaviour is directly interpretable through consideration of our evolutionary past. While the advances in neuroscience offer up many new windows on the brain, we need to be careful about how we use language to bridge the gap between impressive high resolution colour-enhanced images of the neocortex on the one hand and our rather more ill-formed questions about behaviour and experience on the other.

Chapter 12 found us thinking in great detail about what should count as a good theory in psychology and why some theories turn out to be less useful than they might initially appear. Both traditional classical theories of personality such as psychoanalysis and contemporary theories such as the Big Five need to be assessed very carefully in terms of comprehensiveness, parsimony, clarity of constructs, internal consistency, testability, empirical support and heuristic value. We considered also the questions that need to be asked of studies which set out to assess the effectiveness of new treatments for those with psychological disorders.

What, then, can we say about 'thinking psychologically'? We can say first of all that it is a demanding and exciting intellectual challenge. Can any other discipline have such a broad mix of theories, techniques, methods and histories? Does any other discipline have so many connections with so many other areas of human thought? Does any other discipline require its practitioners to think in quite so many different ways, and indeed in quite so many different ways *at once*?

'Thinking psychologically' means thinking about science – and therefore entails thinking about numbers, facts, technologies and discoveries. 'Thinking psychologically' means thinking about philosophy – and therefore entails thinking about truth, logic, deduction, ontology and epistemology. 'Thinking psychologically' means thinking about culture – and hence entails thinking about identity, language, history and power. 'Thinking psychologically' means thinking about meaning rather than about truth, relatives rather than absolutes, and possibilities rather than certainties. Thinking psychologically means all these things, because 'thinking psychologically' means thinking imaginatively about our normally unimaginative understanding of ourselves.

Glossary

Analogy Describing one phenomenon X in terms of another phenomenon Y in order to better illuminate some features of phenomenon X. For example, in psychology the human mind is described in terms of a computer in order to better understand the mind's capacity to handle complex information rapidly.

Affirming the antecedent A common reasoning error in which a possible cause is seen as being a necessary cause. For example, inferring from the fact that someone is dead that he must have been poisoned (simply because poison can kill). Or in psychology, for example, inferring from the fact that there is cross-culture similarity in, say, sexual jealousy that there must be a biological cause of jealousy (simply because if there was a biological cause it could lead to cross-cultural consistency).

Algorithm Generally a procedure for getting to a valid, optimal or logical outcome through the systematic application of a rule. The human mind uses a combination of algorithms and **heuristics** to solve problems.

Analytic A structured type of thinking or reasoning often associated with logic and deduction.

Antecedent A type of premise in deductive reasoning roughly corresponding to 'cause' when applied to reasoning about behaviour.

Behaviourism A historically important form of psychology influential between 1930 and 1960, characterised by a commitment to scientific study of observable behaviour especially animal learning. The experimental procedures and theoretical models of behaviourism were strongly influenced by logical positivism and their apparent success with that philosophy of science continues to influence contemporary psychology.

Bold conjectures Popper's term for hypotheses that are not only surprising in what they predict but which are also falsifiable.

Computationalism An approach to cognitive psychology which emphasises that mental process can be represented by, and in some senses thereby reduced to, a statement of the computations which such processes require.

Conceptual definition A specification of a theoretical construct designed to enable its testing in an experiment.

Conclusion In syllogistic reasoning, the inference which can be drawn on the basis of deduction from the premises.

Concrete operationalisation The practical definition of a conceptual definition as realised in a particular experiment.

Connectionism A new approach to the mind which uses complex networks to explain processing phenomena. Concepts are seen to be represented in a distributed fashion across a network and processed in parallel. The approach is therefore also known as the parallel distributed processing (PDP) approach.

Consequent A type of premise in syllogisms roughly corresponding to effect in reasoning about behaviour.

Contamination In experimental design, when subjects in one condition indirectly get a treatment (including information) that was intended only for another condition.

Counter-analogy An analogy which seeks to demonstrate the limitations of some prior analogy.

Critical psychology A form of radical psychology which criticises traditional psychology's failure to address the systems of language and power which constrain action and understanding.

Curvilinear function A function between two variables such that if plotted on x and y axes yields a curved (curvi-) line (linear) rather than a straight one, indicating that there is no consistent change in one variable as the other changes.

Deduction A form of reasoning that involves deriving specific inferences from a general case. Thus, deriving a specific hypothesis from a general theory involves deduction.

Demand characteristics The often subtle cues which subjects pick up from the social and physical environment about what is expected of them in their role as subject. Experiments seek to minimise demand characteristics in order to protect the internal validity of the experiment.

Determinism The assumption or position that all events are directly caused by preceding events and are therefore in principle predictable from them. In psychology determinism is most evident in biopsychology but is reflected in experimental designs generally.

Discursive psychology A form of psychology which emphasises the defining force of conversation in everyday life rather than causal influences on behaviour.

Dualism The assumption or position that mental and physical entities exist in separate 'planes' or 'realities'.

Emergent property In relation to the **mind–body problem** the assumption or position that the mind emerges from brain activity but cannot necessarily be mapped on to it or reduced to it.

Empiricism The commitment to the need to gather data about the world systematically in order to gain knowledge about it. Thus psychology is typically empirical, while philosophy and mathematics typically are not.

Epistemological anarchy Feyerabend's term for a scientific culture where any and all forms of thinking and methods of enquiry are in principle recognised as valid so long as they get results.

Epistemological pluralism The position adopted in this book which asserts that there is no one single best way to understand human behaviour and thought. Different types of knowledge about behaviour and thought are possible and legitimate.

Epistemology The study of what *knowledge* is, what we can know and what the limits of knowledge are, as distinct from the nature of the reality itself (**ontology**) or how we should study it (**methodology**).

Essentialism The assumption that concepts are defined by intrinsic real properties (rather than by the names they are given).

Ethnocentric The tendency to consider universal that which is true only of one's own culture.

Evaluation apprehension The tendency on the part of subjects to worry about how they will be 'assessed' in an experiment.

Evaluation confidence The tendency on the part of some subjects to enjoy being 'assessed' in an experiment.

Evaluation orientation The tendency of some subjects to feel apprehensive or confident in testing situations.

Evolution The phenomenon whereby successive generations become better suited to their environment. The phenomenon is caused by the process of **natural selection.**

External validity The extent to which an instrument or method yields results which are applicable in the wider world beyond the confines of the original testing situation (for example the psychology laboratory).

Falsifiability Popper's alternative to **verifiability** as the key criterion for all claims in science. While positivists argued that claims need to be capable of being shown to be true, Popper argued that claims needed to be capable of being shown to be false. This put the emphasis on attempting to collect data inconsistent with a theory rather than gathering data consistent with a theory.

Flow diagram A graphical device used to present theories, especially in cognitive psychology, in which boxes typically represent stages of processing, and arrows represent the flow of information through those stages.

Good-subject role An orientation of subjects to experiments where they attempt to be 'helpful' to the experimenter.

Hermeneutic In psychology, the interpretation of meanings of behaviour. Thus a hermeneutic researcher seeks to interpret the significance of action in relation to the contexts of behaviour. Such research interpretations are seen themselves to be the products of particular contexts of enquiry and as such open to further reinterpretation.

Heuristic A rule or procedure which finds a satisfactory answer quickly usually by making assumptions about what superficial aspects of the data imply (see **algorithm**).

Holism The assumption or position that in order to make sense of a phenomenon we need to consider it in its entirety (and not break it down to component parts).

Hypothesis A prediction, usually derived from a theory, which, if supported by results of a study would support the theory.

Hypothetico-deductive A form of reasoning used in science whereby hypotheses are deduced from general theories which have been constructed inductively on the bases of previous findings. If the hypothesis if found to be supported when tested, the theory is taken as supported. If the hypothesis is not supported, the theory in that form should be rejected.

Idiographic An assumption or approach to psychology which emphasises the individualistic, possibly unique, features of personality.

Incommensurabilty Feyerabend's term for the fact that ultimately no two theories can be reduced to terms which would enable an independent test of both.

Individualism The assumption, often unstated, that the most appropriate means of analysing human behaviour is to consider it as produced, experienced and regulated by individuals rather than couples, groups, communities or societies.

Induction A form of reasoning that involves generalising from a set of individual cases to a general conclusion.

Internal validity The extent to which an instrument or method actually does measure or test what it claims to be measuring or testing. Thus a valid shyness questionnaire would have to actually measure shyness (and not something else). Similarly, an experiment to test whether calming music affects recall would actually have to test that hypothesis (and not allow other explanations of any differences in recall to be due to something else).

Iteration A process whereby a procedure is repeatedly applied to the outcome of its own operations.

Liberatory ethics A feminist approach to ethical conduct in psychology which emphases non-manipulation and committed judgements on values rather than simply informed consent and confidentiality.

Linear causality Any situation where Cause A affects Effect B but Effect B does not in turn affect Cause A. For example, radiation affecting the growth of cells.

Logical positivism A philosophy of science which emphasises the importance of directly verifiable claims as the basis of science.

Methodology The means by which any phenomenon is investigated or theory tested. Thus interviews, experiments and participant observation are all examples of methodologies employed in psychology.

Mind–body problem The apparently enigmatic relationship between the mind and its contents and the brain.

Mind–brain identity theory In relation to the **mind–body problem,** the assumption or position that states of mind can be reduced to states of the brain.

Modus ponens A deductive argument in which premises state that (i) if X occurs then Y will occur too and (ii) X did occur and the conclusion is that therefore Y must have happened.

Modus tollens A deductive argument in which premises state that (i) if X happens then Y will happen, and (ii) Y did not happen and the conclusion is that therefore X must not have happened.

Monism In relation to the **mind–body problem,** the assumption or position that mental and physical entities are both expressions of one single underlying reality (usually physical with the mental considered to be merely an 'epiphenomenon').

Naïve dualism In relation to the **mind–body problem,** the assumption or position that the mind and the brain co-exist and that such co-existence is self-evident and unproblematic.

Natural selection The process responsible for the current structure and patterns of species, whereby those species which best match the opportunities of the environment thrive and reproduce at the expense of less suited species.

Necessity A relationship between a condition and an outcome (or cause and effect) where the condition must be true for the outcome to be true or to be brought about (even if the condition is not in itself enough to bring about the outcome). Thus the condition of encoding is a necessary condition for the outcome of remembering (but it is not sufficient as you must still also retrieve it).

Negativistic-subject role An orientation of subjects to experiments where they attempt to be 'unhelpful' to the experimenter.

Nomothetic The attempt to produce general statements about the world such as universal laws rather than observations about individual instances.

Normal science Kuhn's term for the state of research when **paradigms** (the methods and assumptions of an area) are taken for granted and basic principles are applied to different settings. Anomalous data and awkward findings are ignored as technical areas or unimportant details. When the effect of such anomalies becomes too much, the paradigm is overturned during a period of scientific revolution.

Ontology The study of what *actually* exists such as physical being and the nature of the universe as a reality, as distinct from the study of what we can know about existence (**epistemology**) or how we should study it (**methodology**).

Operational narrowing The tendency to make what were originally very general and impressive claims much more narrow and modest in order to test them in an experiment.

Paradigm The procedures, assumptions and methods of a particular area of research which during periods of normal science are taken for granted. For example in psychology using questionnaires to study personality is currently a paradigm.

Participant Term used nowadays in psychology to describe a person who takes part in a study and whose behaviour or experiences are examined. This replaces the traditional term **subject** which can be construed as denying the rights and active role of those being studied.

Particularisation 'The cognitive process of treating some perceptual stimulus as an individual case and not a member of a category.' Advocated by Billig as a balance against the tendency for psychologists to think only in terms of categorisation.

Performative Language's capacity to perform actions as well as simply representing objects. Examples of the performative capacity of language would include promising, apologising, declaring or permitting.

Plasticity In biopsychology, the capacity of the brain to rewire and restructure itself in the light of experience and learning.

Positivism A philosophy of science which emphasised the objective inductive collection of facts. Later replaced by **logical positivism** which emphasised the construction of theories and verifiable hypotheses.

Premises In syllogistic reasoning, essentially the (alleged) facts on which the conclusion is based.

Prototype In cognitive psychology, a mental representation of a typical exemplar of a category which is frequently used in information processing about the category in general.

Psy-complex In critical psychology, the individualistic and mechanistic conception of the mind shared by lay and professional people. Argued by critical psychologists to be a misguided conception.

Reactivity The tendency of subjects to react to the experimenter or the testing conditions and threaten the internal validity of the experiment.

Realism An assumption, characteristic of many areas of psychology, that the objects of study genuinely exist independently of any scientific scrutiny of them. An assumption often contrasted with **relativism** which claims that objects of study are constructed only relative to the methods or concepts applied in such scrutiny.

Reciprocal causality Any situation where A affects B but B also in turn affects A. For example, in a romantic relationship.

Recursion The operation of defining a procedure partly in terms of itself.

Reductionism The assumption or position that in order to make sense of a phenomenon we need to consider its *component* parts and the underlying structures or processes to which it is related. Thus a reductionist understanding of memory as a process might involve examination of component subprocesses of encoding, storage and retrieval. It might also involve examination of the *underlying* biochemistry of memory. The advantage of reductionism is that large complex problems can be broken down in more manageable chunks. The disadvantages are that the whole can be more than the sum of its parts and that the recognition of the contexts and broader functions can be lost.

Relational propositions In a theory the terms which specify the links between **theoretical constructs**. Thus in Eysenck's theory of extraversion the chronic underarousal of extroverts *leads to* attempts to increase arousal externally.

Relativism The assumption or position that objects of study in psychology (or anything else) only exist relative to the methods, concepts and cultural assumptions involved.

Reliability The extent to which an instrument (such as a questionnaire) measures an aspect of the world consistently.

Replicate To carry out essentially the same experiment as a previous researcher in order to check or confirm the results.

Representational A conception of language associated with positivist science whereby words are taken to 'stand for' objects.

Rhetorical That which is calculated to persuade through the particular presentation or organisation of arguments. Billig contends that much argument and debate in psychology is rhetorical in that opposing sides characterise their claims in different ways. The mind is also rhetorical, claims Billig, in the sense that it anticipates how different statements and actions will or will not persuade others.

Schema A mental representation of a general case to help processing of specific instances.

Self-presentation An orientation of subjects to experiments where they attempt to display themselves in a positive light.

Simulations In cognitive science, a program which seeks to reproduce human or other behaviour as it occurs naturally.

Situationism In personality theory, the assumption or position that behaviour is, despite appearances, caused by the situations people find themselves in rather than any internal stable characteristics such as traits or attitudes.

Social constructionism A school of thought in the social sciences, increasingly influential in psychology, which argues that many concepts used to describe and explain human life are illusions ('constructions') of language rather than reflections of any real world.

Source domain In relation to analogies, the concept the analogy is being generated from. Thus in claiming that the human mind is analogous to a computer, the mind is the **target domain** while the computer is the source domain.

Storage In cognitive psychology the capacity of the mind to hold information (usually in a structured manner).

Subject Traditionally, the term used in psychology for a person who takes part in a study and whose behaviour or experiences are examined. However, a subject is often referred to as a **participant** nowadays to encourage recognition of the fact that subjects are human beings and should be treated with respect.

Subject reactance The tendency on the part of many subjects to resent any intimation that their behaviour is predictable.

Subjectivity In critical psychology, the sense of individual identity and separateness from others which gives a sense of personal location in the world but which is in fact an illusion of the way language works.

Sufficiency A relationship between a condition and an outcome (or cause and effect) such that when the condition is true the outcome will necessarily be true or be brought about (even if the condition is not the only way of bringing the outcome about). Thus being completely drunk provides sufficient grounds for being asked to leave a lecture (but not necessary ones – you could be asked to leave if you were sober but started fighting).

Syllogism A form of deductive argument which demonstrates how particular facts (the premises), if true, lead logically to a stated conclusion. Syllogisms of various kinds underlie many claims in psychology relating to why a hypothesis should be tested in a particular way.

Synthetic A fluid type of thinking often associated with imagination and induction.

Target domain In analogies, the concept which the analogy is being generated for. Thus in claiming that the human mind is analogous to a computer, the mind is the target domain while the computer is the **source domain**.

Theoretical constructs The concepts used in a theory. Thus 'mass' and 'energy' are constructs in Einstein's theory of relativity, while 'frustration' and 'aggression' are constructs in some early behaviourist accounts of violent acts.

Theoretical pluralism The position advocated by Feyerabend whereby researchers would simultaneously develop and test several competing theories rather than just one. Theoretical pluralism not only reduces any personal attachments but enables multiple, simultaneous tests of theories in the same experiment.

Theory An account of how some part of the world works. Theories are useful because they integrate data and allow further predictions about the world to be tested (hypotheses). Good theories should demonstrate comprehensiveness, parsimony, clarity of constructs, internal consistency, testability, empirical support and heuristic value.

Variables The measures which vary in an experiment. Thus in a memory experiment, the variables might be the colour of words on the list and the number of words remembered, since subjects would be exposed to varying colours and recall varying numbers of words.

Verifiable That which can in principle be shown to be true. The feature that scientific claims about the world must possess, according to logical positivists.

References

Abrams, D and Hogg, M A (1990) The context of discourse: let's not throw the baby out with the bathwater. *Philosophical Psychology*, **3**, 219–25.

Allport, G W (1961) *Pattern and Growth in Personality*. New York: Holt, Rinehart & Winston.

Allport, G (1985) The Historical Background of Social Psychology. In G Lindzey and E Aronson (eds) *Handbook of Social Psychology*. 3rd edn. New York: Random House.

Altemeyer, B (1998) The other 'authoritarian personality'. *Advances in Experimental Social Psychology*, **38**, 48–92.

Altheide, D and Johnson, J (1994) Criteria for assessing the interpretative validity in qualitative research. In N Denzin and Y Lincoln (eds) *Handbook of Qualitative Research*. London: Sage.

American Psychological Association (1992) *Ethical Principles of Psychologists and Code of Conduct*. APA. www.apa.org/ethics/code.html

Anderson, J and Ronneberg, J (1996) Collaboration and memory: effects of dyadic retrieval on different memory tasks. *Applied Cognitive Psychology*, **10**, 171–81.

Aries, P (1962) *Centuries of Childhood: A Social History of Family Life*. New York: Vintage Books.

Armistead, N (1974) *Reconstructing Social Psychology*. Harmondsworth: Penguin.

Aronson, E (1995) *The Social Animal*. 7th edn. New York: W H Freeman.

Baillargeon, R (1986) Representing the existence and the location of hidden objects: object permanence in 6- and 8-month-old infants. *Cognition*, **23**, 21–41.

Baxter, L A (1992) Root metaphors in accounts of developing relationships. *Journal of Social and Personal Relationships*, **9**, 253–75.

Bee, H (1995) *The Growing Child*. New York: HarperCollins.

Billig, M (1987) *Arguing and Thinking: A Rhetorical Approach to Social Psychology*. Cambridge: Cambridge University Press.

Block, N (1995) On a confusion about a function of consciousness. *Behavioral and Brain Sciences*, **18**, 227–87.

Brewer, M B and Ciano, W D (1994) *Social Psychology*. St Paul: West Publishing.

British Psychological Society (1996) *Code of Conduct, Ethical Principles & Guidelines*. Leicester: BPS.

Brown, L S (1997) Ethics in psychology: cui bono? In D Fox and I Prilleltensky (eds) *Critical Psychology: An Introduction*. London: Sage.

Bryant, P (1990) Empirical evidence for causes in development. In B Butterworth and P Bryant (eds) *Causes of Development: Interdisciplinary Perspectives*. London: Lawrence Erlbaum.

Burr, V (1995) *An Introduction to Social Constructionism*. London: Routledge.

Buss, D M, Larsen, R J, Westen, D *et al.* (1992) Sex differences in jealousy: evolution, physiology, and psychology. *Psychological Science*, **3**, 251–5.

Byrne, R (1971) *The Attraction Paradigm*. New York: Academic Press.

Calvin W H (1993) The unitary hypothesis: a common neural circuitry for novel manipulations, language, plan-ahead, and throwing? In K R Gibson and T Ingold (eds) *Tools, Language, and Cognition in Human Evolution.* Cambridge: Cambridge University Press.

Colby, A, Kohlberg, L, Gibbs, J and Lieberman M (1983) A longitudinal study of moral judgement. *Monographs of the Society for Research in Child Development,* **48**, 1–2.

Cosmides, L and Tooby, J (1987) Evolutionary Psychology: A Primer. Retrieved 28 July 2000 from the World Wide Web: http://www.psych.ucsb.edu/research/cep/primer.html

Costa, P T and McCrae, R R (1988) Personality in adulthood: a six-year longitudinal study of self-reports and spouse ratings on the NEO personality inventory. *Journal of Personality and Social Psychology,* **54**, 853–63.

Couvalis, G (1997) *The Philosophy of Science: Science and Objectivity.* London: Sage.

Craik, F I M and Lockhart, R S (1972) Levels of processing: a framework for memory research. *Journal of Verbal Learning and Verbal Behavior,* **11**, 671–84.

Crombag, H F M, Wagenaar, W A and Van Koppen, P J (1996) Crashing memories and the problem of 'source monitoring'. *Applied Cognitive Psychology,* **10**, 95–104.

Dagher, Z R (1995) Review of studies on the effectiveness of instructional analogies in science education. *Science Education,* **79**, 295–312.

Danziger, K (1985) The methodological imperative in psychology. *Philosophy of the Social Sciences,* **15**, 1–13.

Ellis, A W and Young, A W (1988) *Human Cognitive Neuropsychology.* Hove: Psychology Press.

Ellis, R and Humphreys, G (1999) *Connectionist Psychology: A Text with Readings.* Hove: Psychology Press.

Farah, M J and Aguirre, G K (1999) Imaging visual recognition: PET and fMRI studies of the functional anatomy of human visual recognition. *Trends in Cognitive Sciences,* **3**, 179–86.

Feyerabend P (1975) *Against Method.* London: Verso.

Foucault, M (1969) *The Archaelogy of Knowledge.* London: Tavistock.

Gabrielli, J D E (1998) Cognitive neuroscience of human memory. *Annual Review of Psychology,* **49**, 87–115.

Gardner, H (1983) *Frames of Mind: The Theory of Multiple Intelligences.* New York: Basic Books.

Gardner, H (1998) Are there additional intelligences? The case for naturalist, spiritual and existential intelligences. In J Kane (ed.) *Education, Information and Transformation.* Englewood Cliffs, NJ: Prentice Hall.

Garnham, A and Oakhill, J (1994) *Thinking and Reasoning.* Oxford: Blackwell.

Geertz, C (1979) From the native's point of view: on the nature of anthropological understanding. In P Rabinow and W Sullivan (eds) *Interpretative Social Science.* Berkeley, CA: University of California Press.

Gergen, K (1973) Social psychology as history. *Journal of Personality and Social Psychology,* **23**, 309–20.

Gergen, K (1985) The social constructionist movement in modern psychology. *American Psychologist,* **40**, 266–75.

Gergen, K (1997a) Social psychology as social construction: the emerging vision. In C McGarty and A Haslam (eds) *The Message of Social Psychology: Perspectives on Mind in Society.* Oxford: Blackwell.

Gergen, K (1997b) The ordinary, the original and the believable in psychology's construction of the person. In B M Bayer and J Shotter (eds) *Reconstructing the Psychological Subject: Bodies, Practices and Technologies.* London: Sage.

Gillhooly, K J (1996) *Thinking: directed, undirected and creative*. London: Academic Press.

Gould, S J (2000) *The Lying Stones of Marrakech: Penultimate Reflections in Natural History*. London: Jonathan Cape.

Grady, C L, McIntosh, A, Horowitz, B *et al.* (1995) Age related reductions in human recognition memory due to impaired encoding. *Science*, **296**, 218–21.

Gregory, R (1998) Editorial. Mythical mechanisms (2): Is the brain a computer? *Perception*, **27**, 127–8.

Gruder, C L, Cook, T D, Hennigan, K M *et al.* (1978) Empirical tests of the absolute sleeper effect predicted from the discounting cue hypothesis. *Journal of Personality and Social Psychology*, **36**, 1061–74.

Guildford, J P (1956) The Structure of the Intellect. *Psychological Bulletin*, **53**, 267–93.

Hamilton, V L and Sanders, J (1995) Crimes of Obedience in the Workplace: Surveys of Americans, Russians and Japanese. *Journal of Social Issues*, **51**, 67–88.

Henwood, K L and Pidgeon, N F (1992) Qualitative research and psychological theorizing. *British Journal of Psychology*, **83**, 97–111.

Hernandez, A E, Martinez, A and Kohnert, K (2000) In search of the language switch: an fMRI study of picture naming in Spanish–English bilinguals. *Brain and Language*, **73**, 421–31.

Hofstadter, D R (1979) *Godel, Escher, Bach: An Eternal Golden Braid*. London: Penguin.

Hovland, C I, Janis, I L and Kelley, H H (1953) *Communication and Persuasion*. New Haven, CT: Yale University Press.

Hughes, C and Dunn, J (2000) Hedonism or empathy? Hard-to-manage children's moral awareness and links with cognitive and maternal characteristics. *British Journal of Developmental Psychology*, **18**, 227–45.

Hull, C L (1951) *Essentials of Behavior*. New Haven, CT: Yale University Press.

Johnson, S (1999) The 'horrors' of scientific research. *The Psychologist*, **12**, 186–9.

Kidder, L H and Fine, M (1997) Qualitative enquiry in psychology: a radical tradition. In D Fox and I Prilleltensky (eds) *Critical Psychology: An Introduction*. London: Sage.

Kolb, B and Whishaw, I Q (1998) Brain plasticity and behaviour. *Annual Review of Psychology*, **49**, 43–64.

Kuhn, T S (1962) *The Structure of Scientific Revolutions*. Chicago: University of Chicago Press.

Lumby, J (1995) *The Lancashire Witch-craze: Jennet Preston and the Lancashire Witches, 1612*. Lancashire: Carnegie.

Lutsky, N (1995) When is 'obedience' obedience? Conceptual and historical commentary. *Journal of Social Issues*, **51**, 55–66.

Marcia, J E (1980) Identity in adolescence. In J Adelson (ed.) *Handbook of Adolescent Psychology*. New York: Wiley.

Marsh, P, Rosser, E and Harré, R (1977) *The Rules of Disorder*. London: Routledge & Kegan Paul.

Masling, J (1966) Role-related behavior of the subject and the psychologist and its effects upon psychological data, *Nebraska Symposium on Motivation*, Vol 14, Lincoln: University of Nebraska Press.

McGinn, C (1991) *The Problem of Consciousness*. Oxford: Blackwell.

McGuire, W J (1997) Creative hypothesis generating in psychology: some useful heuristics. *Annual Review of Psychology*, **48**, 1–30.

McGuire, W J (1999) *Constructing Social Psychology. Creative and Critical Processes*. Cambridge: Cambridge University Press.

Meeus, W H J and Raaijmakers, Q A W (1995) Obedience in modern society: the Utrecht studies. *Journal of Social Issues*, **51**, 155–76.

Menon, S R and Kim, S-G (1999) Spatial and temporal limits in neuroimaging with fMRI. *Trends in Cognitive Sciences*, **3**, 207–16.

Milgram, S (1974) *Obedience to Authority: An Experimental View*. New York: Harper & Row.

Miller, A G, Collins, B E and Brief, D E (1995) Perspectives on obedience to authority: the legacy of the Milgram experiments. *Journal of Social Issues*, **51**, 1–20.

Minter, M, Hobson, R and Bishop, P (1998) Congenital visual impairment and 'theory of mind'. *British Journal of Social Psychology*, **16**, 183–96.

Mischel, W and Shoda, Y (1998) Reconciling processing dynamics and personality dispositions. *Annual Review of Psychology*, **49**, 229–58.

Modigliani, A and Rochat, F (1995) The role of interaction sequences in the timing of resistance in shaping obedience and defiance to authority. *Journal of Social Issues*, **51**, 107–24.

Moscovici, S, Lage, E and Naffrechoux, M (1969) Influence of a consistent minority on the responses of a majority in a color perception task. *Sociometry*, **32**, 365–80.

Neisser, U (1967) *Cognitive Psychology*. Englewood Cliffs, NJ: Prentice Hall.

Nelson-Jones, R (1996) *Effective Thinking Skills*. London: Cassell.

Nickerson, R S, Perkins, D N and Smith, E E (1985) *The Teaching of Thinking*. Hillsdale, NJ: Lawrence Erlbaum.

Nightingale, D and Neilands, T (1997) Understanding and practising critical psychology. In D Fox and I Prilleltensky (eds) *Critical Psychology: An Introduction*. London: Sage.

Nisbett, R E and Ross, L (1980) *Human Inference: Strategies and Shortcomings of Human Judgement*. Engelwood Cliffs, NJ: Prentice Hall.

Parker, I (1997) Discursive psychology. In D Fox and I Prilleltensky (eds) *Critical Psychology: An Introduction*. London: Sage.

Perkins, D (1981) *The Mind's Best Work*. Cambridge, MA: Harvard University Press.

Pettigrew, T F (1998) Intergroup contact theory. *Annual Review of Psychology*, **49**, 65–85.

Petty, R E and Cacioppo, J T (1996) *Attitudes and Persuasion: Classic and Contemporary Approaches*. Oxford: Westview Press.

Pinker, S (1994) *The Language Instinct: The New Science of Language and the Mind*. London: Penguin.

Popper, K (1959) *The Logic of Scientific Discovery*. London: Hutchinson.

Popper, K (1963) *Conjectures and Refutations: The Growth of Scientific Knowledge*. London: Routledge.

Posner, M I and Raichle, M E (1995) Precis of images of mind. *Behavioral and Brain Sciences*, **18**, 327–83.

Postma, A, Izendoorn, R and de Haan, E H F (1998) Sex differences in object location memory. *Brain and Cognition*, **36**, 334–45.

Potter, J (1996) Discourse analysis and constructionist approaches: theoretical background. In J T E Richardson (ed.) *Handbook of Qualitative Research Methods for Psychology and the Social Sciences*. Leicester: BPS Books.

Potter, J and Wetherell, M (1987) *Discourse and Social Psychology: Beyond Attitudes and Behaviour*. London: Sage.

Predebon, J (1998) Decrement of the Bretano Müller-Lyer illusion as a function of inspection time. *Perception*, **27**, 183–92.

Preston, J M (1997) *Feyerabend: Philosophy, Science and Society*. Cambridge: Polity Press.

Rescorla, R (1988) Pavlovian Conditioning: It's not what you think it is. *American Psychologist*, **43**, 151–9.

Roazzi, A and Bryant, P (1998) The effects of symmetrical and asymmetrical social interaction on children's logical inferences. *British Journal of Developmental Psychology*, **16**, 175–81.

Robson, C (1993) *Real World Research: A Resource for Social Scientists and Practitioner Researchers*. Oxford: Blackwell.

Rose, N (1985) *The Psychological Complex*. London: Routledge.

Rosenhan, D L (1973) On being sane in insane places. *Science*, 179, 250–8.

Rosenzweig, M R, Bennett, E L and Diamond, M C (1972) Brain changes in response to experience. *Scientific American*, 226, 22–9.

Sapsford, R (1997) Evidence. In R Sapsford (ed.) *Issues for Social Psychology*. Milton Keynes: Open University Press.

Schacter, D L, Norman, K A and Koutstaal, W (1998) The cognitive neuroscience of constructive memory. *Annual Review of Psychology*, 49, 289–318.

Sears, D O (1986) College sophomores in the laboratory: influences of a narrow data base on social psychology's view of human nature. *Journal of Personality and Social Psychology*, 51, 515–30.

Shostrom, E L (1964) An inventory for the measurement of self-actualization. *Educational and Psychological Measurement*, 24, 207–18.

Silverman, I and Eals, M (1992) Sex differences in spatial ability. Evolutionary theory and data. In J H Barkow, L Cosmides, and J Tooby (eds) *The Adapted Mind: Evolutionary Psychology and the Generation of Culture*. Oxford, Oxford University Press.

Smith, E R and Mackie, D M (2000) *Social Psychology*. 2nd edn. Hove: Psychology Press.

Sternberg, R J (1981) Intelligence and nonentrenchment. *Journal of Educational Psychology*, 73, 1–16.

Sternberg, R J (1995) *In Search of the Human Mind*. London: Harcourt Brace.

Sternberg, R J and Kaufman, J C (1998) Human abilities. *Annual Review of Psychology*, 49, 479–502.

Storms, M D (1973) Videotape and the attribution process: Reversing actors' and observers' points of view. *Journal of Personality and Social Psychology*, 27, 165–75.

Thornton, S (1997) 'Karl Popper' Retrieved from the World Wide Web 31 July 2000: http://plato.stanford.edu/archives/sum1998/entries/popper/

Toren, C (1996) Ethnography: theoretical background. In J T E Richardson (ed.) *Handbook of Qualitative Research Methods for Psychology and the Social Sciences*. Leicester: BPS Books.

Turing, A (1950) Computing Machinery and Intelligence. *Mind*, 50, 433–60.

Wareing, M, Fisk, J E and Murphy, P (2000) Working memory deficits in current and previous users of MDMA. *British Journal of Psychology*, 91, 181–8.

Weber, S J and Cook, T D (1972) Subject effects in laboratory research: An examination of subject roles, demand characteristics, and valid inference. *Psychological Bulletin*, 77, 273–95.

Wetherell, M (1996) Life histories/social histories. In M Wetherell (ed.) *Identities, Groups and Social Issues*. London: Sage.

Wetherell, M and Maybin, J (1996) The distributed self. In R Stevens (ed.) *Understanding the Self*. London: Sage.

Wetherell, M and Still, A (1996) Realism and relativism. In R Sapsford (ed.) *Issues for Social Psychology*. Milton Keynes: Open University Press.

Whalsten, D (1999) Single gene influences on brain and behaviour. *Annual Review of Psychology*, 50, 599–624.

Woolgar, S (1988) *Science: The Very Idea*. London: Tavistock.

Woolgar, S (1996) Psychology, qualitative methods and the ideas of science. In J T E Richardson (ed.) *Handbook of Qualitative Research Methods for Psychology and the Social Sciences*. Leicester: BPS Books.

Zimbardo, P G (1971) On the ethics of intervention in human psychological research with special reference to the 'Stanford Prison Experiment'. *Cognition*, 2, 243–55.

Index